Bootstrap Justice

Bootstrap Justice

The Search for Mexico's Disappeared

JANICE K. GALLAGHER

OXFORD
UNIVERSITY PRESS

OXFORD
UNIVERSITY PRESS

Oxford University Press is a department of the University of Oxford. It furthers the University's objective of excellence in research, scholarship, and education by publishing worldwide. Oxford is a registered trade mark of Oxford University Press in the UK and certain other countries.

Published in the United States of America by Oxford University Press
198 Madison Avenue, New York, NY 10016, United States of America.

Library of Congress Cataloging-in-Publication Data
Names: Gallagher, Janice (Janice K.), author.
Title: Bootstrap justice : the search for Mexico's disappeared / Janice Gallagher.
Description: New York, NY : Oxford University Press, 2023. | Includes bibliographical references and index.
Identifiers: LCCN 2022018805 (print) | LCCN 2022018806 (ebook) | ISBN 9780197649985 (paperback) | ISBN 9780197649978 (hardback) | ISBN 9780197650004 (epub) | ISBN 9780197649992 | ISBN 9780197650011
Subjects: LCSH: Disappeared persons—Mexico. | Political persecution—Mexico. | State-sponsored terrorism—Mexico.
Classification: LCC HV6322.33.M6 G35 2022 (print) | LCC HV6322.33.M6 (ebook) | DDC 362.870972—dc23/eng/20220624
LC record available at https://lccn.loc.gov/2022018805
LC ebook record available at https://lccn.loc.gov/2022018806

DOI: 10.1093/oso/9780197649978.001.0001

1 3 5 7 9 8 6 4 2

Paperback printed by Lakeside Book Company, United States of America
Hardback printed by Bridgeport National Bindery, Inc., United States of America

Contents

List of Figures   vii
List of Tables   ix
List of Map   xi
Acknowledgments   xiii
Abbreviations   xix

1. Introduction: Sustained Mobilization and the Fight Against
   Impunity   1

2. The Beginnings: The Formation and Disruption of Legal
   Consciousness   37

3. State and Civil Society Responses to Disappearances
   in Mexico   72

4. The Evolution of Legal Consciousness: Gaining Voice and
   Grappling with the Law   115

5. Legal and Political Opportunities of the Uneven State   164

6. To What Effect? How Sustained Mobilization
   Erodes Impunity   200

7. Conclusion   228

Afterword   245
References   249
Index   263

Figures

Photo 1 The disappeared Trujillo Herrera brothers   xxiii

Photo 2 Alejandro Alfonso Moreno Baca, disappeared January 27, 2011   xxiv

Photo 3 Elvis Axell Torres Rosete, disappeared December 28, 2010   xxv

Figure 1.1 Argument summary   6

Figure 1.2 Political opportunities to combat impunity   13

Figure 1.3 Participatory investigation meeting   17

Figure 1.4 Participatory investigation meeting notes   18

Figure 1.5 Historical origins of "Pulling yourself up by your bootstraps"   21

Figure 1.6 Disappearances in Mexico   25

Figure 3.1 Activists and advocates   74

Figure 3.2 Homicides and disappearances in Mexico   102

Figure 3.3 Mobilization in response to Ayotzinapa   108

Figure 3.4 Participatory investigation meeting notes *Búsqueda* (searching)   112

Figure 4.1 A theory of sustained mobilization   119

Figure 5.1 Case selection   168

Figure 6.1 Judicial results in state-level courts: The 12 cases of disappearances
            with indictments   212

Figure 6.2 Probable perpetrator   213

Figure 6.3 Status of disappeared persons: At least five years after
            disappearance event   214

Tables

Table 2.1 Demographics of NGO Participants versus Non-Participants   43

Table 5.1 Disappearances/Enforced Disappearances 2006–2018   171

Table 5.2 Cases of Disappearances Registered by Local NGO CADHAC   192

Map

Map 5.1   Mexican cartels' map, 2010   169

Acknowledgments

Many debts are accumulated during the course of a project spanning over 10 years and as many places. First and foremost, I am grateful for the overwhelming generosity of time and spirit with which people affected by violence in Mexico talked with me, confided in me, and trusted me with their stories, perspectives, and pain. I am humbled by their decision to open their lives to me, and I hope this effort is a *granito de arena*, a grain of sand, in our collective struggle for justice and dignity. It is impossible to name each of them, but without them there would be no struggle, and no book.

This book began as a doctoral dissertation at Cornell University. I am grateful to my advisors—Ken Roberts, Sidney Tarrow, and Matt Evangelista—who pushed me, from the very beginning, to be methodologically, theoretically, and analytically rigorous, and to follow my impulse to radically depart from my dissertation prospectus when the politics on the ground shifted. Along with my committee's intellectual support, the financial support I received from the National Science Foundation, the Fulbright-García Robles Scholarship, the Inter-American Foundation, and the Einaudi Center for International Studies at Cornell University were essential to developing this book.

At Cornell, I was surrounded by friends whom I came to know as scholars, who saw me through this project, and helped me make the transition into post-PhD life. Phil Ayoub, Jaimie Bleck, Don Leonard, Igor Longvinenko, Tariq Thachil, Simon Velasquez, and Chris Zepeda saw the earliest iterations of this project and helped me shape its progression. Noelle Brigden and Jen Hadden allowed me to tag along with them during their own fieldwork, modeling how to do important, grounded, and rigorous research. Alicia Swords taught me what participant action research was, and the insights and sanity gained from our daily bike rides in Ithaca brought the dissertation over the finish line. Sinja Graf transformed my house into a home while I wrote the dissertation, and filled it with unwavering support, the smell of freshly ground coffee, and critical insights. Along the way, my dear friends Jay Boyd, Julie Kazarian, Alyssa Kelly, Ben Maulbeck, Nikki Royne O'Meara, Juan Reyes, and Cathy Wirth have infused light and laughter into what could sometimes be an arduous process. My Charlton community—Mark, Lee, Deb, Bev—welcomed me as I finished the manuscript.

In Mexico, César Octavio Pérez Verónica guided the early part of this research, as did the staff of the RedTdt, especially Agnieszka Raczynska. Hermana Consuelo Morales invited me into her home and organization, allowing me to embed into the world of human rights advocacy in a way that absolutely would not have otherwise been possible. The human rights lawyers at CADHAC, especially Mar Alvarez, Ana Luna Serrano, and Ana Claudia Martinez, showed me what goes into human rights advocacy and modeled perseverance in the face of tough odds. My experiences with the Movimiento por la Paz con Justicia y Dignidad transformed this project, as well as the past decade of my life. The leadership of the MPJD, in partic- ular Miguel Alvarez, Emilio Alvarez Icaza, Dolores González Saravia, Javier Sicilia, and Brisa Solis, invited me into organizing spaces and trusted me as an ally, for which I am forever grateful. During the course of organizing for the 2012 caravan, I had the enormous pleasure of again working with John Lindsay-Poland, a brilliant and committed advocate and researcher; Ted Lewis, the former head of the Mexico Program at Global Exchange whose vi- sion and deep ties in Mexico and the United States guided this enormous un- dertaking; and Marco Castillo, the co-executive director of Global Exchange, and a visionary activist and talented organizer. The friendships I made in the MPJD are too numerous to recount and continue to buoy me. Sadly, sev- eral friends and allies have passed away: I am especially indebted to Cecilia Bárcenas, Roberto Galván, and Nepuceno Moreno. Nepo vocally denounced the police's involvement in his son's enforced disappearance: his 2011 assassi- nation remains unsolved.

This book took shape as something distinct from a dissertation at Brown University's Watson Institute during my postdoc, where I had the luxury of an outstanding community of scholars, time, and support to develop this manuscript. My fellow postdocs Julia Chuang, Deepak Lamba-Nieves, Duff Morton, Jonas Nahm, Michelle Jurkovich, Elena Shih, and Elizabeth Williams created a vibrant intellectual community that planted the seeds of this book. While at Watson, I benefited from the wise counsel of Rick Locke, Richard Snyder, and Patrick Heller. Lisa Hilbink, Juliana Restrepo-Sanin, Valentina Salas, and Bridget Marchesi helped me take the learnings from this project into exciting new work in Chile and Colombia. Lisa has selflessly mentored me as I transitioned from a graduate student to a scholar, and modeled for me what generosity, rigor, and curiosity look like. Dan Brinks, Sandra Botero,

Jorge Contesse, Yanilda González, Ezequiel Gonzalez Ocantos, Eduardo Moncada, Kim Nolan, and Brian Palmer-Rubin have all offered feedback and encouragement and insightful critiques along the way. Phillip Johnson and David Shirk read early drafts and offered invaluable feedback, making sure I hit the right notes with their deep knowledge of Mexico. Alejandro Anaya, Karina Ansolabehere, Michael Chamberlin and Barbara Frey have been invaluable allies and colleagues who have shared their deep knowledge of and respect for Mexican human rights organizations with me. Perhaps the most generative academic space for this project came in the "Women Studying Violence" workshops held at the University of Notre Dame. Sandra Ley, Abby Cordova, Lucía Tiscornia, Angelica Durán Martinez, and all of the other participants helped me understand what parts of this manuscript could germinate into a fully fledged project, and I am deeply indebted to the space and generosity of spirit these workshops provided.

I benefited from working with brilliant student assistants and researchers over the course of this project. Itzel Cruz helped me learn the ropes of filing information requests in Mexico. My time at Brown brought me into contact with Paula Martinez and Camila Ruiz-Segovia—who approached me to speak at an event following the disappearance of the 43 Ayotzinapa students. They worked tirelessly for me as research assistants, traveling with me to Guerrero to meet the classmates of the disappeared students and their families, and at their behest, we launched a website to document the mobilization and important advances in these cases (ayotzinapatimeline.org). Anthony Ghaly, Laura Weiss and Ana Sandoval picked up where they left off, providing invaluable help with the development of the manuscript. At Rutgers-Newark, I have been welcomed by an incredibly open and generous community of scholars. Nermin Allam, Lisa Hull, Jyl Josephson, Domingo Morel, Norman Samuels, and Mara Sidney have made Rutgers a happy and productive place to work. Georgia Mellos has helped me to navigate Rutgers—and crucuially, how to continue to make research trips. James Jones has made Rutgers feel like a home, and welcomed me into his fabulous community, and together with the brilliant Catherine Tan and Harlem crew, this book took shape in coffee shops and over lunches in New York.

My experience in the MPJD also allowed me to meet two people without which this book would not exist. Francisco Romero is a seasoned human rights lawyer with deep roots in collective struggle who has selflessly continued to work with victims' collectives over the years. I met him as he advocated, pro bono, on behalf of many MPJD victim activists. He has been infinitely patient with me, repeatedly explaining to me the finer points and nuances in the Mexican legal system, helping me understand the inner workings of legal advocacy and responding to endless Whatsapp queries in my quest to understand the intersection of social movements and law in Mexico. Atala Chavez, who became an invaluable ally on the 2012 Caravan, has accompanied me through nearly every step of this process. While Atala appears sparingly within these pages—she is a *co-ayudvante* (legally authorized representative) on Lucía and Alfonso's case, and a psychologist by training—her groundbreaking work with victims' organizations in Tamaulipas and sharp insight into the victim's movement has been crucial in keeping me connected to and grounded with the experience of victims in Mexico, even as I have had to return to the United States. Her ethical clarity and grounded solidarity have been invaluable touchstones for me as I navigate this work, and I am humbled by her investment in and commitment to this project.

My sister, Ellen Gallagher, her wife Allyson Goose, and my dear nephews Jasper and Kai have kept me grounded, fed, and happy during the process of finishing the write-up of this book. My aunt, Judi Kreinick, celebrated the many milestones along the way to finishing this project, patiently cheering me on. Alisha Holland was my daily writing partner through most of this manuscript: perhaps the best realization of the pandemic was that I can indeed be productive working from home—but really only if it was with treasured colleagues who would celebrate the often solitary achievements of academia, offer encouragement, take a deep breath, and offer much-needed perspective (and prodding). Gabi Kruks-Wisner has been an intellectual partner since we traipsed through Nicaragua working for formerly Sandinista organizations in the late 1990s, and we were both lucky enough to benefit from the training and grounded wisdom of Swarthmore professor Ken Sharpe. What a delight it has been to benefit from her guidance as I have finished this project. Whitney Taylor has read nearly every page of this book multiple times, often turning drafts around within hours, and these pages have benefited immensely from her wisdom and instincts.

I met Ana Paula Hernandez during my first summer of research in Mexico in 2010. Ana Paula was the Latin America program officer for the Fund for Global Human Rights, and she opened the doors of the human rights community to me in Mexico. Ana Paula was the person who knew the organizational terrain of human rights in Mexico better than anyone else I have known—and was my go-to person to discuss my evolving understanding of Mexican civil society's response to violence. She brought unrivaled empathy and energy to her work on behalf of victims and facilitated the funding of many of the collectives profiled in this book. Ana Paula was killed in a bus accident in Guatemala in 2019 along with two other human rights activists. I still find myself yearning to talk with her about what this book became. I hope it would have made her proud—she was an incredible ally who knew better than anyone else in Mexico the crucial role of victims organizations. I miss her deeply.

I had the enormous privilege of knowing Sally Merry my entire life. She was the only academic I knew growing up—and I think guided me in ways that I am still realizing. As I found my way to her work, I wondered what seeds she had planted in me that took 30 + years to germinate. As this book came together, I lived with her for a time in her New York City apartment. She helped me hash through the theoretical framing—as well as the imposter syndrome that she suspected was delaying me—over Chinese food and morning coffee. She always accused me of being a closet ethnographer and helped give me the tools, grounding, and confidence to explore new methodologies and epistemologies in this project. When I doubted that I was ready to write this book, Sally asked me if I had something to say that was important, that hadn't been said already, and that I believed to be true. My affirmative answer to these questions, she assured me, meant that I was ready and could do this. Her insistence that this was possible was crucial in bringing this project to completion, and while Sally passed away in 2020, her words continue to ring in my ears. I am indebted to her mentorship and friendship, and this book would not be what it is without her guidance.

Many people ask me how I, a white woman from the suburbs of upstate New York with Jewish and Irish roots, came to devote much of my life to Latin American politics, and specifically to the struggle for justice in Colombia and then Mexico. Much of the answer to this question is, unsurprisingly, a result of how I was raised. My mother is a social worker and psychotherapist, which seems undeniably connected to the fact that I often find myself eliciting people's life stories. My father, who passed away from pancreatic cancer a month before I started to do research in Mexico, was an old school reporter who believed in the crucial role of the fourth estate in holding power to account. While he trained his professional sights on New York State government during his 35 years as a reporter, he taught me the importance of *goo goos* (good government organizations—in the parlance of Albany politics) in promoting a citizen-led vision of what government could and should aspire to. This book is dedicated to both my mom and dad.

Abbreviations

A.C.	Asociación Civil / Civic Association
AEI	Agencia Estatal de Investigación / State Investigatory Agency
BLO	Beltrán Leyva Organization/Cartel
CADHAC	Ciudadanos en Apoyo de Los Derechos Humanos A.C. / Citizens in Support of Human Rights
CEAV	Comisión de Atención a Víctimas / Victims' Attention Commission
CEDEHM	Centro de Derechos Humanos de las Mujeres / Center for Women's Rights)
CEDH	Comisión Estatal de Derechos Humanos / State Human Rights Commission
CENCOS	Centro Nacional de Comunicación Social A.C./ National Center of Social Communications AC
Centro ProDH	Centro por los Derechos Humanos Miguel Agustin Pro Juárez / Miguel Agustin Pro Juárez Human Rights Center
CfC	Ciencia Forense Ciudadana / Citizen-led Forensic Science
CJNG	Cártel de Jalisco Nueva Generación / Jalisco New Generation Cartel
CMDPDH	Comisión Mexicana de Defensa y Promoción de los Derechos Humanos A.C. / Mexican Commission for the Promotion and Defense of Human Rights
CNDH	Comisión Nacional de Derechos Humanos / National Human Rights Commission
DTO	Drug Trafficking Organization
EZLN	Ejército Zapatista de Liberación Nacional / Zapatista National Liberation Army
FrayBa	El Centro de Derechos Humanos Fray Bartolomé de Las Casas, A. C. / The Fray Bartolomé de Las Casas Human Rights Center
Fray Juan de Larios	Centro Diocesano para los Derechos Humanos Fray Juan de Larios / Fray Juan de Larios Diocesan Center for Human Rights
Fray Vitoria	Centro de Derechos Humanos, Fray Francisco de Vitoria, O.P. A.C. / Fray Francisco de Vitoria Human rights Center
FUNDENL	Fuerzas Unidas por Nuestros Desaparecidos(as) en Nuevo León / United Forces for Our Disappeared in Nuevo León

FUUNDEC	Fuerzas Unidas por Nuestros Desaparecidos en Coahuila / United Forces for Our Disappeared in Coahuila
FUUNDEM	Fuerzas Unidas por Nuestros Desaparecidos en México / United Forces for Our Disappeared in Mexico
GIEI	Grupo Interdisciplinario de Expertas y Expertos Independientes / Interdisciplinary Group of Independent Experts
HRW	Human Rights Watch
IACHR	Inter-American Commission on Human Rights
IACtHR	Inter-American Court of Human Rights
INEGI	Instituto Nacional de Estadística y Geografía / National Institute of Statistics and Geography
MP	Ministerio Público / Public Minister (public prosecutor/ investigator)
MPJD	Movimiento por la Paz con Justicia y Dignidad / Movement for Peace with Justice and Dignity
MUCD	México Unido Contra la Delincuencia, / Mexico United Against Delinquency
NGO	non-governmental organization
OAS	Organizationof American States
OHCHR/UNHCHR	Office of the United Nations High Commissioner for Human Rights
PAN	Partido de Acción Nacional / National Action Party
PGJE	Procuraduría General de Justicia del Estado / State Attorney General's Office
PGR	Procuraduría General de la Republica / National Attorney General
PRD	Partido Revolucionario Democrático / Revolutionary Democratic Party
PRI	Partido Revolucionario Institucional / Institutional Revolutionary Party
RedTDT	Red de Todos los Derechos para Todas y Todos / Network of All Rights for Everyone
RNCPD	Registro Nacional Ciudadano de Personas Desaparecidas / National Citizen Registry of Disappeared Persons
RNPDNO	Registro Nacional de Personas Desaparecidas y No Localizadas / National Registry of Disappeared and Missing People
SEGOB	Secretaría de Gobernación / Secretary of the Interior
SEIDO	Subprocuraduría Especializada en Investigación de Delincuencia Organizada / Attorney General's Special Office on Organized Crime Investigation

SEMEFO   Service Médico Forense / Medical Forensic Service
SERAPAZ   Servicios y Asesoría para la Paz A.C. / Services and Assistance for
          Peace A.C
UN   United Nations
WOLA   Washington Office on Latin America

Photo 1 The disappeared Trujillo Herrera brothers: Raúl and Jesús Salvador, disappeared August 29, 2008; Gustavo and Luis Armando, disappeared September 22, 2010

¡AYÚDALE A REGRESAR A CASA!

Alejandro Alfonso Moreno Baca

Sexo: Masculino
Edad: 32 años
Estatura: 1.74 m.
Tez: Blanca
Ojos: Medianos, café oscuro
Cabello: Lacio, castaño oscuro

Fecha de nacimiento: 13/06/1978

Se extravió en el Municipio de Vallecillo, Nuevo León, el 27 de enero de 2011.

REGISTRO: 318/EXT/2011

Te agradeceremos reportar cualquier información

5346.4268
D.F. y área metropolitana

01800.00.252.00
Interior de la República

extraviados@pgr.gob.mx
Vía internet

Este servicio se presta en la Procuraduría General de la República sin ningún costo

PROGRAMA DE APOYO A FAMILIARES DE PERSONAS EXTRAVIADAS SUSTRAÍDAS O AUSENTES

Photo 2 Alejandro Alfonso Moreno Baca, disappeared January 27, 2011

Photo 3 Elvis Axell Torres Rosete, disappeared December 28, 2010

1

Introduction

Sustained Mobilization and the Fight Against Impunity

About 30 of us, all exhausted with aching feet, gathered in a run-down out-door cantina in the center of Mexico City in April 2012. The sound of varied regional accents bounced off the walls—the sing-songy lilt of the Yucatán; the nasal northern inflection, rapid-fire Mexico City slang; and at times my gringo-accented Spanish interjected a question or comment. This motley crew had spent the day in the Mexico's Senate chanting, waiting, listening, chiding, cajoling, and finally cheering when a majority of Mexican senators voted to approve the Victims' Law. We were all part of the Movement for Peace with Justice and Dignity (MPJD) in some way, which had worked hard to get this law passed. Most of those gathered were grieving the murder or disappearance[1] of a loved one. The legislation was a significant victory: it was the first national leg-islation that would aid those whose families had been directly affected by drug war violence.

Lucía, a put-together, well-off woman who would not want me to share her age, warmly embraced her friends in the cantina, alternately comforting and laughing with them. She pulled many of the other mothers aside to check in with them about the status of their cases, the state of their marriages, or health concerns they were having. Her husband, Alfonso, stayed close, but mostly stayed on his phone. Juan Carlos, a stocky man in his early 40s with intense, erratic energy, leaned against the wall locked in conversation with several other *víctimas*—"victims," a contested shorthand label identifying

---

[1] People are considered "disappeared," rather than missing, when there is reason to believe that their absence is involuntary—that is, that they were abducted and/or are being imprisoned and held against their will. "*Enforced* disappearances" are a sub-set of disappearances in which the state (or "persons or groups of persons acting with the authorization, support or acquiescence of the State") is involved in perpetrating the disappearance and also concealing the whereabouts of the disappeared person; this is considered a grave human rights violation and a crime against humanity. See United Nations (2010), "International Convention for the Protection of All Persons from Enforced Disappearance," which was adopted by the UN General Assembly in 2006 and entered into force in 2010.

Bootstrap Justice. Janice k. Gallagher, Oxford University Press. © Oxford University Press 2023.
DOI: 10.1093/oso/9780197649978.003.0001

people whose loved ones have been victimized by violence[2]—about his latest frustrations with state officials. Nancy, a petite woman with blond highlighted hair, heavy makeup, and a shirt with a photo of her missing son silk-screened on it, stood to the side, visibly a little uncomfortable.

Lucía and Alfonso were there because their son, Alejandro Moreno Baca, had disappeared while driving from Mexico City to Laredo, Texas, in 2011. Alejandro, who worked at IBM, had decided to drive to Texas instead of flying because he was nervous that the expensive new computer he was buying in the United States would be damaged on the plane. Juan Carlos Trujillo, who used to make his living running a family business buying and selling gold throughout Mexico, was there because four of his brothers—two at a time, in 2008 and 2010—had been disappeared while traveling for work. And Nancy was there for her 18-year-old son Elvis Axell, who was disappeared from a drug treatment center she had sent him to in late 2010. Though Elvis had been there to seek treatment for his addiction, the center—ironically named Salva Tu Vida, or "Save Your Life,"—was run by a man with deep ties to criminal groups. Right after Christmas, he said he had sent Elvis on an errand with two other patients. None of them have been seen since.

On this day, as we gathered to celebrate the passage of the Victims' Law, I was struck both by how powerful this group had become, and simultaneously, by how utterly powerless they were to find their missing loved ones—the goal that had brought them together in the first place. Members of the group had touched the halls of political power in Mexico and the upper echelons of the international human rights community. They had met with

---

[2] Family members of people who have been murdered or disappeared often identify both themselves and their murdered or disappeared loved ones simply as *víctimas*—victims. While the term "victim" has been challenged by some who want to emphasize the active and empowered role of these family members, the term continues to be embraced and, I argue, re-appropriated by many of the family members of the murdered and disappeared. This re-appropriation has become a way of asserting their common identity (regardless of the perpetrator of the crime or the circumstances of the violence perpetrated against their loved one), articulating common demands for justice, and in asserting that they are victims of crimes—as opposed to complicit. In legal terms, Mexican legislation talks about direct and indirect victims: the 2013 Victims' Law defines direct and indirect victims: "direct" victims are "those persons that have directly suffered some economic, physical, mental, or emotional damage or harm, or in general someone whose legal property or rights have been put in danger as a result of a crime or violations of their human rights." Indirect victims are "family members or persons in charge of a victim who have a close relationship with him or her" (see Ley General de Víctimas 2022). I do not use this legal terminology as I think it establishes an implicit hierarchy in which the suffering of the family members of those who have been disappeared is considered secondarily. Instead, I use the terms "victim"; and "family member of victim" interchangeably throughout the book to refer to both family members of those murdered or disappeared and those who were themselves murdered or disappeared. I use "mobilized victims" at times to specify that I am speaking of victims who are engaged in activism and advocacy.

two Mexican presidents; told their stories to national and international news outlets; and had their cases featured in reports by the most prominent international human rights organizations in the world. Many had visited the United Nations or Organization of American States to give their testimony in Geneva, New York, and Washington. While I never heard anyone say that justice had been served, perpetrators in about a quarter of their cases had been incarcerated, a remarkable feat in a country with impunity rates approaching 100 percent in the more than 85,000 cases of disappearances reported since 2006.[3] They had participated in getting the federal Victims' Law passed, would go on to draft additional federal legislation focused on disappearances, and would help create and monitor new state offices dedicated to finding their loved ones and punishing those responsible for their disappearances. Those assembled would also go on to found numerous victims' organizations, known as *colectivos*, "collectives." Despite these efforts, however, as of the writing of this book, not one of them has managed to locate their missing loved one alive.[4]

This book attempts to make sense of the simultaneous power and powerlessness of people who have been affected by grave human rights violations. Hannah Arendt (1949) considered the power of citizenship to confer "the right to have rights." What happens when citizenship instead confers deeply dysfunctional judiciaries that either cannot or will not guarantee their most basic rights? At its heart, this book asks how people in contexts of normalized rights violations transform into rights-claiming, and ultimately, rights-bearing citizens. I argue that as people go through the process of continually making claims on the state and engaging in mobilization, their understandings of the law, legality, and the state shift, and that with these shifts, their ability to challenge impunity is likewise transformed. By way of

---

[3] The Minister of Human Rights, Alejandro Encinas, reported that 85,006 people had been disappeared between 2006 and April 7, 2021. These numbers differ slightly from the National Registry of Disappeared and Missing People, which registered 80,606 disappeared people between 2006 and April 2021 (see Figure 1.6). Both figures most likely undercount the actual number as many cases are unreported, and some are obscured in the classification of disappearances in other legal categories (e.g., kidnapping; illegal deprivation of liberty).

Individuals criminally responsible for disappearances are almost never held accountable: a UN Committee on Enforced Disappearances report (2021, 5) finds that "impunity is nearly absolute," with between 2 and 6 percent of cases being brought to trial and only 36 total guilty convictions having been issued. A 2020 *Animal Político* report found that out of 11,706 cases of enforced disappearance reported to state or federal authorities between 2006 and 2019, there were only 39 convictions (.33 percent)—"an effectiveness near zero percent" (Angel 2020).

[4] The remains of one woman's daughter had been found and identified with DNA results, though she rejected the results as forensically flawed.

evidence, this book draws from the past 10 years of struggle against impunity in cases of disappearances in Mexico. I focus on the informal drivers of incremental and uneven progress in the battle against impunity: the role of individuals, like those introduced above, and the organizations they form in uncovering what happened to people who have been disappeared; the shifting dynamics between state actors and their criminal allies and the fleeting political and legal opportunities they create; and the king-like power of low-level state agents to open the door to legal progress or keep it slammed shut. I explore the ways these informal relationships and dynamics—fueled by the sustained mobilization of the family members of the disappeared— have meaningfully shaped the accountability landscape and challenged impunity.

Central Concepts and Argument

Law, as Max Weber spelled out, should not respond to the same hierarchies and incentives as politics. In his words, legal rights aspire to be "a source of power of which the hitherto powerless might be possessed."[5] In this view, legal rights and institutions are important precisely because they defy the overarching distribution of power in society. Legal institutions in democracies are, on paper, designed with this in mind, and provisions for judicial independence and discretion, the reliance on precedence, and legal doctrine are tools meant to facilitate the division between power and law (Ríos-Figueroa 2006; Skaar 2011).

Despite these lofty ideals, citizens in every democracy know that law often replicates, reifies, and even deepens existing inequalities. Each time a corrupt leader gets away with malfeasance, or when a person from the upper economic and social echelons or dominant racial caste of society receives preferential treatment, law's vulnerability to existing social hierarchies is revealed. People who have been excluded from power in society, along with their advocates, have realized this vulnerability and have sought to rebalance the scales of justice by pressuring courts to apply the laws on the books more equitably; they have also advocated passage of additional legislation to equip courts with more explicit legal mandates that favor those systematically excluded from power. We have gained an appreciation for their efficacy

---

[5] Weber (1978 [1921]), as quoted in Brinks (2008, 3).

in advancing toward these goals from diverse and varied literatures on trans-national advocacy networks (Keck and Sikkink 1998; Risse et al. 2013), legal mobilization (Epp 1998; McCann 1994; Vanhala 2010, 2012), social accountability (Peruzzotti and Smulovitz 2006), and victim-led movements (Humphrey and Valverde 2007; Wright 2014). The mechanisms through which organized citizens improve legal outcomes in each of these accounts are conceptualized primarily at the collective level: movements influence the actions of state actors primarily through naming their crimes and shaming them for their actions, by recruiting powerful allies, and by taking advantage of political and legal opportunities (Tarrow 2011; Vanhala 2012). Socio-legal scholars, however, demonstrate that legal systems do not respond to collective pressures uniformly. The particular preferences and beliefs of judges (González-Ocantos 2016; Hilbink 2007) and the resources (Brinks 2008) and institutional role (Michel 2018) of individual claimants are all crucial to understanding why law, at times, rises to the challenge of conferring the status of rights-bearing citizens to the "hitherto powerless"—and why, all too often, it fails to do so.

This book unpacks the relationship between mobilization and impunity by focusing on the evolving thinking and actions of those most intimately affected by violence. I build most explicitly on the work of González-Ocantos (2016), who explores how and why the thinking of *judges* (and judicial bureaucrats) changes over time—and connects these changes in thinking to eroding impunity. I flip the focus in the citizen-state interaction. I look at how and why the thinking of *victim claimants* evolves—and likewise connect how the changes in their thinking lead to the erosion of impunity. I argue that as people participate in ongoing mobilization and claim-making over time, (1) their legal consciousness shifts, and with these shifts, (2) their understandings of and ability to challenge impunity are likewise transformed.

Observable Outcomes/Actions

As illustrated in Figure 1.1, *sustained mobilization* includes both sustained claim-making and collective action. I understand *claim-making* as "citizens' efforts to secure established rights and entitlements" (Gallagher, Kruks-Wisner, and Taylor forthcoming). In the context of the past decade in Mexico, claim-making has included filing reports of disappearances with multiple

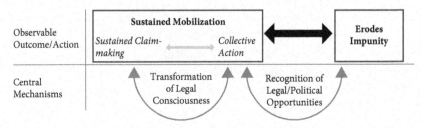

Figure 1.1 Argument summary

state and international legal entities, engaging in ongoing participatory investigatory meetings with state officials, and undertaking investigatory activity independently and in collaboration with state agencies. I understand *collective action* as action taken by a group of people in pursuit of a common goal or objective. Collective action, as used in this book, includes both commonly understood contentious actions like protests, hunger strikes, and sit-ins/occupations, and also innovations to the contentious repertoire, including independent searches for the missing and caravans—mobile protests employed to shine a light on distinct local contexts and/or physically bring together geographically distant communities.

Impunity, while observable, is more complicated as a concept than often assumed. Impunity is generally understood and defined as the state's failure to punish; that is, as the failure to establish individual criminal accountability for a given crime or crimes (Engle et al. 2016; Haldemann and Unger 2018). Does it follow, therefore, that by holding the individual perpetrator of a crime legally accountable, impunity is eliminated? Both internationally accepted principles and victims' movements tell us, definitively, that it's not that simple.

In 1997, on the heels of the Cold War and amid a context of new genocidal violence in Rwanda and Bosnia,[6] the UN Human Rights Commission created a Set of Principles for combating impunity[7]—a framework which lays

---

[6] These principles build on a 1988 decision by the Inter-American Court of Human Rights, which found that "the State has a legal duty . . . to use the means at its disposal to carry out a serious investigation of violations committed within its jurisdiction, to identify those responsible, to impose the appropriate punishment and to ensure the victim adequate compensation" (Velásquez-Rodríguez v. Honduras, par. 174).

[7] The 38 Principles define impunity as "the impossibility, de jure or de facto, of bringing the perpetrators of violations to account—whether in criminal, civil, administrative or disciplinary proceedings—since they are not subject to any inquiry that might lead to their being accused, arrested, tried and, if found guilty, sentenced to appropriate penalties, and to making reparations to their victims." These principles were updated in 2005, and have never been formally adopted by the Human Rights Commission/Council or the General Assembly. According to Haldemann and Unger

out the obligations of states to alleviate impunity. These obligations include not only guaranteeing the right to justice but also the right to truth, the right to reparation, and the right to a guarantee of non-recurrence.[8] In the language of the Principles:

> Impunity arises from a failure by States to meet their obligations to investigate violations; to take appropriate measures in respect of the perpetrators, particularly in the area of justice, by ensuring that those suspected of criminal responsibility are prosecuted, tried and duly punished; to provide victims with effective remedies and to ensure that they receive reparation for the injuries suffered; to ensure the inalienable right to know the truth about violations; and to take other necessary steps to prevent a recurrence of violations." (UN Principles to Combat Impunity 2005: General Obligation, Principle 1)

Within the right to know, victims' rights in particular are specified: "Irrespective of any legal proceedings, victims and their families have the imprescriptible right to know the truth about the circumstances in which violations took place and, in the event of death or disappearance, the victims' fate" (UN Principles to Combat Impunity 2005: Part II, Section A, Principle 4).

The concept and language of impunity have been vernacularized[9] within countries struggling with widespread violence and dysfunctional domestic judicial systems. Impunity is used by victims of violence to talk not only about their desire for the perpetrators to be punished, but also to call for a full account of violent crimes, to demand that the state take measures to prevent future violence, and that the state provide comprehensive redress for crimes already committed. At times, criminal responsibility can actually feel quite beside the point and disconnected from justice. This is expressed clearly by

---

(2018, 10), "[The impunity] principles are best seen as flexible instruments of guidance with the potential to gradually acquire, through widespread usage, quasi-legal recognition."

[8] "Non-recurrence," synonymous with "non-repetition," refers to the international legal concept that states are obliged to take all necessary steps to ensure that a grave rights violation does not happen again. It is often referred to in the transitional justice literature as the "Never Again" promise (see Davidovic 2021).

[9] "Vernacularization" is generally understood as the process by which international human rights ideas are translated into terms appropriate for local contexts (see Merry 2006).

Nancy Rosete, whom I introduced earlier. After the perpetrator of the disappearance of her son was imprisoned, she told me:

> I felt like the lawyers were saying to me "look *señora*—look what we achieved!" But I answered them—"And? And my son? Where is my son?" It doesn't help me that this man is locked up—I have forgiven him. I am looking for justice; I am looking for my son.

In this book, I adopt a broad and inclusive definition of combating impunity and ask what role victims of crime play in advancing the rights to truth, justice, reparations, and non-recurrence. My decision to employ this broader definition of combating impunity was inductively derived: after working with the family members whose loved ones were killed or disappeared more than a decade ago, it was abundantly clear that their understanding of what it takes to address impunity is not limited to legally punishing those responsible. While people's understanding of impunity varies widely, among the hundreds of families I interviewed, the right to know *dónde están*—where are they?—lies at the heart of their demands.

Central Mechanisms

While the aforementioned concepts are observable and measurable, the processes and mechanisms[10] through which claim-making and collective action lead to an erosion of impunity are more difficult to observe. Complicating matters further, and as illustrated in Figure 1.1 by the double-headed arrows, these processes are non-linear and often cyclical in nature: claim-making transforms legal consciousness, which in turn shapes both collective action and the ability of victims to recognize political and legal opportunities. To ground these complex and iterative processes empirically, I rely on life history interviews and longitudinal ethnography conducted in both social movement and institutional contexts over the past decade.

---

[10] McAdam, Tarrow, and Tilly (2001) define mechanisms as "delimited changes that alter relations among specified sets of elements in identical or closely similar ways over a variety of situations" (24).

Transforming Legal Consciousness

Like most victims' families in Mexico, each of the families profiled in the book was apolitical prior to the disappearances of their loved ones: neither they nor their disappeared loved ones (that they know of) had ever been to a protest, joined a social movement, or lobbied a politician. Over the course of the past decade, they have transformed into vocal advocates, determined activists, and social movement participants or leaders. How do we explain their transformations? Existing explanations of why people mobilize are useful in understanding why individuals make claims, protest, or join social movements at one point in time—most often when they *begin* to mobilize— including their previous experiences with the state (Wood 2003); the relative benefits and costs (Ostrom 2000); whether their life circumstances allow them to mobilize (McAdam 1986); and whether others in their social networks are mobilizing (Kruks-Wisner 2018). Wood understands the underlying reasons for *ongoing* mobilization as rooted in their evolving political culture—their "values, norms, practices, beliefs, and collective identity" (19), while Kruks-Wisner finds that as people's socio-spatial exposure changes, what people imagine is possible likewise shifts. I lean into both of these insights to understand ongoing claim-making and collective action, homing in on the ways that ongoing mobilization itself shifts people's reasons for, capability for, and forms of mobilizing.

As I sought to make sense of the transformation of the many people I had gotten to know during the course of this study, I found that the literature on legal consciousness articulated a crucial part of their stories by unpacking the everyday ways in which people think of themselves in relation to the law and legality.[11] In Ewick and Silbey's (1998) pioneering study of how New Jersey residents respond to conflict and rights violations, they outline three primary ways that their respondents think about themselves in relation to the law: "before the law," when they view the law as distant, reliable, and ultimately just; "against the law" when they see the legal system as aligned against them—the law is harsh, unjust, and arbitrary; and "with the law," when they

---

[11] Merry (1990, 5) defines legal consciousness as "the ways people understand and use the law . . . the way people conceive of the 'natural' and normal way of doing things, their habitual patterns of talk and action, and their common-sense understanding of the world." Ewick and Silbey (1998) elaborate: legal consciousness is "a reciprocal process in which the meanings given by individuals to their world become patterned, stabilized, and objectified. These meanings, once institutionalized, become part of the material and discursive systems that limit and constrain future meaning making. . . . Through language, society furnishes images of what those opportunities and resources are: how the world works, what is possible, and what is not" (39).

see the law as a game with individual actors to be manipulated, navigated, and, ultimately, won. I found that these paradigms illuminated the ways in which people I knew and had interviewed thought of themselves in relation to the law when they began mobilizing—though I realized each had shifted their way of thinking, speaking, and acting over time.

The literature on legal consciousness understands legality as "enduring"— in other words, as relatively stable and fixed throughout someone's life— because it is "embedded in and emerges out of daily activities" (Ewick and Silbey 1998, 17). Interestingly, scholars of legal consciousness draw on episodes of conflict in their studies[12] to reveal the "quotidian character of law and legality" because

> when the routine and the mundane *seemed to break down* . . . we believed that people's interpretations and accounts of these problems would re-veal their unarticulated understandings of the mundane: in short, that the taken-for-granted would reveal itself in its breach. (Ewick and Silbey 1998, 28, emphasis added)

What happens, then, when a traumatic experience wholly refigures the rou-tine and mundane? When a moment of conflict does not merely *reveal* the underlying relationships, understandings, and values that people had coming into the conflict—but *transforms* them? How does our understanding of legal consciousness change when the nature of the grievance is bigger: when it challenges where people live, how they make their living, what they do every day, their relationships with their family, and how frequently they interact with state institutions and personnel?

I argue that in the face of the traumatic aftermath of disappearances, the legal consciousness of victims who choose to engage in sustained mobili-zation is transformed. As victims meet, clash with, and build relationships with a variety of state officials situated throughout the expansive state ju-dicial and political bureaucracy, reified and unitary understandings of the state may become dislodged. Like many middle-income countries, the ter-rain of the Mexican state is highly uneven: its "reach, visibility and accessi-bility" (Kruks-Wisner 2018, 5) vary drastically within its territory. Because

---

[12] Merry (1990), for example, looks at lower courts and the ways in which people use them to sort out family and neighborhood conflicts; Nielsen (2000) looks at offensive public speech and how people think it should be dealt with, or not, by the law; Sarat (1990) looks at welfare applicants in the aftermath of being denied benefits.

of this, victim activists engaged in sustained mobilization will likewise begin to think of both individual officials and particular agencies, states, or localities as more or less helpful to them in their efforts to dislodge impunity. Their experiences, observations, and reflections will lead them toward an understanding of legality as an "ensemble of legal actors, organizations, rules, and procedures" (Ewick and Silbey, 1998, 131). That is, they will be led to a "with the law" perspective and away from the "before" and "against" the law perspectives. Shifts in thinking beget further transformation: as they shift their vision of legality, they are spurred to acquire more knowledge and skills to strategically engage with state actors, which in turn convinces them further of law and legality as a contested, thoroughly human arena.

Recognizing Legal/Political Opportunities, and Eroding Impunity

Why do the ways in which victims think about themselves in relation to the law matter for understanding the erosion of impunity? Intuitively, we know there is a connection between how people think and act. As Taylor (2018) explains:

> Behavior is the manifestation of how an individual understands themselves relative to their social contexts. . . . [O]ne's understanding of the world— which, again, is socially constructed but individually held—encourages and discourages certain sets of actions, rendering X thinkable and doable, while Y unthinkable and therefore undoable. (346)

I argue that the disruptive nature of disappearance reconfigures what is thinkable, imaginable—and therefore doable. As victims develop a more nuanced understanding of state officials and institutions, they are increasingly able to strategically navigate the uneven terrain of the state. This process of transformation dynamically affects both individuals and collectives: individuals learn through direct experience as well as from talking with each other about possible political and legal openings; they move fluidly between actions that are more effective on their own (usually involving their own cases) and those which are more likely to be successful if they are undertaken collectively (e.g., accessing state officials); and collectives draw upon the ever-growing and evolving savvy of their members. Through sustained mobilization, common contentious repertoires have evolved that are employed by both individuals and collectives: (1) confronting the state, (2) leveraging political pressure to access state officials, (3) strategically navigating the state's judicial bureaucracy, (4) locating allies within the state, and (5) participating in independent searches for their loved ones.

This contentious repertoire has evolved iteratively; it has been shaped by and has also shaped the legal and political opportunities to combat impunity in Mexico. Prior to democratization in 2000, the Mexican state's terrain was more uniform, and as a result, there were many fewer political opportunities for victim-led advocacy. After the current wave of violence began in 2006, human rights organizations at first guided civil society's response to the violence, filling one of two roles: they positioned themselves either as *activists*, who critique the state, use more confrontational tactics, and strenuously contradict the state's narrative criminalizing victims, or as *advocates*, who collaborate with state officials to investigate disappearances.[13] As the victims' movement coalesced, however, small victim-led collectives emerged in every state affected by violence. These collectives were able to draw on knowledge and repertoires both from the individuals within their organizations and from the cumulative experience of collectives and more established organizations throughout the country. Unlike established human rights organizations, which needed to develop an identity as activists *or* advocates to have external credibility, victims' collectives developed a nearly irreproachable political legitimacy that let them pick and choose which strategies to deploy depending on the political context. They were able to draw from *activist strategies*, which include vocally denouncing and critiquing the state and engaging in confrontational action; and *advocacy strategies*, building relationships with officials within the state who are potential allies. These collectives use their political legitimacy and legal standing as victims[14] to develop and strategically deploy these evolving contentious repertoires.

What has the strategic deployment of these strategies looked like in practice? And how has it affected impunity? In Figure 1.2 I present a stylized account of how the uneven terrain of the state is perceived by mobilized victims, and the corresponding outcomes that are possible if they mobilize.

When victims develop a "with the law" perspective, they increasingly see legality "as an arena in which actors struggle to achieve a variety of purposes"

---

[13] In prior work (Gallagher 2017), I argue that activists and advocates play distinct roles in breaking through tenacious patterns of impunity, with activists upping the political costs of investigatory inaction, and advocates facilitating the flow of investigative information between victims and state investigators. These concepts are elaborated on and updated in Chapter 3.

[14] Mexican victims have legal standing to participate in the processes involved in their cases under a provision known as *co-ayudvancia*. See Michel (2018) for an in-depth exploration of the origins, functioning, and impact of this legal innovation.

Perceived Motivation of State Official(s)	State Alliances	
	Stable	Unstable
Cynical	Impunity	Strategic Prosecution
Solidarity	Searching	Erosion of Impunity

Figure 1.2 Political opportunities to combat impunity

(Ewick and Silbey 1998, 131). This view of the law orients victims to seek to achieve whatever inroads against impunity are possible in any given setting. Said differently, it predisposes them to a strategic and pragmatic approach. While mobilized victims weigh a number of factors when deciding how and where/to whom to direct their mobilization and claim-making, I focus on two key contextual variables: how victims perceive the motivation of state official(s), and state alliances. When victim activists perceive that state officials' *motivations* are *cynical*—that is, self-interested at the expense of their professional duty to serve the public—they will pursue different strategies and expect different outcomes from those they would anticipate when they perceive state officials as acting out of a sense of *solidarity* with them. These perceptions are most often associated with an individual—an investigator, judicial bureaucrat, or high-level official—though their assessment may extend to an entire branch of the attorney general's office—for example, when the person in charge is viewed as acting decisively against them or on their behalf. The perceived motivations of most officials, of course, lie on a spectrum between these two ideal types, but I find that these are analytically useful categories to help us understand the importance of perceived enemies and allies within the judicial bureaucracy, which is often viewed from the outside as a coherent entity with interchangeable officials. In short, the (perceived) motivations of individual state bureaucrats matter for challenging/maintaining impunity.

Next, I shift my unit of analysis: I think about how different types of *state alliances*—both alliances *within* the state (i.e., between judicial officials and politicians; or between members of competing political parties), and also *between* state officials and members of organized crime/drug trafficking organizations (DTOs)—can create opportunities to erode impunity. I find that the dynamism within criminal and collusive alliance networks creates unexpected political opportunities. Scholars of both social movements (Tarrow

2011) and political violence[15] commonly think of elite divisions opening up political opportunities when political parties compete, when there are disagreements within leadership teams, or when different levels and/or sectors of elites disagree (i.e., inter-governmental with national; or local business interests with local elected officials). I add the divisions between and among state officials and members of organized crime as an additional category and argue that shifting alliances between these groups can lead to substantive political and legal openings to challenge impunity. Similar to the motivations of state officials, victims need to perceive these legal openings in order to take advantage of them—something they become better at doing with more experience and as their legal consciousness evolves.

As Figure 1.2 illustrates, given the Mexican context of normalized collusion between the state and DTOs, when state alliances are stable and victims deem state motivation as cynical, *impunity* is likely to be tenacious. Victims may engage in activism and searching independent of the state, though they may be actively deterred due to security concerns. While victims may make limited efforts to engage in advocacy, they learn quickly that this is not viable: advocacy requires an openness on the part of the state to negotiating with victims and building relationships. As I discuss in Chapter 3, impunity has evolved to be the norm throughout the Mexican justice system, particularly in cases of disappearances. Because of this, with cynical state officials and stable alliances, it will be difficult to disrupt the processes that guarantee impunity.

When victims perceive that either state alliances are unstable or state motivations are not entirely cynical, I argue that opportunities for cracks in the wall of impunity emerge. That is, when it is clear to victims that political dynamics are shifting or that state officials are willing to act in solidarity with the disappeared, this can meaningfully disrupt impunity. All political opportunities are not equal, however.

- When state officials are perceived as acting in *solidarity* with victims in otherwise *stable* (and corrupt) political alliance environments, it may be possible to nonetheless advance the right to truth by *searching* for the disappeared—while intentionally limiting any investigation into the circumstances or perpetrators of the disappearance. This is often done

---

[15] In the Mexican context, for example, Trejo and Ley (2020) explore how changes in state and national-level political parties open (and close) political opportunities and affect violence.

by searching for remains in mass graves, and matching the DNA profiles of remains with the DNA of the family members of the disappeared. Victims recognize that activist tactics in these environments are risky— as are any calls to investigate the circumstances of the disappearance or to hold the perpetrators legally responsible. In such environments, "quiet advocacy" has been possible, resulting in the identification of the remains of the disappeared. With "quiet advocacy," meetings between victims and state agents may occur, but they will happen without public documentation or notification, and the results will not be publicized.

- When state officials are perceived to be *cynically motivated* and state alliances are *unstable,* I argue that advancing the right to justice through *strategic prosecution* is the most likely outcome. Strategic prosecution means that certain perpetrators may be vulnerable to prosecution while others won't be. For example, an incoming political party—which has likely publicly taken up victims' call to address violence and impunity in their campaign—may decide to prosecute former officials who are members of a competing political party in order to appear to be making good on their campaign promise. Or, as the control of the plaza shifts either because of state-sponsored attacks or intra-DTO power struggles, members of newly disempowered DTOs may become vulnerable to prosecution if their fall from power also erodes their protective rela- tionship with state officials. In both instances, political logics are driving prosecution and impunity—not the merits of any particular case. In this scenario, victims may continue to deploy activist strategies to call for an end to impunity, but they will most likely be crowded out of meaningful advocacy except in cases of disappearances that the cynical state actor views as politically expedient (i.e., the perpetrator is a political enemy). Victims may indeed calculate that some prosecution is better than none and choose to support the politically driven prosecution(s).

- When state officials who are perceived to act in *solidarity* with the victims are located in environments with *unstable* political alliances, the *erosion of impunity* on multiple fronts may be possible. When, for example, an incoming governor and/or an attorney general is perceived as an ally, they may actively incentivize and reward state agents who sincerely in- vestigate disappearances and even pursue prosecution against those responsible. Disappearances may be investigated immediately, and the highest possibility of people being found alive exists. In this environ- ment, both activist and advocacy strategies may be employed: there is enough political space for victims to denounce judicial dysfunction and widespread impunity, and there are state allies available to partner with and establish participatory investigations. In this more open political and security environment, victim collectives may deploy the full range of tactics they have developed both as a group and as individuals advocating on behalf of their cases. This may allow them not only to advance their right to truth and justice but also to craft agreements and legislation that address the right to non-recurrence and reparations.

In each of the scenarios described, concrete advances in victims' quest to address impunity are possible in ways that were not imaginable 10 years ago. One central investigatory innovation in the past decade has been necessary to enable each of these forms of combating impunity: *mesas de trabajo*, which I loosely translate as participatory investigations.

When outsiders imagine what justice looks like in cases of serious human rights abuses and deadly violence, they may picture a standard courtroom with an impartial judge adjudicating a case argued by opposing lawyers; and investigators interviewing individual witnesses and assembling their case, forming hypotheses and lines of argument based on their evidence. The reality of investigations into disappearances in Mexico does not resemble this. While the content of these meetings varies significantly, the scene illustrated in Figure 1.3 is typical. Representatives from different local, state, and federal bureaucracies are seated at a table with the victim's family member and a member of a victims' collective. At these meetings, family members of victims, their civil society allies, and members of different state agencies make agreements about who will undertake different investigatory actions including searching for a disappeared person in a specific location; obtaining cell phone records; negotiating the logistics of search parties; discussing protectionary measures for the family members; and reviewing relevant legislation. When I began this research in 2011, the form of these participatory investigations was still being forged at great cost by several organizations in states hard hit by violence in the north of Mexico.[16]

---

[16] These organizations included two Chihuahua City, Chihuahua, organizations: Justicia para Nuestras Hijas (Justice for Our Daughters) and Centro de Derechos Humanos de las Mujeres (CEDEHM, Center for Women's Rights) (see Gallagher 2015; Michel 2019); Ciudadanos en Apoyo de los Derechos Humanos (CADHAC, Citizens in Support of Human Rights) in Monterrey, Nuevo León; and Fuerzas Unidas para Nuestros Desaparecidos en Coahuila/en México (FUUNDEC/ FUUNDEM, Forces United for Our Disappeared-Coahuila/Mexico) in Saltillo, Coahuila. CEDEHM

Figure 1.3 Participatory investigation meeting. A meeting between state officials and victims' collective representatives, Acapulco, Guerrero, December 13, 2016

Source: Comisión de los Derechos Humanos del Estado de Guerrero, in response to author's information request

The document shown in Figure 1.4 is an example of meeting notes from a participatory investigation. Based on my experience observing these meetings personally in Nuevo León and within the federal prosecutors' office as well as interviewing victim advocates about their experiences in these meetings in an additional seven states, these notes appear very typical of what happens in these meetings. Although the notes are handwritten, they are fairly formal. They report that this participatory investigation meeting was held on August 3, 2019, to discuss the investigation into the September 2017 disappearance of a young man in Baja California. These notes, documenting one of eight meetings that day, recount that those assembled have met

pioneered participatory investigations in response to the 2009 Inter-American Court on Human Rights (IACtHR) Campo Algodonero ruling. Prior to 2014, it was common for victims' collectives to hold marches, go on hunger strikes (as we will see Nancy do in Chapter 4), and set up *plantones*— essentially, encampments—outside government offices in order to pressure the state to agree to hold these meetings. International organizations, including the UN High Commissioner for Human Rights, Human Rights Watch, along with national organizations like the MPJD, were often able to broker meetings between local victims' collectives and state officials and make some modest investigatory advances (Gallagher 2017). In places where there have never been participatory investigations or where we have seen alternation in personnel and administrations, mobilization may still be necessary to persuade the state to establish these meetings with the local victims' collective.

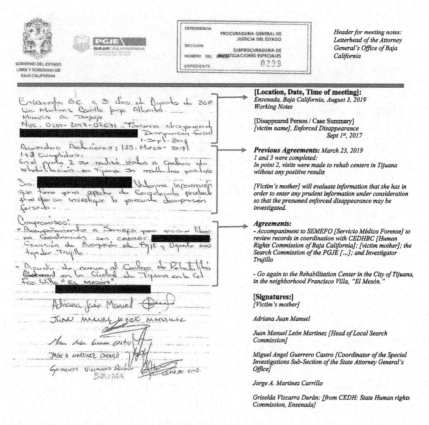

Figure 1.4 Participatory investigation meeting notes
Source: Information provided by the Procuraduría General de Justicia del Estado, State Attorney General's Office, in response to author Information Request to Baja California government

previously, and that two of the three agreements made previously have been achieved (though it does not state what those agreements were). They make new agreements: in this case, Investigator Trujillo from the state attorney general's office (PGJE), in coordination with someone from the State Human Rights Commission of Baja California, will accompany the disappeared man's mother to the Forensic Medical Office, where DNA and identifying information about unidentified corpses is presumably held and where they will search for the remains of her son. They will also go to the "El Mesón" Rehabilitation Center in Tijuana. It is unclear from this document what the purpose of that visit is: it could be to check the records to see if her son was or is there. It could also be to investigate a lead about a possible perpetrator linked to this location. While most of the actions taken in this particular case appear to be aimed at locating the victim, the case notes from other participatory investigations held the same day point to more investigative actions, including getting a new *ministerio público* (public prosecutor), assigned to a case; continuing to interview possible witnesses; sharing audio recordings and analyzing phone calls; and checking social media profiles of people who may have known the victim.

Initially, hopes were high for participatory investigations—and outcomes were promising. Human Rights Watch wrote in 2013 that

> in the state of Nuevo León, where government officials and prosecutors, responding to pressure from victims' families and human rights defenders, have broken with a pattern of inaction and incompetence, and begun to seriously investigate a select group of disappearances. Their efforts have helped win back the trust of victims' relatives and, with it, their collaboration, which has proven critical to identifying new leads and gathering valuable evidence. . . . [T]he approach provides a blueprint for overcoming some of the greatest obstacles to resolving disappearance cases. (Human Rights Watch 2013)

The early promise of participatory investigations led to their widespread adoption, and as I discuss in Chapters 3 and 4, they have become central to most victims' collectives' work and strategy. One critique of participatory investigations has been that they require an immense amount of work on the part of the victims' family. What can we say about what victims have been able to accomplish through their exhaustive efforts combating impunity?

Bootstrap Justice: From Rights-Claiming to Rights-Bearing Citizens

As I discuss above, states are obligated to guarantee their citizens' rights to justice, truth, non-recurrence, and reparations. While Mexico has done a remarkable job of codifying this broad array of rights into law, giving them constitutional priority, and rendering elegant Constitutional Court decisions (see Gallagher and Contesse forthcoming), Mexico is also largely incapable of and/or unwilling to make good on these promised rights. This gap between increasingly well-codified rights and their implementation is not something particular to Mexico: others have referred to the phenomenon as a "de jure-de facto gap" (Gallagher et al. 2022) or the "parchment-practice gap" (Kapiszewski et al. 2021). Understanding what citizens do in contexts where this gap is particularly wide—where formal legal processes are deeply dysfunctional and where these "guaranteed" rights are routinely violated with little consequence—is the focus of this book. Citizen action in the face of normalized rights violations range from resigning themselves to rights non-fulfillment, often referred to as "lumping" their grievances; to dedicating themselves to changing the state's behavior through mobilization and/or repeated claim-making; and finally, to attempting to fulfill the right/redress the violation themselves or through collective action and alternative forms of justice.

Apart from lumping, these responses require enormous effort and initiative on the part of citizens—and are why, in part, I entitled this book *Bootstrap Justice*. "Pulling oneself up by their bootstraps" is understood in the United States context as an individual changing their life circumstances—most classically, lifting themselves out of poverty—by sheer force of will. The roots of the expression, however, reveal its double-edged meaning. Linguists believe that "pulling oneself up by their bootstraps" originated in the 19th century and was used derisively to refer to someone who "claimed some ludicrously far-fetched or impossible task,"[17] like the one shown in Figure 1.5. By the 20th century, however, it had worked its way into the American lexicon to earnestly celebrate the rugged individualism of those who succeed and arise from difficult circumstances.

Our current understanding of someone pulling themselves up by their bootstraps is problematic: if some can single-handedly raise themselves out of their difficult circumstances, this implicitly lays the failure to overcome the impossible at the feet of each individual, attributing these failures to shortcomings in their character and/or effort. Inherent to its conceptualization is a willful ignorance of the structural and institutional barriers to personal achievement. *Bootstrap Justice*, then, expresses both the seemingly ludicrous idea that it is possible for a person to manifest justice through force of will and without state involvement; and also honors the initiative and ingenuity of families forced to create their own versions of justice in the face of incapable and unwilling institutions.

---

[17] See discussion at https://www.barrypopik.com/index.php/new_york_city/entry/pull_yourself_up_by_your_bootstraps/.

Figure 1.5 Baron Münchhausen, a historic character, performing the impossible—thought to be one of the origin stories of the expression "Pulling yourself up by your bootstraps."

The idea of bootstrapping—taking on a seemingly impossible task—also helps to explain families' persistence against the resistant state. Simmons (2016) and Wood (2003) remind us that the decision to mobilize and thoughts about how to respond to rights violations are rarely rational—instead driven by people's values, emotions, and the societal contexts in which they are immersed. Building on their insights, I argue that claim-making persists in spite of state unresponsiveness when the nature of the grievance is particularly compelling and disruptive to a person's life, and when the stakes of, and pleasure taken, in asserting one's agency are high. I posit that with very few exceptions, people who experience the disappearance of a loved one have the urge and impetus to do something. The nature of the disappearances—a person missing with no explanation; the possibility that they may be alive and suffering; the preclusion of closure—propels family members to action. That action often includes some type of interaction with the legal and security arm of the state—calling the police, going to report the crime, or going to one of the myriad state offices tasked with attending to victims of violence, including the State Human Rights Commissions, Victims' Committees, or

Search Units. The behavior of these state entities is, again, nearly always unsatisfactory: the outcome people seek is the return of their loved ones, and this almost never happens. The urgent unmet need to find their loved ones paired with the incompetence and/or inaction of the state has created the conditions in Mexico for ongoing claim-making, with no end in sight.

How does rights-claiming relate to becoming a rights-bearing citizen? While the state is the ultimate arbiter of rights, we know that different rights place distinct demands on the state. Much of this book is concerned with the right to justice—that is, the right of each person who has been disappeared to have the perpetrators of their disappearance brought to account and held criminally responsible. This right is thought of, traditionally, as being carried out nearly entirely within the state's apparatus. While cause lawyers (Sarat and Scheingold 2006) and private prosecutors (Michel 2018) have found ways to institutionally insert victims and advocates within legal proceedings, the protagonists of investigation and prosecution are still considered to be state judicial officials. With other rights tied to combating impunity, rights fulfillment is less clearly entirely dependent on, or even possible solely relying on, the state: the right to non-recurrence is an enormous, ambitious one requiring the collaborative transformation of society; the right to truth may seem like a sub-right of justice (since investigating is part of the right to justice), but truth can also be unearthed by the independent fact-finding of journalists and victims themselves. The right to reparations is most often facilitated by the state, but it is spurred by, and often necessitates the involvement, of non-state, civil society actors (see De Greiff 2008).

If the state is largely (or even partly) responsible for providing a right, does it follow that for a citizen to become rights-bearing, the state would have to act? Not necessarily. An individual or group can do much of the work necessary to secure a wide range of rights: not only in rights areas generally considered to be positive rights (work, housing, health, etc.), but also in those considered negative rights like safety and security. To what extent, then, can individuals fulfill the rights necessary to obviate impunity—independent of, or in spite of, the state? In other words—is it possible to bootstrap justice? As I illustrate throughout the book and especially in Chapter 6, the answer is—partly. While the overwhelming majority of disappeared people are never found, advances—in what victims can expect to learn about their disappeared loved one, and the possibility that some judicial processes might move forward if the family members of the disappeared person engaged in sustained mobilization—have grown considerably in the past decade through the efforts of the victims, though these advances are appreciable only in comparison with the blanket impunity that is the norm in Mexico. As is most likely true for individuals who are seen as having pulled *themselves* up by their bootstraps, the most successful outcomes in fact rely on a (metaphorical) *village* coming together—including the committed family members of the disappeared person, their civil society supporters, and allies within the state.

Mexico Context and Puzzle

How did it fall to the family members of the disappeared in Mexico to attempt the herculean feat of bootstrapping justice? In this section, I briefly zoom out to understand how the political system in Mexico came to normalize rights violations and impunity, leaving victims to fend for themselves.

For eight decades, Mexico's presidency was occupied by the PRI, or the Institutional Revolutionary Party, which was famously dubbed the "perfect dictatorship."[18] Beginning in the 1920s, the party maintained control by appeasing their key constituencies—workers, farmers, the urban poor, and the military—through allocating political favors, government jobs, and public goods. Cracks first began to appear in this cooptation strategy after the 1968 Tlatelolco massacre, in which scores of students were gunned down by the military as they protested PRI government policies just as Mexico was preparing to take the world stage to host the Olympics. Government repression continued through the Mexican Dirty War, which lasted roughly from the 1960s to 2000. It was a low-intensity conflict and mirrored the logic of many other Latin American dictatorships: opposition leaders particularly in areas with robust histories of resistance, such as the state of Guerrero and Mexico City, were most heavily targeted. According to the official report issued by the Mexican government, there were 645 disappearances, 99 extrajudicial executions, and more than 2,000 cases of torture during this period.[19] While the scale of this repression was fairly limited compared with other 20th-century dictatorships in Latin America, it nevertheless inspired a small

---

[18] Famed Peruvian writer Mario Vargas Llosa, visiting Mexico in 1990, said, "I do not believe that Mexico can be exonerated from the tradition of Latin American dictatorships. . . . Mexico is the perfect dictatorship. . . . It is a camouflaged dictatorship: It has the characteristics of the dictatorship: the permanence, not of a man, but of a party. And of a party that is irremovable," (El País 1990).

[19] Figures are from the National Security Archive (2006).

core of human rights organizations, based primarily in Mexico City. These organizations became well versed in the practices of naming and shaming state-perpetrated and politically motivated repression and would bring this experience into their response to the increasing violence that began after 2006.

Mexican civil society has historically been coopted by or dependent on the state, with unions and civic organizations serving more as a base for PRI party support than any true alternative locus of power. As the PRI's control started to crumble toward the end of the 20th century, more independent-minded members of civil society focused their energy on ensuring free and fair elections. These efforts were boosted by the ostentatious displays of state incompetence in managing the economy and corruption scandals in the aftermath of the 1985 Mexico City earthquake and the fiercely contested (and probably fraudulent) 1988 presidential election. When the PRI finally lost the presidency in 2000, much of civil society breathed a sigh of relief: they had succeeded in pushing Mexico to hold free and fair elections, and many believed that they would finally reap the benefits of liberal democracy. Many went to work for the government, or received government funds to consult on projects they expected to flourish in Mexico's democratic spring.

The PRI's 2000 electoral defeat marked a new era in Mexican politics, but newly democratic Mexico quickly disappointed most of its citizens. The PRI's rule had left a state bureaucracy bloated with employees but short on governing capacity. Under the six-year term, of Vicente Fox (2000–2006), the Mexican state's shortcomings were clear. Despite Fox's campaign promises and efforts at reform, unemployment, crime, and corruption rose; inequality deepened; and the economy stagnated. Behind the scenes, a crisis was growing. Mexican DTOs were capitalizing on the fragmentation and weakening of Colombia's drug cartels, growing richer and more powerful than ever before. When President Felipe Calderón took power in 2006, he confronted a highly decentralized country, with deeply corrupt officials, especially within local police forces and judicial systems. Although his motivations are subject to debate,[20] his approach to confronting the weak state and growing DTO power was clear: he sent the military into cartel hotspots with an explicit strategy to take out the leaders.

Calderón's strategy resulted in a sharp rise in a very different type of violence than Mexico had seen during the Dirty War. Where the government

---

[20] See Trejo and Ley (2020) for in-depth discussion of Calderón's motivations.

succeeded in taking down cartel leaders, highly visible violence erupted in many of Mexico's cities, as destabilized cartels engaged in grisly and open combat for control of the *plaza,* or the right to control the selling and trafficking of drugs in a given locality. As part of their struggle for territorial control, warring DTOs deepened pre-existing relationships with state officials and also built new alliances with all levels of law enforcement, notoriously coopting local and state police forces. This often meant that the line between violence perpetrated by state and criminal actors was blurry, or even non-existent.

Victim profiles also differed from those during the Dirty War. The victims caught in the crossfire were largely not politically active, and most were average working-class young men and women.[21] The government's official rhetoric during Calderón's term was that victims of violence *estaban en algo,* they were involved in something nefarious, and therefore were largely to blame for bringing violence upon themselves. The near total lack of investigation into homicides and disappearances, however, made this line of reasoning impossible to substantiate.

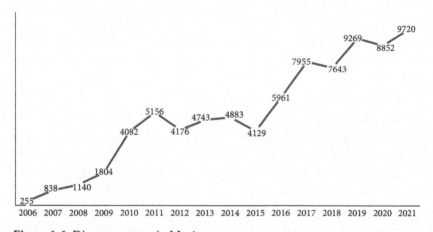

Figure 1.6 Disappearances in Mexico

Source: Registro Nacional de Personas Desaparecidas y No Localizadas

---

[21] Ansolabehere, Frey, and Payne (2021) do an in-depth analysis of victim identity in Mexico. They find that disappearances target "disposable" populations, which, they argue, are considered to be disposable by the state, "first, because of their marginal social status, and second, because the narratives in the region link disappearances to criminality, thereby rhetorically justifying their disappearance" (86).

As shown in Figure 1.6, this wave of violence resulted in an unprecedented and escalating number of disappearances and revealed a justice system incapable of holding accountable the perpetrators of violence against civilians. By the end of Calderón's term in 2012, more than 16,000 people had been disappeared. This number grew to more than 54,000 under Peña Nieto and has continued to climb under current president López Obrador.[22] In nearly all of these cases, the victims have not been found, and perpetrators have not been held accountable. While this book focuses on the inroads that have been made into this near-blanket impunity, it is vital to remember that cases being investigated at all—much less victims being found alive or identified by their remains—are still very much the exception to the rule.

As this violence continued to increase after 2006 under Calderón, the Mexican state, civil society, and the human rights community were caught largely flat-footed. In my early interviews with state officials in 2010 and 2011, nearly all of them used words like "unprepared" and "overwhelmed," and many spoke of the steep learning curve they were experiencing in responding to the spiraling violence. The human rights organizations had previously focused only on cases where the state was the clear perpetrator—in other words, cases fulfilling the standard definition of human rights abuses. Taking on these new kinds of violence would require "a change in identity," as the head of one of the largest human rights organization in Mexico told me in a 2013 interview.[23] The larger civil society community remained centralized in Mexico City, focused on other issues like health care, voting rights, and education. These are vital issues for the country to address, but they did not reflect or respond to the rise in lethal violence that had erupted in northern border states and in several central Mexican states where cartels were based and/or were key to the drug transit route. While the logic seems outdated now, at that time human rights and civil society organizations simply didn't realize the scale of the problem of disappearances, or didn't feel that *les pertenecía*, that is, that it was their responsibility to respond.

Toward the end of the Calderón administration, the tens of thousands of family members whose loved ones had disappeared found themselves with little institutional support. In social movement terms, conditions were

---

[22] *Registro Nacional de Personas Desaparecidas y No localizadas* (RNPDNO), https://www.gob. mx/cnb/documentos/informe-sobre-busqueda-e-identificacion-de-personas-desaparecidas-en-el-pais?state=published.

[23] The notable exceptions to this were the civil society and human rights organizations in Chihuahua. Many organizations had emerged in response to the femicides of the 2000s, providing a more institutionally dense environment to support victims of violence than in any other state.

inauspicious for mobilization. It was difficult to counter the government's framing that those affected by violence were involved in crime themselves and therefore not deserving of justice. Few organizations agreed to support the victims' family members, and these consisted mainly of small faith-based human rights organizations headquartered in border states, often with meager budgets and staffs of fewer than 10 people. Political and economic elites were somewhat split, with party loyalties divided between many state governors and the president; however, they provided a fairly unified front in support of Calderón's militarized approach to confronting drug traffickers. Engaging in mobilization presented a possible threat to the safety of family members, with newly empowered DTOs unpredictably exacting violent re-venge on those who challenged them.

Against the backdrop of this movement-averse environment, the loosely organized Movement for Peace with Justice and Dignity (MPJD) emerged in 2011.[24] After Juan Francisco Sicilia, a medical student, athlete, and son of prominent poet and public intellectual Javier Sicilia, was senselessly murdered, mass protests erupted. With the rallying cry *estamos hasta la madre*—roughly, "we've had enough," more than 100,000 Mexicans gathered in Mexico City's *zocalo* (central plaza) to demand an end to the violence.[25] While the MPJD itself would fade, it played a part in seeding many of the more than 100 victims' collectives currently active in at least 18 of Mexico's 32 states—most of which emerged during Peña Nieto's administration, and which hold some version of participatory investigations with state officials. After the high-profile disappearance of 43 students from the Rural Ayotzinapa Teachers' College in 2014, as the early experiences in Northern Mexico became more widely known—and as violence and in particular the number of disappearances continued to grow throughout Mexico— the frequency of participatory investigations grew throughout Mexico. It was not that these meetings were granted automatically, but as states sought to mollify the clamoring for justice of increasingly active and empowered local victims' organizations, participatory investigations became a more widely

---

[24] There had been previous protests, notably after the disappearance of business leader Fernando Martí's son in 2008; in the wake of the tragic 2009 fire that killed 49 children at the ABC daycare center in Hermosillo; and following the 2010 massacre of 16 teenagers in the Villas de Salvarcar neighborhood in Ciudad Juárez. The MPJD was the first to organize the family members who had been disappeared throughout the Mexican territory, and to channel the outrage over a single event into a sustained, broad-based movement.

[25] As with most protests, accounts of crowd size vary significantly.

used option. The outcomes of these participatory investigations are a significant focus of this book.

Empirical and Methodological Strategy

This book is epistemologically plural: I use an interpretivist lens as a researcher "making meaning out of the meaning making of other humans" (Pachirat 2015, 427), and a positivist approach to understand how the actions people take, whether individually or collectively, affect certain outcomes. Put simply, I construct an interpretivist conceptual base and then use those concepts to make positivist causal claims.[26] These approaches, while quite different, are not incompatible. Richard Nielsen, who memorized parts of the Qur'an during his fieldwork as he sought to understand why some clerics radicalize and others don't, "found that the interpretive practices I adopted in my fieldwork were essential to helping me produce solid *positivist* political science in my book" (Neilson 2020, 40). Wedeen (2010) agrees, and argues that "interpretive social science does not have to forswear generalizations or causal explanations and that ethnographic methods can be used in the service of establishing them. Rather than fleeing from abstractions, ethnographies can and should help ground them" (255).

In order to ground both the interpretivist and positivist claims made in this book, I have spent the past decade gathering a broad range of qualitative data. I conducted research in 18 of Mexico's 32 states and spent the most time in Mexican states that experienced relatively high levels of violence and/or in which mobilization flourished, including Chihuahua, Coahuila, Guerrero, Mexico City, Nuevo León, Tamaulipas, and Veracruz. In all, I conducted over 250 interviews, spent about three years immersed in intensive ethnographic observation, filed hundreds of information requests with state and federal government bodies, constructed an original case-level data set in collaboration with a non-governmental organization (NGO), and also conducted a randomized representative survey. For the past decade I have known the families profiled in this book and countless others who began to mobilize with the MPJD. The longevity of these relationships affords me a longitudinal understanding not only of institutional trajectories and outcomes, but also of

---

[26] I used a positivist approach to select my cases and to analyze the patterns and variation I observed in impunity at the individual, collective, and state level.

how the people involved in these struggles shaped and defined strategies, organizations, and institutions. These relationships, together with my position as an outsider, allow me to draw lessons from the experiences of Mexican citizens seeking justice within a system not designed to provide it. The arguments and evidence presented in this book were made possible through these long-term commitments to relationships in the field of inquiry. And of course, these insights would not be possible without the generous sharing of time, trust, and insight of the family members of the disappeared.

Case Selection

While my fieldwork gave me a broad understanding of the dynamics of mobilization and impunity in Mexico from 2006 through 2020, I relied in part on the positivist logic of comparative research design (Przeworski and Teune 1970) to answer the question of how people in places where rights violations are normalized transform into rights-claiming and rights-bearing citizens. I decided to anchor the empirics presented in the majority of this book in an in-depth study of three families. As I explain further in Chapter 2, I selected the families of focus for this book based on the logic of most different comparison: Nancy, Juan Carlos, and Lucía and Alfonso are from dramatically divergent class backgrounds, and their loved ones disappeared under quite different circumstances. They also vary in the extent to which they acted alone.[27] Despite having no prior political experience, these families all engage in sustained mobilization following the disappearance of their loved ones between 2008 and 2011. This research design enables me to understand the common dynamics operating across these cases: to understand, in other words, what was shared across their processes of transformation.

Implicit in my research design is the presumption that legal consciousness, while socially constructed, varies individually (Taylor 2018), and that focusing on individual processes of transformation is central to understanding

---

[27] I consider Lucía and Alfonso as a couple rather than as individuals, because they processed, strategized, and acted as a unit: I cannot think of a time when I attended a participatory investigation session, a march, or a social movement meeting that one attended without the other. Juan Carlos often is accompanied by other family members, most commonly his mother, María Herrera, known affectionately as Doña Mari. However, Doña Mari, Juan Carlos, and other brothers, including his brother Miguel, mobilize in different spaces, with different methodologies, and according to distinct logics. Nancy, while supported by members of her family, mobilizes without the accompaniment of other family members.

the erosion of impunity. But social movements are deeply entwined in individuals' transformation: they are the sites in which individuals' socio-spatial situating shifts most dramatically; where contentious repertoires are learned and diffused; and in which individuals like those profiled here exert collective agency to access state officials, draft new laws, and join together to search for their loved ones. In other words, understanding how individuals become rights-claiming and -bearing citizens is explicable only by looking also at the work of these movements.

Because the movements that individuals participate in are interconnected with how they capitalize on political opportunities, I also include a brief case study of how victims' collectives situated in three different Mexican states work to strategically erode impunity. As I explain in Chapter 5, I focus on the political dynamics within the states of Nuevo León, Tamaulipas, and Veracruz. These cases were chosen for what they share: in each of these states, power alternated due to the entrance of a governor from a different political party during the time of study. Additionally, each state had been controlled by the Zetas—a DTO renowned for ruling through brutality and intimidation rather than appealing to the sympathy of the local population—in the early 2010s. These commonalities meant that the modalities of DTO violence and disappearances were somewhat similar. This most similar research design allowed to me gain an understanding of what drove the disparate outcomes we see in these states.

Ethnography and Ethics

To understand how the families of focus, and so many like them, transform into rights-claiming and, ultimately, rights-bearing citizens, I primarily used an interpretivist lens to analyze ethnographic data—an approach especially well-suited to the "how" questions central to the operation of mechanisms in contentious politics. As Fu and Simmons (2021) explain, "How questions differ fundamentally from variation-finding questions because they invite researchers to discover new variables, processes, and causal connections apart from explaining an observed variation" (1698). This approach helped me to understand victim activists—rather than leading NGOs, judges, or politicians—as the central and important actors in understanding the Mexican justice system. As Jourde (2013) tells us, "ethnography invites researchers to see and question political relations and political sites that are generally unseen, or 'unidentified,' by main-stream political science but which are nonetheless meaningful" (201). While my ethnography centered on groups of victims affected by violence, it also branched into relational ethnography that focuses on "processes involving configurations of relations among different actors or institutions" (Desmond 2014, 554).

In addition to ethnography carried out over the course of a decade, I used an interpretivist approach to analyze a series of life history interviews I conducted (Klandermans and Staggenborg 2002). In the life history interviews, lasting between 10 and 25 hours (over the course of several sessions in each case), I asked only a few guiding questions, encouraging interviewees to tell me about their early life; the events leading up to and fol-lowing the disappearance of their loved one; and their path toward becoming involved in activism and advocacy. I prompted respondents to expand their answers to my questions about my themes of focus: contact with state agents; experiences with agency in their personal and professional relationships and in their interactions with state agents; and reflections on their involvement with social movements. I interpreted their answers and wove them together with my longitudinal ethnography to make sense of the shifts over time in the ways they understood themselves and legality.

Underlying my methodological choices was a constant, central ques-tion: how does one ethically conduct research with traumatized people? To answer this, I found myself relying largely on my training and experience as a human rights accompanier. I had worked as an accompanier in Colombia between 2006 and 2008 prior to beginning graduate school. I understood my role in that position to be to deter violence against those who were organizing by leveraging the safety that my positionality as a white woman from the United States conferred upon me. In the Colombian context, local human rights organizers requested international accompaniment because they believed the Colombian government—whose militarization was partly financed by and politically championed by the United States—would be less likely to kill, disappear, or incarcerate them if there were international witnesses, especially from the Global North. In the course of this work, I accompanied organizations of families with disappeared children.

When I began this project, I didn't realize how relevant this training would be. While it has been undertaken by practitioners in a range of fields, González (n.d.) who works with family members whose loved ones have been victimized by state violence in Brazil, Colombia, and Argentina, proposes that accompaniment should be adopted as a research methodology. She defines accompaniment as "a strategy defined by regular, extended presence alongside an individual, based on deep listening, bearing witness, providing support, and centering the needs, experiences, and priorities of the person being accompanied" (10). In her understanding, accompaniment "shares interpretivist ethnographers' focus on 'meaning making,'" values immersion, and requires embeddedness, empathy, and solidarity (11). Key to the aims of accompaniment research, according to González, is avoiding retraumatizing already traumatized populations.

The key empirics in this project emerged through applying an accompaniment lens to my ethnographic and interview work. The most meaningful, and research-productive, experiences have occurred when my work can be useful to victimized people and to me as a researcher, and when publicizing these findings is safe and potentially advances the agenda of the individuals and organizations involved in creating it. Three experiences in particular stand out: first, in 2012, I took a brief hiatus from my dissertation research to be a full-time organizer with the MPJD, the national victim's movements. I accepted the MPJD's invitation to be the (unpaid) co-coordinator of a 33-day, 27-city caravan that the MPJD organized in the United States. The caravan of 125 people, nearly all from Mexico, most of whom were directly affected by the violence of the war on drugs, built relationships with US communities affected by the drug war and made their case to the US public and policymakers on the importance of decriminalizing drugs, curbing money laundering, stopping the flow of weapons to Mexico, and fixing our broken immigration policies. This intense experience allowed me to know the victim activists well and planted the seeds of this book's argument: as I realized the scope of claim-making and mobilization activities each individual was involved in, I became convinced that without telling their stories in more depth, we could not understand disappearances in Mexico. Second, for several months in 2013, at the invitation of the director, I embedded with Ciudadanos en Apoyo a los Derechos Humanos (CADHAC, Citizens in Support of Human Rights), the largest human rights organization in Nuevo León at the time. I worked in a small office alongside three of their lawyers, stayed with the director in her home, accompanied them to the meetings they had with state officials, and agreed to update and systematize the case files they had into a database. These empirics and experiences are directly recounted in Chapters 5 and 6, and undergird my analysis throughout the book.

Third and finally, over the years I came to realize that testimony and telling one's story in depth was a central part of the repertoire of most victims and in fact part of combating impunity: by telling their truth, they hoped to sensitize both the public and state officials to their plight—and by so doing, encourage truth, justice, and non-recurrence. This realization led me to conduct in-depth interviews and to include the real names and images of Lucía and Alfonso, Juan Carlos, Nancy, and their disappeared loved ones. After I had a full draft of this manuscript, I returned to Mexico to present the book to the key respondents and to revisit what they wanted included in the manuscript. I compiled each section of the book in which they were mentioned or their stories were shared, translated the text back into Spanish, and sat with each of the families in their homes. I asked them to check the text not only for accuracy but also for anything they wanted deleted for any reason, including their fears that it could pose a security risk. I gave them the choice, again, to opt out of the project for any reason—that is, I asked them if, after seeing what would be published, they wanted to withdraw their participation or have it anonymized. As I sat anxiously and drank coffee and nibbled on Mexican pastries, each of them sat with me and read the draft of all the sections that mentioned them (which surprised me—each was about 25 single-spaced pages and fairly dense). Each corrected details within their narratives—mainly concerning their early lives—but none asked for any substantive changes or omissions. Juan Carlos showed the draft to several of his children—telling them tearfully, "This is what dad does."

Plan for the Book

Chapter 2 lays the theoretical and empirical foundation for understanding how legal consciousness shifts over time and also illustrates the ways in which disappearances as a grievance propel mobilization. This chapter begins by reviewing the central explanations in the extant literature of why people mobilize— the "pleasure in agency" participants experience and the relative costs and benefits; demographic and life circumstances; and the nature of the grievance. Into this mix of understanding why people mobilize in difficult contexts, I explore the role of legal consciousness, that is, *the way a person thinks*—about the law, cooperation, their own sense of agency—in shaping whether and how they mobilize.

The heart of the chapter explores the lives and ways of thinking of the three families introduced in the beginning of this chapter—Nancy, Juan Carlos, and Lucía and Alfonso—before and in the immediate aftermath of their loved ones' disappearance. By exploring the ways in which each family related to and thought about the state prior to the disappearance of their loved one, we set a baseline for understanding how their subsequent engagement with the state diverges from their early experiences. I make the case that none of the families would be considered particularly likely to mobilize prior to the disappearance, given the high costs and minimal possibility of success, the disruption this activity poses to their lives, and their lack of exposure to social movements. I illustrate their divergent perspectives prior to the disappearance of their loved ones and trace the ways in which these dispositions are borne out in their immediate reaction to the disappearance. While I find that no single way of thinking about legality made them more (or less) likely to mobilize, I show that the "with the law" perspective led to more immediate strategic action. Finally, I present each disappearance event in great detail. In the particular tragedy of each event, I argue that we gain insight into how the nature of disappearances as a grievance shapes mobilization: its cruelty and impetus for action lies in the ongoing uncertainty and possibility that their loved one's well-being may be contingent on their own actions.

Chapter 3 sets the historical and political context of impunity and disappearances in Mexico, tracing the shifting terrain of political and legal opportunities for people affected by disappearances and the corresponding opportunities for activism and advocacy. I discuss the historical background of state-perpetrated disappearances in Mexico during the Dirty War and the birth of the Mexican human rights movement in response—as well as early and ongoing tensions between Mexico City–based human rights organizations and victim-led organizing efforts often located far from the capital city. I argue that after formal democratization in 2000, the political opportunities shift markedly: while advocacy is increasingly possible, the state's diminishing control over lethal violence, worsened by its weak and decentralized judiciary, overwhelms Mexico's legal and political institutions. Mexico's human rights organizations likewise find themselves unprepared for the unprecedented crisis in lethal violence and shifting dynamics in repression as the lines between state and non-state perpetrators of violence blur. This leaves victims of violence with scarce organizing resources to draw from. In response, we see a burgeoning of local collectives, with more than 100 emerging in response to the crisis of disappearances in Mexico in the past several years. While the victims' collectives are independent, coalition organizations, conferences and social media allow them to coordinate mobilization strategies and experiences.

Chapter 4 traces the transformation of legal consciousness among the three families profiled as they evolve from apolitical citizens to prominent activists and advocates. By following the claim-making and mobilization trajectories of Nancy, Juan Carlos, and Lucía and Alfonso, I show that as their understandings of legality evolve, so to do their abilities to challenge the inner workings of impunity. I map the pathways each took from the moment of the disappearance to becoming involved with social movement organizations; giving their testimony for the first time; and meeting with state officials. The chapter progressively puts individual stories in relation with one another— both *theoretically*, as the ways they think and act begin to converge, and *in practice*, as they meet each other in the national victims' movement. I show that despite their initial divergent legal consciousnesses, sustained mobilization draws them to think more similarly over time—gravitating toward a strategic and nuanced understanding of the law. As the ways they think converge, they are also drawn to a common contentious repertoire, which includes (1) confronting the state with contentious action; (2) partnering with social movements to access state officials; (3) strategically navigating the state's judicial bureaucracy; (4) locating allies within the state; and (5) participating in independent searches for their loved ones. Theoretically, the chapter argues for a more prominent emphasis on legal consciousness in our understanding of why people mobilize and how their thinking and actions change over time.

Chapter 5 details how organized victims navigate the legal and political opportunities to erode impunity by employing the shared repertoires discussed in Chapter 4. The chapter first explores the powerful role of *ministerios públicos*, public investigators/prosecutors, in determining the investigatory fate of searches into disappearances. Next, I turn to state-level case studies. In each case, I explore how local organized victims' organizations respond to the political and legal opportunities created by changes in the alliances within the state and between the state and criminal actors, as well as the political openings produced by institutional allies, to undermine impunity. I show that in Tamaulipas, a state with long-standing and stable patterns of collusion between the state and DTOs, searching for disappeared people is, surprisingly, possible, due to state allies and advocates who engage in low-profile negotiations with the state. In Veracruz, victims' collectives put disappearances and impunity on the map, but are then sidelined after party alternation. A cynical and politically driven new attorney general engages in the strategic prosecution of his political rivals—though their convictions are short-lived. Finally, in Nuevo León I show how victims engaging in both activism and advocacy are able to strategically build and use their relationship with a sympathetic attorney general amid a lull in DTO violence to erode impunity.

In Chapter 6, I explore the impact that sustained mobilization has had on impunity in Mexico. I argue that sustained mobilization has led to significant and measurable changes in four types of outcomes: legislative, institutional, judicial, and movement. *Legislatively*, two significant pieces of legislation are directly attributable to the victims' movement, along with numerous other state developments. *Institutionally*, these laws created new judicial and governing bureaucracies charged with attending to the crisis of disappearances. *Judicially*, I show how in the most auspicious environment for accountability, Nuevo León, sustained mobilization has resulted in significant inroads into collusive impunity, but I also show the limits of what is possible in Mexico's justice system. I also closely review the case results of Nancy, Juan Carlos, and Lucía and Alfonso, detailing how their mobilization affected the judicial status of their cases and their conceptions of justice. Next, I show how the capacity of *movements* has grown in the past decade, establishing repertoires of contention, building networks of support, developing the ability to provide psycho-social support, and the capacity to conduct independent searches. I argue that while woefully far away from rights fulfillment, these advances have resulted in a substantive closing of the gap between promised and delivered rights. For those who have engaged in sustained mobilization, I argue that they have become rights-conscious, and in some ways rights-bearing, citizens.

In the concluding chapter, I reflect on the challenges of studying violence and the reasons I chose to write a book spanning many levels of analysis, and focused on family members of victims of disappearances. I then summarize the methodological and conceptual contributions of this book, as well as the implications of my findings. I draw out the implications of these findings for policymakers and funders, and call for a recognition of the central place of victims of violence in challenging impunity and propose a series of measures to support, legitimate, and protect their work. I close by returning to the stories and reflections of Nancy, Juan Carlos, Lucia, and Alfonso.

2

The Beginnings

The Formation and Disruption of Legal Consciousness

In seeking to understand *how* people become rights-claiming and ultimately rights-bearing citizens, part of the answer is that they decide to mobilize. This begs the question—*why* do they decide to mobilize?

In this chapter, I do two things: first, drawing primarily from the life histories and ethnography conducted with members of three families touched by disappearance, I explore how each family thought about the state and legality—that is, their legal consciousness—prior to the disappearance of their loved one; follow them as they recount the disappearance of their loved one; and show the ways in which their consciousness is borne out in their immediate reaction to the disappearance. I argue throughout the book that legal consciousness shifts in the process of sustained mobilization—which then affects people's actions (rights-claiming) and outcomes (rights-bearing): this chapter sets the baseline way of thinking of each of the three families. Second, I explore different explanations of why people mobilize—and while I don't answer this question fully, I point to the insufficiency of existing literature in explaining sustained mobilization. I present each disappearance event in great detail, and in the particular tragedy of each event, I argue that we gain insight into how the nature of disappearances as a grievance shapes mobilization. Its cruelty and impetus for action, I find, lies in the ongoing uncertainty and possibility that their loved one's well-being may be contingent on their own actions.

Why mobilize? For these families and so many I have met with, the answer to this question is painfully obvious: I am protesting, marching, on hunger strike, searching, yelling, sitting in, and meeting with state officials to achieve one very simple goal: to find my son. My daughter. My husband. My sister. While the impetus to find one's missing loved one is nearly universal, only a fraction of those affected by disappearance go on to mobilize.[1] How do

---

[1] I use the term "mobilize" as an umbrella category to capture the variety of activities one might take in response to the disappearance of a loved one, including *legal* mobilization, turning to the law

Bootstrap Justice. Janice k. Gallagher, Oxford University Press. © Oxford University Press 2023.
DOI: 10.1093/oso/9780197649978.003.0002

we understand the mechanisms and processes through which this impulse transforms, for some people but not others, into sustained mobilization? I draw on theories of both individual and collective action to understand why victims of disappearance mobilize. I address four questions: (1) Does an *analysis of benefits, risks, and the "pleasure in agency"* (Wood 2003) *that people experience by participating in mobilization* favor involvement? (2) Is there something about a person's *demographics and life circumstances* that makes them more likely to mobilize? (3) Does *the way a person thinks*— about the law, cooperation, themselves—make them more likely to mobilize? (4) Is there something about the *nature of the grievance*, that is—about disappearances themselves—that spurs mobilization? I make the case that none of the families of focus would be considered particularly likely to mobilize prior to the disappearance given the high costs and minimal possibility of success, the disruption it poses to their lives, and their lack of exposure to social movements. Despite this—they have engaged in sustained mobilization for more than 10 years. What explains this?

Approaches to Understanding Mobilization

Most approaches to understanding why people mobilize look at aggregate levels of political participation and mobilization. Since this chapter is focused on why *individuals* mobilize, here I ask to what extent prominent existing theories help us understand why some people mobilize and others don't— and also why mobilization looks so different for different people. In other words, for neighbors who have a loved one who has been disappeared, how do existing theories explain why one neighbor reports the crime, seeks out the state investigators, and takes part in demonstrations; another searches for their loved one and goes on a hunger strike; and another stays home?

Costs, Benefits, and Pleasures of Mobilization

Mobilizing for justice in a state that nearly guarantees impunity to the wrongdoers carries a high cost and non-obvious benefits. With impunity

---

to pursue redress; participating in *social movement* mobilization; and taking *independent* investigatory and non-institutional actions with the goal of finding their disappeared loved ones.

rates in cases of disappearance unknowable, but reasonably calculated to be approaching 100 percent, and with mobilization posing considerable risk to personal security, financial well-being, and family stability, there are clear deterrents to the mobilization we have seen in cases of disappearances. These realities undoubtedly help to explain why the levels of mobilization are fairly low: with more than 85,0000 disappearances since 2006, the annual Mother's Day March, the largest national march focused on disappearances, generally has fewer than 2,000 participants. In interviews with family members of the disappeared, they often talked about the reasons their family members didn't mobilize: "My husband isn't here because he doesn't think it will change anything" (interview in 2011). "My friend also has a [disappeared son]. But she doesn't say anything, just stays in—she says she has her other kids to worry about and pushing this will only cause problems" (interview in 2013). "My family doesn't talk to me because I [continue to mobilize]. . . . [T]hey think we won't find my son, and that me being in the newspaper and on the news will attract the attention of the bad guys (*los malos*)" (interview in 2016). The costs of mobilization accumulate and some of the perceived benefits of mobilization wane over time: as time passes, family members are acutely aware that the possibility of finding their loved ones—and especially of finding them alive—diminishes significantly while the risks to personal safety increase as victims build visibility by engaging in sustained mobilization.

What are the benefits of mobilizing, and are they uneven across individuals? Mobilization scholars have helped us think through the reasons that groups of people mobilize beyond benefits which accrue to individuals. Looking at why certain communities tended to support the El Salvador leftist insurgents, Wood (2003) finds that people decide to participate in potentially costly and dangerous mobilization because of the "emotional and moral motives," namely, the pleasure they derive from asserting their agency—and on the "value they put on being part of making history" (19) in defiance of what we think of as a rational cost-benefit analysis. Interestingly, she finds that people are more likely to participate in costly action if they have directly experienced state behavior that violates rights which they see as central to their well-being.

Does thinking through the costs, benefits, and pleasures of mobilization help us understand why some may mobilize while others don't? While some of the benefits of participating in victim mobilization are undoubtedly "public goods"—that is, they accrue to all people regardless of whether they mobilized—many people mobilize because they perceive there are what Mancur Olson (2009) famously deemed "selective incentives": that is, because they will benefit from mobilization in ways that those who don't mobilize will not. Empirically there is some evidence to support that those who mobilize will experience better judicial outcomes than those who don't: I argued in a previous study that cases that were the target of mobilization in two Mexican states were more than twice as likely to be investigated than average cases (see Gallagher 2017). The costs of mobilization are also, in effect, selective disincentives. Take, for example, a woman who had been observing the excavation of a mass grave as part of the process of searching for her husband. She received texts from an anonymous number telling her to stop her search. When, despite the threat, she returned the next day to the mass grave, she received threats via text and voice memo in which they made it clear that they knew where she lived, what car she was driving, and were watching her movements—and they threatened her with violence if she continued. This ended her mobilization. It is common knowledge that mobilized victims face this kind of danger, and that it clearly can deter mobilization. As Wood (2003) reminds us, however, individual actions are not only explicable solely, or even primarily, through rational calculations: some individuals participate in high-risk activism because they derive fulfillment from struggling for justice, defying authority, or successfully asserting their agency through struggle.

Thinking through the costs and benefits of mobilization, in sum, helps us explain the relatively low levels of mobilization of family members of the disappeared. However, including an examination of individuals' values and emotions—and as I will argue, ways of thinking—moves us closer to understanding why similarly situated individuals engage in long-term mobilization while other do not, and it directs our attention to thinking about the cultural embeddedness and particularity of decisions to mobilize.

The Nature of the Grievance: Disappearances as Mobilizers

Enforced disappearances are, under international law,[2] considered a "continuous" crime. Unlike a murder, which happens at a distinct moment in time, disappearances are a crime experienced by the victims (if alive) and the victims' families in an ongoing way. The Office of the UN High Commissioner

---

[2] See the United Nations International Convention for the Protection of All Persons from Enforced Disappearance, which entered into force in 2010, Article 8, Section 1b.

for Human (OHCHR) Rights describes the pernicious effects of this crime against humanity as follows:

> A disappearance has a doubly paralyzing impact: on the victims, frequently tortured and in constant fear for their lives, and on their families, ignorant of the fate of their loved ones, their emotions alternating between hope and despair, wondering and waiting, sometimes for years, for news that may never come. . . . The family and friends of disappeared persons experience slow mental anguish, not knowing whether the victim is still alive and, if so, where he or she is being held, under what conditions, and in what state of health. Aware, furthermore, that they, too, are threatened, that they may suffer the same fate themselves and that searching for the truth may expose them to even greater danger. (United Nations 2009)

While the OHCHR describes disappearances as "paralyzing," in nearly every one of the more than 80 countries that have experienced widespread disappearances, we have seen the mobilization of groups of families of the disappeared, the Madres de la Plaza de Mayo in Argentina in the 1970s being the first and best known (see Dewhirst and Kapur 2015). We have not seen similarly consistent and high levels of ongoing mobilization in countries that have confronted other crimes against humanity as defined by the International Criminal Court, including murder, mass imprisonment, torture, and rape.[3]

Simmons (2016) investigates how the material and ideational nature of a grievance—in her case, the threat to the subsistence goods of water and corn in Bolivia and Mexico, respectively—shapes the nature and form of contention. She finds that when access to these subsistence goods is threatened, they spawn impassioned responses not explained without considering them as embedded within the local cultural and historical context. Given these findings, she calls for social movement scholars to "study the way in which the content of a movement's claims shapes its emergence and composition" (2). I take up this call by looking closely at the events preceding the disappearance, the disappearance itself, and the ways in which the everyday actions, ways of thinking, and priorities of the families profiled here

---

[3] I would argue that we do see consistent and sustained mobilization across national contexts in the face of enslavement and apartheid, not coincidentally the two other crimes against humanity which are most clearly continuous in nature.

are affected by the disappearance event. While Simmons focuses on the variability of meanings ascribed to subsistence goods in different cultural and national contexts to explain mobilization, I point to the universal disruption and trauma of disappearances. Insofar as the family unit remains the anchoring institution of most modern societies, I argue that the disappearance and subsequent ongoing uncertainty and suffering of the remaining family members present a nearly universal impetus to mobilize.

Focusing solely on the nature of disappearances as a grievance, however—and its universal impetus to mobilize—overpredicts mobilization.[4] This sharpens the central question of this chapter: what enables some people, and not others, to continuously act on the impetus to mobilize in the wake of the disappearance of their loved one?

Biographical Availability and Exposure to Mobilization Networks

Social movement scholars have emphasized that people with more financial or temporal flexibility—individuals' *biographical availability*—will play a significant role in whether they mobilize. McAdam (1986, 70) defines biographical availability as "the absence of personal constraints that may increase the costs and risks of movement participation." This concept has been operationalized in four main ways—marital status, parenthood, employment, and age (Beyerlein and Hipp 2006). This is fairly intuitive: if people have a job with flexible hours, are wealthy, have spouses able to support them financially, no young kids at home, or they are retired—it makes sense that each of these qualities would make it more possible for them to mobilize.

Reliable data about those who do not mobilize is by its nature is hard to come by: those who don't mobilize are not at protests or public gatherings, and state records are sealed. In order to address this data problem, I worked with CADHAC, the leading local human rights NGO in Nuevo León at the time, to construct a database of all cases of disappearances that they had received during the four-year period in which disappearances spiked: 2009–2012. While 321 people came to CADHAC during this time to report the disappearance of a loved one, only 53 became involved with CADHAC's advocacy activities. To understand the demographic profile of those family members

---

[4] Thanks to Whitney Taylor for this conceptualization of the relationship between these concepts.

of victims who become active members of the organization, I reviewed the case files of everyone who had reported a disappearance during this period and coded them for demographic information (see Table 2.1).

The demographics of the victims' relatives in the two groups are quite similar. NGO participants tended to be slightly older than non-participants and were more likely than non-participants to work at home. This makes sense, since participating with the NGO is difficult if a person is employed given that many advocacy activities occur during the day and are therefore more accessible to retired individuals or to people who do not work outside the home. Overall, however, these data indicate that a static understanding of biographical availability is insufficient to explain who mobilizes and who doesn't: the minor differences in the demographics of the two groups doesn't explain why some became mobilizers and others non-mobilizers. The individual stories I present in this chapter, however, do give us insight into the mechanisms and processes at play for those who choose to mobilize. The family members in each of the three stories would appear biographically "unavailable" for mobilization at the time of the disappearance of their loved ones: Nancy struggled financially and worked outside the home; Juan Carlos ran a business; and Alfonso ran several businesses. The disappearance leads each of them, however, to transform their "biographical availability." Despite

Table 2.1   Demographics of NGO Participants versus Non-Participants

	Demographic Information of Family Member of Victim Reporting to the NGO					Demographic Information of Disappeared Person	
	Age	Weekly Household Income	% Women	Average Schooling 2=Finished Junior High, 3=Finished high school	% who do not work outside the home	Age of Victim	Weekly Income of Victim
NGO Participants N=53	51	$131	71%	2.59	54%	30	$146
NGO Non-Participants N-268	44	$148	82%	2.61	45%	29	$162

Source: Author's analysis of original data. 2019

structural and logistical barriers, as I narrate here and throughout the text, each drew on other family and community resources to become biographically available, and they have gone on to dedicate their lives, nearly full-time, to searching for their loved one and advocating for justice.

Apart from biographical availability, several additional areas of scholarship look at whom people interact with to explain why some mobilize and others don't. Scholars of state-society relations have urged us to think about socio-spatial positioning of people: Kruks-Wisner (2018) examines whom people interact with to understand the form and frequency of citizens' claims on the state. She finds that "claim-making is more likely among citizens who traverse social and spatial boundaries of caste, class, neighborhood and village" (207). Social movement scholars have long looked to whether people have access to mobilizing networks and resources to explain when movements might emerge, while legal mobilization scholars have similarly looked at whether potential claimants have access to "rights advocacy organizations, supportive lawyers, and sources of financing," all of which help overcome the informational and material obstacles to pursuing legal redress (Epp 1998, 23; Botero 2015). While none of the individuals in this chapter had any links to or awareness of social movement or rights advocacy organizations prior to the disappearance of their loved one, I find the concepts of personal networks and socio-spatial mobility useful in understanding why certain individuals mobilize.

What people do for a living, their family situation, whom they interact with, and whether they have contact with civil society organizations help explain why some people do or do not mobilize. But we are still left wondering why similarly situated neighbors—similar jobs, similar income, similar relationships within their community—act differently in the face of disappearances.

Legal Consciousness and Mobilization

If mobilization is spurred by the particular experience of disappearance but doesn't result in universal mobilization; is not explicable primarily through an analysis of people's biographical availability nor their social networks prior to the disappearance; and entails immense cost and scant tangible benefits— what does explain why some people (and not others) mobilize when faced with the disappearance of their loved one? Wood (2003) and Kruks-Wisner

(2018) direct our attention to the individual-level cultural, political, and social drivers of ongoing mobilization. I apply their insights as I seek to understand how individuals shift the ways in which they think about themselves in relation to power, legality, and each other as they experience trauma and the impetus to mobilize.

I ground the following accounts of these subjects' lives and decision-making within the theoretical framework of *legal consciousness*, which as I discussed in Chapter 1, is commonly understood as "the ways people understand and use the law . . . the way people conceive of the 'natural' and normal way of doing things, their habitual patterns of talk and action, and their common-sense understanding of the world" (Merry 1990, 5). While the way each thought about the law before the disappearance is captured only imperfectly through memory, in narrating their lives and specific actions, we gain an understanding of their varying degrees of trust in legal systems or legality. As Ewick and Silbey (1998, 29; 32) explain, "Legality is a pattern in relationships that is enacted daily in the interpretive schemas people invoke to make sense of their own and others' actions and in the human and material resources, capacities and assets that make action possible."

I draw centrally from Ewick and Silbey's (1998) foundational work, which presents three ideal types of legal consciousness: "before the law," "against the law," and "with the law." Those who understand themselves as "before the law" view law as clean and reliable: "law is majestic, operating by known and fixed rules in carefully delimited spaces" (28). Those who understand themselves as "against the law" see legal orders as harsh, unjust, arbitrary, and capricious; "a net in which they are trapped and struggle for freedom" (184). Those who understand themselves as "with the law" fundamentally see the law as a game, contest, or struggle: "an ensemble of actors, organizations, rules and procedures with which they managed their daily lives" (131).

The behavioral expectations for each of these categories are intuitive: those who see the law as majestic and just will use institutional means of redress and will believe they work; those who see themselves as against the law are unlikely to make legal claims (Taylor 2018) and may actively seek to avoid the law; and those who see themselves as "with the law" would be most likely to strategically engage in both institutional and non-institutional actions, like mobilization, to make the "game" of the law work for them.

One note about the "truth" of the narratives presented here: as Wedeen (2010) tells us, "There is no perfect correspondence between reality and representation" (264). That is, while ethnography teaches us many things about the way in which people construct meaning in complex social and political environments, it is ill-suited to discerning the objective "truth" of any particular claim. As such, I want to remind the reader that what I present throughout the book are the words and perspectives of the people I know and have interviewed over the course of a decade. I have not triangulated among different parties to verify their stories and memories. It therefore goes without saying that when Juan Carlos recounts the fantastic story of finding money stashed in the walls of his house, or when Nancy recounts her disillusionment with a social movement organization, these are statements of their own opinion and memory. This is by design: to make sense of how each person understands their own process of mobilization, rather than aiming to verify any "objective" truth, I am much more interested in what the memories they highlight and how they structure their own recollections teaches us about how they understand themselves and their environment.

Before the Disappearances

We most often think about those who mobilize when they are already involved. Do we find the seeds of their activism in their early lives?

Nancy: "I Was Raised with So Much Fear"

Nancy's life had always been hard, and all of the contact she had with the police or the state had consistently made things harder for her. Nancy, the oldest of four children, was born in 1974 to her 16-year-old mother and a father who would go on to have seven other children with three different women. Her father worked with the judicial police, a body widely considered at the time to be among the most corrupt sub-sectors within the corrupt Mexican police. Nancy learned early that the police would, at best, give her father a slap on the wrist in response to his frequent drinking and well-known history of violent domestic abuse. Nancy, her brother, and mother all bore the physical and emotional scars of his beatings and attempted to flee several times. Yet each time they tried to leave, traveling to other states where they hoped they couldn't be found, Nancy's father's colleagues helped him track them down. By the time Nancy was eight years old, she remembers:

It wasn't love I had for my father—rather it was fear. It wasn't that I wanted to live with him, rather that I had to live with him. Even if it would be calm for a while, I never knew when the situation would change again and he would start to beat us again—beat us hard, with a belt, with a stick, with whatever he found. Once they called the police on my dad, but he was only held in jail overnight and the next day it was all worse—he hit us worse. And so we returned to live with the fear.

When her father was finally suspended from his job as a judicial policeman because of his drinking and violence with both his family and on the job, he found another job as a municipal policeman. Her father's violence, along with events outside the family's control—their Mexico City home was destroyed by the historic 1985 earthquake, and they ended up bouncing from shelter to shelter—meant that Nancy's family was constantly moving. This exacerbated her tendency to keep to herself and not make close ties to her classmates. She describes herself as asocial, quiet, a little nerdy, and very obedient as a young student. She understands this early submissiveness as deriving, in part, from her mother. "My mother was not a warrior. . . . [S]he was submissive, a coward, [and] it was our neighbors' and my mother's family who finally called the police on my father."

Despite the fact that Nancy was a diligent and hard-working student, she ended up leaving school when she was 16 years old after falling sick with typhoid. Though her father dangled the possibility of paying for Nancy to finish her education at a private school, in the end he required that Nancy stay home to help raise her younger siblings. He also obliged her to learn to sew to help him with his side business. Determined to continue her education, Nancy would sneak off to school when her dad was working and plotted to escape from her house. When she met her first boyfriend Rafael, she saw her chance. In disguise and in the middle of the night, she sneaked over to his house and convinced him to take her with him to another state. She was 18.

Nancy hoped her life with Rafael would be a fresh start. Soon after moving away from home, Nancy became pregnant. While she had tried to hide the location of her new home from her father, he soon found her. When he learned she was pregnant, her father showed up at her new home and tried to force her to have an abortion. He tricked her into going on a car ride with him and instead brought Nancy to a clinic where they performed clandestine abortions. When Nancy realized what he was trying to do, she ran from the parking lot. Her son, Elvis Axell, was born in 1993.

While Rafael and Nancy's partnership had initially been a peaceful contrast to her early life, Rafael soon became jealous and paranoid that Nancy was seeing other men. He began drinking and beating Nancy, which got them thrown out of the room they were renting and left them homeless after Elvis was born. Nancy was able to rent a small room for the three of them by selling *nopales* (cactus) in the market with her infant son strapped to her chest: she realized she could buy the cactus cheaply in the central market and sell them at a markup near her house. She saved this money so she could leave Rafael, who had begun beating her more and more frequently.

Nancy did the best she could to raise Elvis Axell in a positive environment. After leaving Rafael she moved with Elvis to a working-class bedroom community of Mexico City, called Coacoalco in Estado de México (EdoMex, Mexico State). Here, most families worked in the service sector or factories in Mexico City and commuted through the city's traffic for up to four or five hours a day. Nancy found a job in the neighborhood as a seamstress at a small factory. Since she had learned to sew to help her father as a teenager, the factory was impressed and let her work from home so she could take care of Elvis. Nancy enjoyed the work and grew close to the managers, who, she felt, treated her like a daughter. A conflict with a co-worker ultimately forced her out. Later, she found work as an attendant at a gas station, which is where she met her second husband.

While economically Nancy had achieved some stability, her family and environment continually presented challenges. After rarely going out to clubs in her youth, one night when she was living in Coacoalco, Nancy ventured out with some friends to a neighborhood party. There, she was drugged, she believes with rohypnol, raped, and became pregnant as a result. Determined to take control of her own life, this time she opted to have an abortion. When I asked her if she reported the rape to the police, Nancy responded that she "never considered" reporting it—"for me, the police had caused me nothing but pain."

Nancy had a fraught relationship with her family, who lived nearby. Needing help with child care, Nancy reluctantly left Elvis with her mother when she went to work. As Elvis entered his teenage years, he often spent time after school with his grandmother. It was there he was exposed to alcohol and cigarettes for the first time. When Nancy tried to discipline her son, he would go and stay with his father and his father's girlfriend, both of whom were drug users. Elvis met his first girlfriend at his father's house. She was several years older than he was and had been using drugs for several years. By 15, Elvis was regularly using drugs—sniffing cement mix, which was cheap and readily available, along with regularly smoking marijuana. Nancy felt her son was out of control: she noticed that all of a sudden he had a new cell phone, then a new sweater—things she knew no one around him could afford. Soon after, she got a call: Elvis's good friend had been arrested after being accused of mugging a couple. The couple said her son had run away and escaped but that he had also been part of the holdup. Nancy was frightened that Elvis, whom she saw as earnest and naïve, was being drawn into a familiar downward spiral of drug use, teenage parenthood, unemployment, crime, and chaos. She was determined to do anything she could to stop this cycle.

Against the Law: How do we understand Nancy's early life experiences through the lens of legal consciousness? Nancy learned early that the law, embodied in her abusive policeman father and his network of law enforcement enablers, was capricious and vengeful, and that it was systematically employed to limit her freedom and threaten her physical safety—constituent experiences of those who view themselves as "against the law." When she was young, this danger limited her independence: "Because I was raised with so much fear, I always thought I had to strictly obey all discipline," she told me. Despite viewing her mother as a "coward," Nany witnessed her mother attempt to resist this control and flee from her father. Her mother's failure to escape the "net in which they [we]re trapped, and within which they struggle[d] for freedom," (Ewick and Silbey 1998, 184), in the form of her father using his law enforcement contacts to find his terrified family, taught Nancy at a young age about the reach and power of the legal and security system.

Nancy resisted the control and threat posed to her by this system with early acts of defiance: sneaking off to school, escaping her home, and defying her father by having her child. When this pattern of violence and control recurred in her relationship with her first husband, she again found ways to resist: leaving him and figuring out how to support herself and her young son. While we tend to think of overt acts of resistance to the law when imagining how someone "against the law" will resist the power that oppresses them, Ewick and Silbey remind us that "a resistant understanding of legality . . . is expressed in silences, refusals, and absences as well as in acts of defiance and disruption" (188–189). After she is raped, we see Nancy apply her understandings of the perniciousness of law by avoiding the legal system—she has learned that the legal authorities make things worse, and she seeks to absent the law from her life whenever possible. When her son begins to be in trouble with the law and substance abuse, Nancy's "against the law" orientation manifests in what she does not do: she doesn't turn to Elvis's school or teachers, nor to any state agency for help.

Lucía and Alfonso: "I Lived in a Disneyland"

Lucía grew up in Parral, Chihuahua, a middle-class mining town in the north of Mexico as the only child of a single mother. She was the goddaughter of a well-off family who owned the hardware store in her small town and who introduced Lucía as part of the family when they went out. Because of this, Lucía lived a comfortable, if quite sheltered, early life. She prided herself on being a "good," well-behaved girl, and she saw that this gained her social favor. "I didn't give anyone any problems, and because of this, I was always invited to go out all over the place." Lucía felt that being around so many adults from an early age made her more mature than her peers. As part of her early education, she would read the newspaper every day. As a teenager she helped with the administration of the hardware store, something that would serve her well as she went on to be a secretary in the local government's social security administration, and later as she helped her husband with his various business ventures.

Alfonso, who married Lucía in 1976, was raised in Oaxaca, where he and his twin sister were the fourth and fifth children of seven. Alfonso's father was a scrappy entrepreneur who rented out extra space in their house as a crash pad for local workers and counted every penny the family spent. Alfonso showed an interest in business early and a willingness to work hard: He cleaned the toilets of the boarding house and learned how to fix the appliances and heating by the time he was 10. Alfonso's parents instilled in him respect for meticulous record-keeping and frugality: his mother documented every single peso that Alfonso's education had cost them. Alfonso moved to Mexico City when he was 19 to study mechanical engineering. When he graduated in 1973, he was offered a job in Parral, Chihuahua.

Lucía and Alfonso met when he came into the hardware store and opened a line of credit. Lucía's reputation as an upstanding and even-tempered young woman with an eye for administering an office or business was key for Alfonso. He imagined their life together as one in which he would play the provider role, and Lucía would tend to the home. After a brief courtship, he asked her to marry him, telling her he had a blender, a stove, and all they needed to build a home. They were soon married in a church ceremony in Parral. Alfonso decided to hold the reception in the evening, when appetizers and drinks were acceptable fare, as opposed to the more elaborate and expensive ceremonies that included the large midday meal, common in his home state of Oaxaca. The couple maintained close relationships with Alfonso's family, often driving their Volkswagen bug more than 20 hours for a weekend to visit his family. Two of his sisters even accompanied them on their honeymoon.

They soon moved to Mexico City, where Lucía continued to work as an assistant with the state social security agency. After two years of marriage, Alejandro was born, and Lucía's mother moved in with them to help care for her first grandchild. Two years later, their second son was born, and four years after that, their third son joined the family. Lucía left her job to care for the children. She prepared their lunch when they came home from school, took them to their after-school activities, and attended their important events, which Alfonso often couldn't make because of his busy schedule at work. Alfonso managed the family's finances and major decisions. He built them a house exactly to his specifications, managed their extensive real estate investments, and booked the family vacations. Alfonso's business ventures flourished in Mexico City. He oversaw major construction and renovation projects at many of the country's top companies and also managed properties he or his family members had bought. He was in charge of making sure all renovation projects were up to code, and he was valued for his dedication to detail, trustworthiness, and ability to deliver projects on time.

Alejandro, their oldest son, was an eager reader and from an early age, he pored over the books his parents bought him about history, science fiction, and technology. Lucía remembers him pushing the family to take him to the Museo de Antropología in Mexico City, where he had memorized all the names of Mexico's different Indigenous communities by the time he was seven. As a teenager, he became fascinated by computers and interactive computer games, and he built friendships with gamers he met online. He enrolled at the Tec de Monterrey, an expensive private university, but later transferred to UNITEC, a less prestigious school. After a tech business venture he had launched together with his classmates from the Tec failed, he went to work for IBM. Though Alejandro had been living with friends, after taking the job at IBM he moved home, at his parents' insistence, after breaking his leg. They were eager to take care of their eldest son during his recovery.

Lucía had never thought of what she wanted to do with her life per se. She had spent it caring for people and was accustomed to following her husband. In Lucía's words, before the disappearance of Alejandro, "It was an ideal life—marriage, economic prosperity, stability, and children. It was a beautiful dream made reality. We were very satisfied. It was the life anyone would want." Alfonso echoed these sentiments: his sons were employed and seemed happy. What else could he want?

Before the Law: Legal consciousness is often linked to class position, with the upper classes most likely to understand themselves as normal and not disadvantaged, and legality as a benevolent but distant latticework of rules that justly orders their lives. Poor people are more likely to view the law as something that oppresses them and therefore should be resisted or manipulated. While legal consciousness is not something a couple necessarily shares, Lucía and Alfonso both sense that there are rules that govern society and that by complying with them a person is assured happiness and success. They are both best understood as seeing themselves as *before the law*, though from very different vantage points. For Lucía, prior to Alejandro's disappearance, "legality" and interactions with the legal system were not only outside of her scope of experience but also outside of what she understood as her allotted position as a well-off wife and mother. She told me that before the disappearance "we lived in a Disneyland. Sure, we lived in a country in which I knew there were problems—poverty, violence. But we lived blindly. I thought—I am an honest woman; I work honestly . . ." While she doesn't complete the thought, Lucía's supposition was that living and working honestly insulated her and her family from the problems of her country and guaranteed her an orderly, peaceful life. This is emblematic of someone who considers the law as "external, unified and objective" (Ewick and Silbey 1998, 75), without questioning the mechanisms that produce this order.

While Lucía saw herself and her family as falling under the umbrella of a system that generally rewards honest and good people, Alfonso viewed their success and happiness as a direct result of his actions and agency. His frugality, investing, and planning had served him well: the natural order of things, as Alfonso saw it, was justly enacted. Because he worked hard within this logical, impartial system, he had succeeded and guaranteed his family a good life. For Alfonso, legality was a disembodied but prevailing order, devoid of particular experiences, state agencies, or people in general. In reflecting on his life prior to Alejandro's disappearance, I prompted him several times to reflect on the government or law—and he resisted talking about any specific experiences, consistent with someone who sees the everyday embodiments of law as disconnected from the overarching concept of legality. In my fourth attempt to ask him about experiences with state agencies, he told me that he had avoided working with the state in his contracting business: "They're bad at paying; they're corrupt. So that the work actually goes forward after the bidding and estimates from here to there—you have to throw money in. I had the luck and blessing to never have the necessity of working for the government." While his assessment of government officials reveals his skepticism of the state, this is largely disconnected from his understanding of how things should and do work: corrupt officials are an aberration of society's order and a distraction from the impartial and omnipotent forces that reward assiduous planning and preparation.

Juan Carlos: "For Me It Was Always a Hustle"

Juan Carlos was born in a place where people generally don't stay. Pajacuarán is a poor town of about 10,000 people in the state of Michoacán which most people leave for the United States. The great majority there live off of what their loved ones send back from the United States, and the others get by on what they can grow and sell. Juan Carlos's mother, María came from a large, well-known family of meat sellers and was one of the few people born in Pajacuarán who stayed. The first of eight children, she finished elementary school and then planned to become a nun. But then, as her sons told me, "the devil arrived"—in the form of their father—"and she fell in love." Juan Carlos's father worked in the countryside and hadn't gone to school. Though he had been married with eight children at the time they met, when his wife died, he quickly married María, and went about adding to his family: they had eight additional children over a period of 10 years. At first, the couple struggled economically. María's parents helped them buy a truck, and she began to prepare food and sell it on the street. After an unexpected windfall—they found money packed into the floors of their adobe house—the family opened a grocery store in their village, bought new trucks, and started a delivery service. With these earnings, they paid for many of the 16 siblings to attend a private Catholic school.

Juan Carlos started to work in the family's stores when he was five or six years old. At this point, there were about 15 of them living in their house. The blended family, known as the "Trujillo-Herrera" family at school, was close, with each sibling "adopting" another, taking responsibility for each other. Juan Carlos was hyperactive and always getting into trouble. His father hit him every day and sometimes gave him more severe beatings when he woke to find Juan Carlos slipping bills out of his wallet so that he could buy toys. Juan Carlos remembers, "I was always a little strange. I always did things a little differently. Maybe it's because I wanted attention, or I didn't have enough to do. But without fail, my dad would come home, and he'd hit me." Their father became more violent and controlling with the family over time, leading him and María to eventually separate. This divided the family, with most of María's biological children going to live with her. To cut costs, Juan Carlos's father stopped giving any money to María and pulled Juan Carlos out of Catholic school. The economic situation at his mom's house soon became desperate, with barely enough money to feed María and her eight children.

School had been his salvation. Juan Carlos remembers being close to at least four teachers. Around the time of the separation, when he was about 10 years old, he was falsely accused of harassing a classmate and temporarily expelled. For Juan Carlos, this was a turning point. He wondered why the teachers he had been close to hadn't defended him. When the school realized they had made a mistake one of his teachers called to apologize, but it was too late. He was stung by the betrayal and started acting out and missing school. He took extra jobs, for a time missing school to work long days in a local factory, where he would be paid 60 pesos, about $3, for a full day's work. He also began to steal bicycles. "My life began to unravel—I started to buy chickens and to go to cock fights. I was basically a juvenile delinquent."

When he finished middle school at 12, Juan Carlos's formal education was over. He wanted to keep studying, but there was no money. Two other brothers, one only 11 years old, had already headed to the United States after helping themselves to some of their dad's money. After paying about $700 each to a coyote, a migrant smuggler, they were taken across the border on a party bus that regularly went between the United States and Mexico.[5] After returning to an aunt's house in Sonora, they sent for Juan Carlos. It was there he began to learn about business. Though Juan Carlos tried to return home to Pajacuarán, he couldn't get settled and decided to join his brothers in the United States. Juan Carlos arrived in Oakland, California, outside of San

---

[5] This was before the militarization of the border that President Bill Clinton led in the 1990s, and also long before the "Secure Fence Act" (2006) in George W. Bush's presidency, at a time when it was much easier to cross the border than it is now.

Francisco. There, he worked in construction while his brothers worked at a meat processing factory and a chain clothing retailer. He rotated through a series of jobs, including selling Bibles, furniture, and cars.

In 2001, Juan Carlos was deported to Tijuana from the United States. He had intended to stay in Mexico just long enough to save up enough money to pay another coyote to cross back into the United States, and he went home to Michoacán where he knew he had a place to stay while he saved up. But once at home, he got a job selling furniture and quickly became the best-performing furniture salesman in the company. He decided to stay put. He purchased a truck and began his own business buying and selling furniture. Soon, he had invited his family to join him: his mother, four brothers, and his aunt began to help him. Together, they bought another truck—and Juan Carlos decided that in addition to buying and selling used furniture, he would add silverware and gold. Starting with one truck, they soon had three, and buying and selling used gold became the cornerstone of their business. They learned how to identify the different qualities of gold, to melt down the jewelry or other gold pieces they bought, and to turn them into bars of gold which could then be sold for much higher prices. By 2005, they had 22 trucks, 120 employees, and were operating in much of Mexico.

With the Law: From an early age, Juan Carlos learned that successfully navigating the intersection of money and law held the keys to his and his family's survival. He saw this modeled at home with the windfall of money in their house, which they did not report to the authorities, as well as with his neighbors and older brothers, who skirted immigration laws as they traveled to and from the United States to earn money. As he got older, he applied this gamesmanship in his own life. Stealing bicycles, crossing the border, and working while undocumented in the United States all necessitated that he understand the rules of the game, how to avoid punishment, and what to do when caught. His willingness to violate rules and his ability to avoid getting in trouble most of the time is testimony to his ability to play the game of legality, and not be cowed by the oppressive power of the law, nor awed by its power.

Alfonso, profiled above and who I understand as seeing himself "before the law," also adeptly negotiated the intricacies of the legal system. How are they different? Alfonso takes as a given that the rules of the game are omnipotent and fundamentally stable and good, and that if he operates within them he will succeed. Juan Carlos understands rules as constructed by people with certain interests in order to achieve their desired objectives. To achieve his own goals, he must flout the rules and make them work for him. There is no moral content or objective good in the given rules of the game for Juan Carlos, and therefore challenging them carries no moral cost, nor does it challenge an order that would have been beneficial to him.

Unlikely to Mobilize: Biographical Availability and Personal Networks

What do the ways of thinking and life circumstances of these three families at the time of the disappearance of their loved one teach us about the likelihood that they will mobilize? Given their divergent ideas of legality, we might expect Juan Carlos to be the most likely to mobilize, as he had shown in his life prior to the disappearance of his brothers that he was willing to challenge, push, and violate the law when he deemed it necessary. His "with the law" legal consciousness contrasts with Lucía and Alfonso's "before the law" and Nancy's "against the law" perspectives, both of which usually deter mobilization—the former because the just, natural order of things doesn't require mobilization; and the latter because if the entire system is aligned against you, mobilization cannot be expected to improve things.

While their ways of thinking about the law might lead us to believe that only Juan Carlos might mobilize, their life circumstances would seem to preclude all from mobilization, except for Lucía. Prior to Elvis's disappearance, Nancy and her husband both worked at a gas station and struggled to make ends meet. While Alfonso was relatively wealthy, he worked long hours managing his renovation company and investment properties. Juan Carlos was in charge of the complicated and growing family business of buying and selling gold, which demanded his constant attention. Only Lucía was not working outside the home at the time of her loved one's disappearance, and at home she had both her mother and helpers who came in to assist her with ironing and housework. Her household's savings and investments meant that she had both the time and financial resources to devote to searching for her son.

In addition to their relative biographical unavailability, these three families shared another characteristic that made them, according to the extant literature, unlikely to mobilize: none of them had ever been to a protest, had contact with a social movement, or even belonged to a civil society

organization previously, nor did they know anyone who had. While their social circles would become central in their response to the disappearance, as
will become clear in the following sections, it is important to note that they
were outside mobilizing networks and structures at the time of the disappearance of their loved one. Thus the question: how did these people, none of
whom thought about the state or social movements as natural allies in pursuing redress prior to the disappearance of their loved ones and whose lives
were already quite busy, end up becoming leaders, advocates, and activists
for victims of disappearances?

Facing Disappearance

Despite vastly divergent life circumstances, between 2009 and 2011 Nancy,
Alfonso, and Lucía, and Juan Carlos all faced what had been previously unim-
aginable: the disappearance of a close family member for no apparent reason.
The following narratives recount the immediate circumstances surrounding
these tragic events. These narratives serve three purposes: throughout each
section I connect the legal consciousness, social position, and biographical
availability of each person and reflect on how it impacted their initial mobilization. These approaches are additive, not exclusive. This close tracing
of the individual-level decisions give us insight into the critical moments of
transformation, allowing us to understand the mechanisms and processes
through which these ways of thinking, usually seen as stable and static, begin
to shift. Second, the intricacies of the disappearances themselves reveal the
specific challenges this crime presents: the difficulty of taking any action
when you fear that it might endanger your loved one if that person is still
alive; the challenges of investigating with no physical evidence nor a defi-
nite idea of where the disappearance occurred; and the extreme anxiety that
goes along with reacting to a disappearance quickly in the crucial hours and
days following the event. Third, these disappearances, while not scientifically
representative of disappearances in Mexico, do provide a snapshot of the
perpetrators and victims of disappearances as well what the available options
were for family members to pursue redress for disappearances in Mexico in
the early days of the current crisis of disappearances. These narratives reveal how the muddy lines between state and DTO involvement play out in
the disappearances themselves, and how the family members experience this
collusion.

Elvis Axell: Disappeared While in Drug Treatment, 2010

Nancy thought that a clinic called Salva Tu Vida, or "Save your life," sounded like the right place to send her son Elvis. Nancy had felt like things were finally turning around for her. After a turbulent childhood and a highly conflictive relationship with her policeman father, she was making a home for herself, her second husband, and her 17-year-old son, Elvis Axell. Elvis was regularly using marijuana and sniffing glue, and he had narrowly escaped being arrested on a robbery charge. As we would expect of someone who conceptualizes themselves as "against the law," Nancy wanted to do everything she could to make sure Elvis didn't fall into the Mexican justice system. She hoped that drug treatment would be what Elvis needed to finally set him on a stable path.

Nancy looked online for treatment facilities near their home. At the Salva Tu Vida rehabilitation center, about half an hour from Nancy's home near Mexico City, Nancy met with Fernando, the charming director, who assured her that Elvis's life would improve dramatically and permanently as a result of the residential treatment he would receive. While she had no frame of reference, she was impressed by the orderly and renovated facilities and the testimonials of other young men who spoke of how their lives had been transformed by treatment and proudly ticked off their months of sobriety. While Elvis wasn't convinced that a drug treatment center was right for him, he told his mom that he trusted her judgment and promised to give it his all. Though paying for treatment was not easy, Nancy was determined to do whatever it took to get Elvis on the right path. She was setting in motion plans to pawn her television and stereo when her husband, who was against sending Elvis to treatment, nonetheless offered to exchange the couple's only valuable asset—the new car he used for work—in lieu of payment for a six-month stay at the drug treatment center.

Fernando, the treatment clinic director, had explained that a crucial component of the program was to make the drug user aware of the dire consequences of their addiction. The first step was a highly unconventional check-in process: Salva Tu Vida staff would storm her house at an agreed-upon time and take Elvis to the center in the middle of the night. The experience would symbolically mark a dramatic break with Elvis's past behavior, Fernando explained to Nancy, and prevent him from resisting treatment. Nancy made the arrangements, and left the door unlocked on the appointed night. Treatment center staff arrived at 2:00 AM on the appointed date in June

2010, entered Elvis's room, and carried him off. Nancy recounted watching this happen. She told me she was surprised that Elvis didn't struggle, and pushed down feelings that something was wrong. Fernando was the expert, she thought, and Nancy hoped this was the right choice for her son.

Nancy did not see Elvis for the first three months, which she was told was an important part of the treatment protocol. Elvis seemed to be responding well to treatment, and Nancy was pleased with his progress—and by Fernando's assurances that Elvis was healing and recovering. Elvis was managing the kitchen at the treatment center, was "promoted" to floor manager, and then to "staff," which meant he was allowed to interact with the public. Nancy and Elvis communicated even during the first three months through notes they would hide in the dirty laundry: Nancy would pick up Elvis's dirty clothes on Friday, and he would often include a note—"I love you mommy; I miss you"—tucked in between his dirty socks. He would also wait for her to come—one time making her a paper flower and quickly dropping it in her purse as she came to do the laundry pickup. In a diary that investigators later recovered, Elvis recorded his top five reasons for wanting to be sober every day, and each entry included reasons about his mom: "Because my mom is proud of me. Because I love my mother." For Nancy, this would later serve as evidence that Elvis, wherever he was, hadn't run away because he was angry with her.

After three months, she went to the treatment center for the planned "confrontations," where families would discuss the issues that led to the patient's addictions. She was told that these confrontations got heated and sometimes involved yelling and even nearly coming to blows. Nancy and Elvis, however, found that they had little to yell about. Elvis regretted using drugs and said he would be ready to come home when the treatment ended. When he spoke in front of the therapy group, he thanked his mom for bringing him to treatment and said he was proud of himself for the progress he had made. From then on, Nancy visited Elvis every week for family counseling until he was scheduled to be released. Elvis reported that he was clean and sober and looking forward to starting anew. Nancy, Elvis, and Fernando agreed that he would come home on New Year's Day, 2011.

The first sign that something was wrong came via a telephone call from Fernando just two days before Elvis was scheduled to be released. He called to say that on the night of December 28 he had sent Elvis to pick up a new patient in the city of Matamoros, located in the neighboring state of Tamaulipas, along with two other patients, and they had yet to return. Nancy was immediately alarmed—how could it be that her son had not only been permitted to leave, but had been sent away from what she understood was a secured treatment center, without her permission? She started to panic, calling Fernando multiple times. She wondered if her son and the other patients would serve as the "muscle," like those who had scooped her son up from his bed in the middle of the night. Nancy had a gut feeling that something was desperately wrong: "I started crying hysterically in my house. . . . [F]rom that moment it came to me like a burning in the body that something was happening, something had . . . something was happening."

Nancy went back and forth with Fernando over text and phone calls. Fernando initially promised he would go and look for Elvis, but he changed his mind at the last minute, saying it was too dangerous to travel at night. On December 31, a day traditionally set aside for family celebration in Mexico, Nancy went alone to search hotels along the route her son would have passed on the way to Matamoros. She had Elvis's picture in hand and asked everyone she could if they had seen the three boys. She also called a missing persons hotline, but no one fitting her son's description had been hospitalized or detained by the police in the preceding days. She didn't know what else to do.

That night, Nancy told her extended family what was happening:

> There was no celebration as such, and I told them everything, and we started sharing information, we all started crying. We started to think: What if he sent them to deliver drugs? What if he made them work as drug mules? What if he killed them? What if he sold them to drug trafficking? What if he sold them to organized crime? We talked until dawn, and there was no more celebration as a family. Everyone was just crying.

While Nancy had not thought of any of these possibilities prior to Elvis's disappearance, she had begun to hear stories of more violence in the news, and she knew that there were gangs involved in the local drug trade. These dynamics had seemed distant to her: her family's problems had seemed particular to their specific circumstances, and she hadn't been aware of the larger dynamics affecting her state. The conversation with her family jarred her. She was plunging into a world she knew nothing about and in which her strategy of hunkering down and working hard to provide for her and Elvis was no longer viable.

After that day, the earth began to shift for Nancy. Fernando began to change his story: He started acting hostile and claimed the three missing boys had escaped, stolen his truck, and were out partying. He told Nancy not to go look for him because he thought he knew where they might be and who they might be with. At one point, he told them that he had found the boys—and that getting them back was, as Nancy remembers, "nothing more than a question of getting the address where they are and going and picking them up." But that promise, like so many others Fernando made, proved false.

Nancy was conflicted about how to interact with Fernando. She knew she needed his cooperation if she was going to find her son. He was, after all, the one who had sent the boys on this errand; "he had the experience; he was the responsible one," she told me. At the same time, she felt a creeping awareness that Fernando was untrustworthy at best, and at worst complicit in Elvis's disappearance and actively covering it up. The things her family said kept echoing in her mind: had he sent them on an errand for the clinic? Or was Fernando involved in drug trafficking in some way, and had he involved the boys in some scheme? Later it would come out that Fernando was involved in both human and drug trafficking—but at this point, all Nancy could do was to speculate.

In addition to feeling guilty that she'd put her son in harm's way by sending him to rehab, she feared that bringing in state authorities would make things worse—that it would spur Fernando to harm her son if, God willing, he was still alive. What paralyzed her most was the impossibility of knowing how her actions might affect the odds that her son would be found alive; of how going to the police might affect his well-being; of what, if anything, could compel Fernando to come clean about his involvement and what he knew about the disappearance.

She finally held a family meeting, saying she'd decided that she wanted to report her son's disappearance, but that she didn't know what the fallout would be. Nancy told them that calling the police could potentially put them all in danger, cause legal problems, and even result in their imprisonment. She needed to know who in her family she could count on. They were all in. With a heavy heart, Nancy finally went to the police on January 5, six days after Elvis's disappearance.

Nancy's reluctance to report Elvis's disappearance to the police, and her reliance on herself, rather than a network of friends or an organization, were all seeded by her early experiences and understanding of herself as "against the law." We also see the nature of disappearance clearly as a particularly pernicious form of violence in her accounting: her world and that of her family immediately and dramatically shift as she realizes her only son is missing.

We see the "double paralyzing impact" of disappearances referenced by the OHCHR—though the paralysis for Nancy is brought about by her deep anxiety that if she pushes Fernando too hard, or not hard enough, it will further jeopardize her son's well-being. In this early reaction, there is no hint that Nancy will come to be a prominent activist, though her ability to turn to her family despite their history of difficult and conflictive relationships does suggest a baseline of family support that might enable her to shift her biographical availability and dedicate significant time and resources in the search for her son.

Alejandro: Disappeared in Transit to the United States, 2011

Lucía and Alfonso held a special meal on January 25, 2011. They had hoped to dissuade their 32-year-old son, Alejandro, from driving to Laredo, Texas, where he had arranged to pick up a large and expensive computer he had bought online. In early 2011, as Alejandro was planning his trip, reports of brutal violence in Monterrey, an industrial hub and economic powerhouse within Mexico, had just begun to emerge. On January 1, 2011, the local newspaper reported that for "the first time in the history of the state . . . a body appeared hanging in the streets in public—an organized crime practice that has been observed in states like Tamaulipas and Chihuahua" (as quoted in Villarreal 2021). But Alejandro was determined: he didn't want to fly with the computer, concerned that it would be damaged in transit, and he also wanted to stop and see a friend on the way in Monterrey. Alejandro Moreno Baca decided that in January 2011, driving through Monterrey en route to Texas was a reasonable risk to take.

Alejandro left Mexico City a little before 7:00 AM on January 27 for the roughly 12-hour trip to Laredo. At 4:00 PM, he met his friend in Monterrey and went out to eat. He got on the road to Laredo around 7:00 PM and was communicating via text messages with his parents. The last communication Lucía received from her son was a text sent from outside Monterrey. It read: "Mom—hold on, I'm stopping at a *puesto de revision*," referring to a checkpoint, which was most likely run either by federal forces or by the brutal Zetas DTO. Being stopped at checkpoints is fairly routine in Mexico, so Lucía didn't think much of it.

When Alejandro stopped responding to Lucía and Alfonso's texts that evening, they thought maybe he just didn't have cell phone coverage.

By the morning of January 29, they'd found out that Alejandro had never shown up at his friend's house in Texas, and they were immediately concerned. Lucía, Alfonso, and Diego, their youngest son, caught the first flight to Monterrey out of Mexico City and set about activating their network of friends and colleagues, many of whom they knew through Alfonso's work and their children's friends. As they tell it, a series of "angels" then began to help them, which they needed because, as Alfonso said, "it was a world we knew nothing about." They formally reported Alejandro missing at 8:00 PM that same night in Monterrey and left DNA samples at the state prosecutor's office. The next morning, they set out to Nuevo Laredo, in the neighboring state of Tamaulipas, where Alejandro would have crossed the border. There, they filed another formal *denuncia*, legal complaint, with the attorney general about Alejandro's disappearance and also with the federal police for the robbery of Alejandro's vehicle.[6] The commander there told them, according to Alfonso, "'Sir, don't worry: your son will be returned within three months. The car will probably be around, [it's] probably being driven around the countryside.'"

On their way back from Nuevo Laredo, on Sunday, January 30, three days after they had last heard from Alejandro, a policeman at the toll booth told them to be sure they got back home while it was still light out because the region was dangerous. They decided to stop in the small town of Sabinas Hidalgo, where they had been told that any car that had been in an accident along the highway between Monterrey and Nuevo Laredo would be brought. Sabinas was an eerily deserted town. There, the *ministerio público* (MP), the public prosecutor—the state official charged with administering justice in the town—was locked in his office and agreed to open the door only after they convinced him they were searching for a missing family member. He showed Lucía and Alfonso how he kept his desk hidden from the windows so that he would be safer from gunfire. Shaken, they went to make copies of Alejandro's picture to give to the MP. The woman at the copy store told them that her cousin had also been disappeared. She urged them to stay positive: it turned out that her cousin had been taken and was returned alive two months later. Feeling like they were being watched and noticing there was

---

[6] A formal report of a crime in Mexico is called a *denuncia*. After a *denuncia* is made, an *acta circunstanciada* is written, roughly translated as a detailed report. Since 2011, the law has changed, and now after a *denuncia* is filed, a *carpeta de investigación*, an investigation file, is opened.

only one way in and out of the town, they vowed never to go back. Lucía wondered aloud at the time—"my God, where are we?"

That evening they arrived back in Monterrey and kept busy, doing anything they could think of that might help locate Alejandro. Their network of "angels" continued to come through: an old friend of theirs had a contact in Nuevo León's government who figured out how to give them access to the photo records of the toll booth. Lucía and Alfonso pored through these photos until they found three photos which showed Alejandro's car passing through the toll booth on the evening of January 27. Three photos were taken at 8:54 PM on January 27, showing the arm of the person in his car—which Lucía and Alfonso believe to be Alejandro's—paying the correct toll. Before they went back to Mexico City, Lucía and Alfonso went back to this toll booth and asked the people working if they could help them. The woman working at the toll booth gave them an additional key piece of information: she told them another family had stopped by asking the same questions about their daughter and her boyfriend—a policeman—who had disappeared on the same highway eight days before Alejandro. While she told them she couldn't give them this couple's information by law, she left her desk briefly, intentionally leaving her notebook open. Lucía and Alfonso copied their contact information and went to the family's house and introduced themselves. In time, they would come to work closely with this family, bringing them to the local human rights organization and joining forces in the investigation.

On this first trip they also checked the morgue for anyone fitting Alejandro's description, ending the evening at the military barracks. A military officer agreed to talk to them but wouldn't let them in. Instead, he talked to them under a tree outside the military installation. While he didn't give them any leads, he vowed to help them. Later that same night, Lucía called a number her other sons had found online, which she believed to be the number designated for citizens to call the army with their concerns. The young man who picked up aggressively asked how they had gotten the number. When Lucía explained why she was calling, he told her, as she remembers, that she should be careful " 'because everyone, everyone—from the police to the investigators to the politicians was *coludido* (colluding with DTOs)'.... And he [the young man telling us this] was with the army! Imagine it. We were discovering the horror which we had been plunged into and which we are still living today." He then told her to lose that number and never call again.

The next morning, Lucía and Alfonso decided to return to Mexico City: they hoped and believed that Alejandro had been kidnapped and waited for a call at home for asking for ransom. Better to be back in the city, they reasoned. The call never came.

As people who saw themselves as "before the law," Lucía and Alfonso's first reactions to their son's disappearance were to go to the state—which they did in an exhaustive fashion characteristic of Alfonso's thorough and systematic way of doing things. They made multiple *denuncias*, sought contacts at attorney generals' offices in three states: Mexico City, Nuevo León, and Tamaulipas, and reached out to the army. Despite Alfonso's specific belief that some *individuals* within the state were corrupt, this did not map onto a system-wide critique: he believed that the state was responsible for investigating this disappearance and was initially determined to do everything possible to enable the state to do their job. Lucía jumped into an active and supportive role in this initial phase, foreshadowing her journey from home to the public sphere. Calling the military helpline was already new territory for her: she had never before sought state assistance, but like her husband, she appeared to believe that this early action should be state-focused.

With Lucía and Alfonso, we also see the importance of economic prosperity in their immediate mobilization activities. Their wealth facilitates their biographical availability: they were able to drop everything, buy flights, rent a car, and pay for lodging in Nuevo León without concern for the cost nor concern that Alfonso's employment would be affected. While they had had no contact with social movements prior to Alejandro's disappearance, we also immediately see the importance of their social network: the "angels" who activate to help them emerge from a web of people with access to elite social circles, which in turn confers upon them the ability to access multiple federal and state agencies.

Juan Carlos: Tragedy of Out-of-State Plates, 2008 and 2010

"We had rules: not to go out, not to drink, stay in known hotels, and not to work at night or tell anyone in the hotels we were staying at what we did for work." These were the measures that Juan Carlos and six of his brothers agreed to take when they traveled for work to keep themselves safe. They traveled from town to town across Mexico buying and selling people's gold jewelry, which they would then melt down and sell for a profit. They knew this put them in a risky situation because they carried large amounts of cash, and the people they interacted with knew that.

They didn't realize, however, that traveling around the country also put them in a different kind of danger: they were crossing the invisible but consequential boundaries of different DTOs, and at times, wandering into active battlegrounds. On August 28, 2008, brothers Raúl (19) and Salvador (24) and five of their employees, arrived in the small town of Atoyac de Álvarez, Guerrero, a town just north of Acapulco that was a convenient and frequent stop on their way home. They ran into another one of their brothers, Rafael (29 at the time), who had also stopped in Atoyac on his way home after a day of buying and selling gold. Earlier that day, there had been a violent confrontation between two local offshoots of major Mexican cartels, during which a group affiliated with the Beltrán Leyva Cartel had killed the wife and daughters of "El Nene," the *jefe de plaza* (local DTO boss) of the Granados, a local group aligned with the Familia Michoacana cartel. In response, El Nene[7] sent his men after anyone in the vicinity who seemed suspicious, including anyone not from Atoyac.

The Trujillo Herrera brothers Raúl and Salvador and their five employees knew nothing of this when they arrived that evening. They had all spent their morning buying and selling gold in Oaxaca, where they'd had a successful day—managing to buy more than a kilo and a half of gold. Raúl convinced Salvador to stop in Guerrero on their way back to Michoacán because he wanted to see a dancer he had been dating there. Despite the rules, the group settled into a hotel they weren't familiar with and went to El Diamante, a local bar where the dancer worked, to relax. When they arrived, the dancer was sitting with another man. When she left the man's side to be with Raúl, he was visibly upset and left. While it seemed inconsequential at the time, it later became clear that this jilted man was one of El Nene's men, and that this was one possible explanation for what may have set the ball rolling for the evening's tragedy.

As the night wore on, Raúl and Salvador went back to their hotel with the dancer, their five employees, and some other friends. Older brother Rafael stayed at the bar after they had left, talking to the bartender. The bartender told Rafael about the cartel fighting that day and urged Rafael to tell his younger brothers to be careful because El Nene would take revenge. More specifically, she told Rafael that El Nene would *"levantar gente."* While *"levantar"* literally means "to pick up," it would soon come to be widely

---

[7] "El Nene's" given name is Rubén Granados Vargas. He would go on to be arrested in 2009 and then again in 2017 for his involvement in cartel activity (de Dios Palma 2017).

known as a euphemism for disappearing people. But in 2008, Rafael didn't know that. He understood the bartender's caution as a warning that police would be on the roads looking to "pick up" suspects.

After Raúl and Salvador headed back to the hotel with their five employees,[8] Rafael never saw any of them again. Around 10:30 the next morning, Rafael called Salvador. There was no answer. When he called Raúl's phone, Salvador answered, but Rafael could tell he was speaking from some distance to the phone—as if someone else was holding the phone near him. Salvador's voice seemed off to his brother, and while Salvador said they were on their way back home to Michoacán, Rafael knew something was wrong. Later, it would be determined that at noon that same day a call was placed from Salvador's phone to El Nene's brother. However, a thorough investigation into this phone and these calls has never been conducted.[9]

Rafael called his boss and older brother Juan Carlos, who was back home in Pajacuarán, an eight-hour drive away. Juan Carlos sprang into action as best he could from home. After contacting the families of the other missing men, he started trying to reach the Atoyac police and to figure out how to get in touch with the *jefe de plaza*. While he didn't know who controlled the *plaza* in Atoyac specifically, he understood the regional security dynamics well enough to immediately seek out the state and non-state actors who controlled the local security context. He repeatedly called the local police, but no one would talk to him over the phone. Juan Carlos asked Rafael to go to the police station and meet with the local police chief. When Rafael finally spoke with the police chief, he declined to take any action, instead suggesting that the brothers file a formal report. Juan Carlos later came to believe that the chief of police had been involved in the disappearance and that he had known his brothers were in Atoyac. According to what witnesses told Juan Carlos, the previous evening local police had gone to the bar and asked workers there who the truck with out-of-state plates belonged to, "but no one," according to Juan Carlos, "not SEIDO, not anyone, has wanted to investigate this."

In the meantime, word came that El Nene's men had set up a roadblock on the highway that Rafael would take out of town. This was not the kind of contact with the *jefe de plaza* that Juan Carlos was looking for, and he realized

---

[8] The five disappeared employees, all from Pajacuarán, are Rafael Cervantes Rodríguez, Fabio Higareda Viña, Luis Carlos Barajas Días, José Luis Barajas Alcázar, and Joel Franco Ávila.

[9] Nearly all details of this event were narrated by Juan Carlos, with cross-checking and inclusion of several additional facts made with the assistance of attorneys at Centro ProDH, a leading Mexican human rights NGO (see Chapter 3 for further information about Centro ProDH).

the focus needed to be on ensuring a third brother didn't go missing that day. While Rafael kept insisting he wasn't leaving Atoyac without his brothers, he was finally convinced that staying was too risky for his personal safety, and he was able to slip out of town on a back road. Knowing Rafael had safely escaped Atoyac but convinced that he wouldn't be able to negotiate or reason with El Nene, Juan Carlos set about frantically cold-calling government officials. Through his persistence he would manage to get meetings with the Michoacán attorney general and governor in the first month after the disappearance. None of these contacts, however, led to any significant investigatory leads.

Tragically, Juan Carlos's experience navigating the crucial hours and days following a disappearance did not end with the disappearance of Raúl and Salvador in 2008. Two years later, he received another dreaded call: his brothers Gustavo and Luis Armando had stopped responding to texts.

In early September 2010, short on funds and frustrated by their inability to make any progress finding their brothers, the family decided that while Juan Carlos and his brother Miguel would continue to search, the other brothers would return to their gold-buying business. On their very first trip outside of Michoacán, brothers Gustavo and Luis Armando, along with a cousin and nephew who had joined the business, headed to Veracruz. They were on their way to the town of Vega de la Torre, Veracruz, when they took a detour down a side road because the bridge on the main road had been knocked out by a hurricane. They were then detained at a joint army and state police checkpoint, the municipal police of Poza Rica were called, and Gustavo and Luis were separated by the municipal police into two different police vehicles. At the time, and without their knowledge, there was a standing order in Veracruz: any car with plates from Michoacán would be stopped, and its occupants detained. The head of the municipal police of Poza Rica, widely known by his DTO nickname "El Indio,"[10] ordered the men to be turned over to them.

Juan Carlos's sister-in-law called him at 4:00 PM that day. She'd tried calling Gustavo and Luis Armando but no one was responding. When she called again, no one spoke, but she heard strange sounds in the background. Juan Carlos and Rafael, recognizing the signs of a disappearance from their prior experience, immediately headed to Poza Rica, checking hospitals and jails on

[10] "El Indio's" given name is Javier Amado Mercado, and he was later imprisoned for his leadership role with the Zetas (Animal Político 2011).

their way. This time they didn't seek out local authorities. "It was obvious for us from what we had learned from the first disappearance, where the police were involved, and even [with] . . . high level contacts . . . with the President of Mexico, Senators, Attorneys General and investigators . . . that they hadn't been able to bring back my brothers."

Juan Carlos stayed in Veracruz, looking for his brothers. His search would eventually bring him into contact with members of organized crime, unscru- pulous private investigators, and low-level state police as he continued to ask, ¿dónde están?

From the time of the first disappearance, Juan Carlos reacted to the disap- pearance of his brothers strategically and in a way consistent with someone who regards themselves as "with the law": he did not expect that going to officials would work on its own, nor did he shy away from a system he knew to be corrupt. Rather, he pursued contact with and tried to negotiate with the local actors whom he understood to have control over the security of Atoyac: the local police, and the head of the local DTO. In Chapter 4, I will explore more fully how these initial instincts evolved. For now, it is signif- icant to note that by the time of the second disappearances in 2010, Juan Carlos's understanding of the operation of power and legality in Mexico had evolved to the point that it was clear to him it would not be productive to in- volve the state.

In Juan Carlos we also immediately see a shift in his life circumstances: since he is the head of the family business, he has the resources and flexibility to channel his own and his family's time and capacity into looking for his brothers. Like Nancy and Lucía and Alfonso, there is no hint, initially, that he will turn to social movements or civil society organizations. Similar to the others, the disappearances are an inflection point where all the family's activities and focus are considered to have happened before or after: the disappearances are a pivotal tragedy in his life which upend his business, his family, and fundamentally alter the trajectory of his life.

Conclusion

In each of these narratives, the disappearance of their loved one provokes an immediate reaction that has a feeling of inevitability: when Elvis goes missing, how could Nancy do anything else but search the hotels where he may have stopped? How could Lucía and Alfonso not drive the same highway their son did, contacting authorities and looking for clues as to what might have happened to him? Since Juan Carlos understood that some mix of local police an DTOs controlled the town where his brothers were taken, how could he do anything but contact them? Considerations of the risk to themselves, the cost of their reaction, and the impact their actions will have on their livelihood are absent in these first responses.

Digging into these reactions, however, we uncover the seeds of these responses: Nancy's resistance to contacting authorities led her to conduct her initial investigation on her own. Lucía and Alfonso's faith in a society which, in the end, is bound by order and the state, led them to seek out state agents at every level, and their personal network expanded their ability to respond. Juan Carlos's understanding that his brothers' fate would be determined by the politics of power in the *plaza* led him to pursue state and non-state recourse from the moment of the disappearance, and his familiarity with making the law work for him led him to be resourceful as he pursued meetings with high-level state officials.

We also see how considerations of whether and how to mobilize (or not) are filtered through the lens of each family's legal consciousness and factored into each family's decision-making. Nancy avoids contact with the authorities, in part fearing the reaction of another authority figure—the head of the treatment center, as she believes him to be involved. Lucía and Alfonso return to Mexico City instead of remaining near Monterrey so they can wait for a ransom call. Juan Carlos weighs the need to get his remaining brother out of harm's way versus having a trusted interlocutor present at the scene of the crime.

In taking time to consider these calculations of each family, we also can see a glimmer of their particular cruelty. Nancy's agony over whether her tone and actions might push her son's presumed abductor to cause her son more harm. The powerlessness and desperation of Lucía and Alfonso as their oldest son disappears without a trace somewhere in northern Mexico. Juan Carlos's terror as he navigates communication within a dangerous context while trying to make sure another brother escapes harm.

While these stories are horrific, they have become tragically common in Mexico since 2006. In the overwhelming majority of cases of disappearances, my fieldwork has taught me that the initial response of the families has some resemblance to those I have profiled here. A dreaded phone call. An initial search. In nearly every case—there is an initial impetus to find the disappeared person. There is nearly always a consideration of whether to call police; to contact those who last saw the person. But most often, considerations of the risks, danger, and futility are enough to deter people from reporting crimes in Mexico[11]—much less engaging in ongoing mobilization. What was different in these cases that facilitated the families' ongoing mobilization?

In other words, what have we learned in this chapter about what enables some people, and not others, to continuously act on this impetus to mobilize in the wake of the disappearance of their loved one? After looking closely at how the particular nature of disappearance moved the very different families to action, we followed this impetus as it was channeled through each person's existing perspective on legality, the state and themselves—in other words, their legal consciousness. We also saw how the costs and benefits of mobilization, personal circumstances and resources, and social networks shaped their actions immediately following the disappearance. I argue, however, that the true north guiding this trajectory was family members' way of thinking about the law.

In Chapter 3, I turn to the overall political and social movement context in Mexico at the time of these disappearances to lay the necessary groundwork for understanding what challenges, resources, and options for mobilization Nancy, Lucía and Alfonso, and Juan Carlos had. In Chapter 4, I return to these three cases and continue to pull the thread of legal consciousness. I examine how each person's ways of thinking and actions evolved over time and as they met others affected by the same tragedy, reflecting on shifts in their relationship to state agents, legality, and contentious politics. I look at how changes in each person's ways of thinking enabled them to continue their search—and facilitated changes in their calculations about the benefits and risks of mobilizing, life circumstances, and social networks.

---

[11] In an analysis of the Encuesta de Victimización y Percepción sobre Seguridad (ENVIPE), the annual national victimization survey, México Evalúa found that an average of 92.8 percent of crimes were not reported in Mexico between 2010 and 2019. 64.1 percent of those who didn't report a crime said that they didn't report a crime because it was "attributable to [state] authorities," and 36.3 percent stated that reporting a crime was a "waste of time" (México Evalúa 2020, 74; 76).

3

State and Civil Society Responses
to Disappearances in Mexico

It's now clear that Mexico isn't a place where *no pasa nada* [nothing
is happening], because of people like you who are struggling. This
is not easy—we are trying to reclaim territory which is subsumed
under the ocean of impunity. And we're doing it by constructing
chapels of hope—that's what this struggle is. And that generating
this space goes further than what we do as individuals or even
collectives—is extraordinary.

> —Emilio Alvarez Icaza, MPJD leader (now Senator) March
> 23, 2012, speaking to a victims' collective after a
> participatory investigation meeting with the Nuevo León
> state officials.

When Nancy, Lucía, Alfonso, and Juan Carlos took the first steps to mobilize
in response to the disappearances of their loved ones, they encountered a political landscape unequipped to support them. They found state institutions
mired in bureaucratic inertia, with little capacity to investigate the whereabouts of their missing loved ones, and even less willing to find and prosecute those responsible. When these families later turned to civil society, they
encountered human rights organizations in Mexico City that worked largely
on cases involving state violence against activists—which excluded their
loved ones. As they encountered others who also had missing loved ones,
in time they began to realize that the existing avenues for redress weren't
working—and that they must be part of crafting new approaches and organizations and in pushing state institutions to reform.

This chapter is about how the family members of victims went from being
isolated, unknown, and relatively powerless—to protagonists not only in the
legal cases of their disappeared loved ones, but in victims' collectives and
within national politics. Chapters 2 and 4 tell the story of the evolution of
victims' mobilization, power, and agency at the individual level. This chapter

Bootstrap Justice. Janice k. Gallagher, Oxford University Press. © Oxford University Press 2023.
DOI: 10.1093/oso/9780197649978.003.0003

complements these individual-level journeys by contextualizing them within the political, institutional, and social landscape that confronted the families of the disappeared in the 2010s, tracing how it came to be, and how it evolved and adapted to the emerging crisis of disappearances during the Calderón (2006–2012) and Peña Nieto (2012–2018) administrations. Much of the information will be familiar to those well acquainted with Mexico's history and current political context; however, the specific history of disappearances as a modality of violence and the response of social movements to these disappearances is less well known.

In social movement terms, this chapter pays close attention to the evolving legal (Vanhala 2012) and political (Meyer and Minkoff 2004; Tarrow 2011) opportunity structures in Mexico; it lays out how civil society mobilization responded to different threats and repressive tactics from the state, in particular to the democratization of Mexico in 2000 and the subsequent jump in violence related to the drug war (2006–present). The analysis is divided into three distinct time periods. Each one (1) summarizes key developments in the security and governance practices of the Mexican state; (2) explores the changing nature of both the phenomenon of and the response to disappearances; and (3) situates mobilization in response to disappearances within the larger context of civil society organizing. Each of these time periods highlights the historic and ongoing tension and synergy between two distinct but complementary forms of social movement mobilization: *advocates* who opt to work with the state as a necessary tactic to reach their goals, and *activists* who critique state inaction and complicity in the commission of human rights violations and eschew collaborating with the state. I argue that Mexican state-society relationships in the area of human rights shifts from almost completely adversarial prior to 2006—with activism the only viable strategy—to one in which advocacy is increasingly possible. After the PRI's electoral defeat in 2000, *asociaciones civiles*, ACs (civic organizations) led by professional organizers fulfilled activist or advocate roles. After 2012, and especially after the 2014 disappearance of 43 Ayotzinapa Rural Teachers College students, I illustrate how the emergence of victims' collectives blurred this activist/advocate binary. The proliferation of these collectives marked a departure from professional social movement organizations and organizers setting the agenda for and leading the struggle for human rights in Mexico, and a new era of political power, legitimacy, and autonomy for family members of victims of violence.

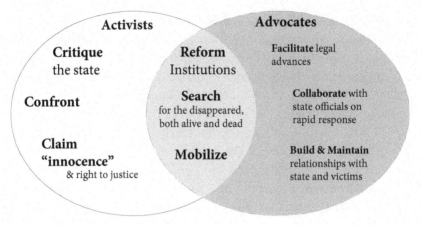

Figure 3.1 Activists and advocates

Activists, Advocates, and Substituting for the State

Central Concepts

Social movement scholarship has helped us gain insight into the structural conditions that explain why groups of people mobilize around certain grievances, at certain times, and using certain organizing tactics, or contentious repertoires,[1] like marches, sit-ins, and strikes (McAdam et al. 2001; Meyer and Minkoff 2004; Tarrow 2011). I argue in previous work that an important category of difference among social movements is their attitude toward and interaction with the state (Gallagher 2017). In this chapter, I employ and update this framework, arguing that social movement *organizations* (usually ACs) that work with victims of violence have tended to mobilize into two distinct ideal types: *activists* and *advocates*. As illustrated in Figure 3.1, *activists* take a consistently critical view of the state, publicly confronting the state and asserting their right to justice; *advocates* facilitate dialogue and the exchange of information about key aspects of legal cases with state investigators.

In the early 2010s, I argue that *activist* organizations challenged systemic normative biases that criminalized victims of violence and prevented them from obtaining justice. Activists contested state narratives that blamed

[1] As coined by Charles Tilly in 1977, repertoires of contention are understood by social movement scholars to be the socially and culturally available forms of collective action for social movements at any given time and place.

victims, reframing the victims of lethal violence as innocent subjects who deserved justice[2]. Activists also imposed a political cost to impunity for judicial and state officials through the well-documented practices of public naming and shaming (Schmitz 2002; Ron, Ramos, and Rodgers 2005; Franklin 2008; Murdie and Davis 2012). Activists in both the early 2010s, and previously, during Mexico's Dirty War, were most often institutional outsiders—NGOs, social movements, informal political collectives. They often had little contact with state officials, or the contact they did have was hostile and contentious. This tension was often unavoidable, since the state insisted on criminalizing victims. Even when the state was willing to engage with activists—activists often demurred, believing that negotiating with a corrupt state that had shown itself more than willing to criminalize them was not productive. Instead of negotiating with the state, activists concentrated on building the political costs of impunity by mounting national and international pressure campaigns. In order to channel this pressure onto the officials tasked with prosecuting the vast majority of disappearances cases, activists were omnipresent at what I call the judicial decision-making site (JDMS)—the physical location of officials tasked with investigating or prosecuting cases (see Gallagher 2019). Since the vast majority of disappearance cases in Mexico are processed in state, as opposed to federal, judicial systems, JDMSs are usually in the state capitals.

Meanwhile, I argue that *advocate* organizations in the early 2010s, and still in many states within Mexico, played the role of interlocutor by addressing the informational deficiencies that often plague investigations into lethal violence by facilitating regular communication and the exchange of crucial investigative information with state judicial officials. Advocacy organizations provide legal accompaniment to family members of the disappeared and include local NGOs, cause lawyer associations, and international and inter-governmental organizations.[3] An advocacy organization can serve as a bridge between the state and those directly affected by violence, but it must have legitimacy with both sets of actors to occupy this role effectively.

[2] A previous version of this figure was included in Gallagher 2017. The most significant change to this updated figure is the inclusion of "search" as something both groups engage in—a fairly recent innovation in the contentious repertoire discussed at length in Chapters 4 and 5. The descriptions of activists and advocates in this section draw from and update the theoretical categories presented in the 2017 article.

[3] If organizations are not headquartered locally, it is vital for them to have an ongoing physical presence at the JDMS, as the in-person relationships they build with judicial officials, members of civil society, and families of victims are keys to their effectiveness.

Advocates gain access to state officials through multiple channels: activist pressure may increase the political cost of impunity and open the door for advocates; and efforts to reframe criminalized victims as political subjects worthy of justice may shift the ideational environment of investigators, state officials, and judges.[4] Advocates are often either former activists or victims' collectives who are brokered into new, collaborative relationships with state officials by outside actors after waves of intense activist pressure. For example, in a 2019 interview, Jan Jarab, the head of the UN Human Rights Office's Representative in Mexico at the time, told me, "We have worked for them [victims' collectives] to become the interlocutor; [and then] we are standing with them when they have been legitimized."[5] Once they have gained access to the state, advocates use their access to generate and follow up on investigatory leads, to call for rapid state responses to new threats and violent events, and to pressure the state into allocating resources for searching for the disappeared.

How has the shifting political opportunity structure in Mexico shaped the emergence of activist and advocate organizations, and the more recent emergence of victims' collectives that engage in both activism and advocacy simultaneously? How do the paired developments of a democratic opening and spiraling lethal violence spur certain types of organizing and frustrate others?

I have argued previously (Gallagher 2017) that organizations can effectively occupy only the activist or the advocate role—and that these categories are mutually exclusive. In order to build relationships with their members and, in the case of advocates, with potential allies within the state, they must have a coherent mission: either they are activists critiquing the state by naming its deficiencies and shaming it for inaction, or they are advocates seeking ways to mitigate harm through negotiating and strategically partnering with state actors. Advocates jeopardize their relationships with state actors and their ability to play interlocutor if they are openly critical of the state. Activists, on the other hand, betray their role critiquing the

---

[4] See González-Ocantos (2016) and Hilbink (2007) for a discussion of the vital role the ideational environment plays in the decision-making of judicial officials. I argue that over the course of investigations, relationships can be built that not only facilitate the flow of investigative information between the two parties but also change the way that usually hostile parties relate to each other and think about their respective roles in the judicial process, ultimately driving changes in state attitudes toward victims, as promoted by activists.

[5] Jan Jarab, interview by author, via Zoom, September 11, 2019.

state and are inevitably accused of selling out or being co-opted by their base if they negotiate and collaborate with the state.

What became clear with the flourishing of powerful independent victims' collectives after 2011, and even more so after 2014, however, is that individual victims or organizations led by and made up of only victims are now able to shift fluidly between activism and advocacy. Why can individuals or victims be both activist and advocates, while organizations cannot? State actors are now, after years of struggle and pressure, more open to perceiving them as politically legitimate and authentic. Organizations, which the state has grown to know over time, demand accountability and critique inconsistency; for victims, the people directly affected by disappearances, expectations are different. While victims of early drug war violence were dismissed or criminalized by state actors, as they gained political power it became more difficult for the state to deny victims the right to be angry; indeed this anger is a powerful tool that I have often seen shame investigators and officials into action, when it would get their lawyers or representatives thrown out of the room. Said differently, the state's willingness to grant victim activists more leeway in their behavior stems largely from (1) the activism and advocacy of the past decade to challenge the criminalization of victims; (2) the undeniable gravity and prevalence of disappearances; and (3) the (previously) apolitical profile of most family members of victims.

In the remainder of this chapter I explore the evolution of Mexico's national-level political and security context, and discuss how it shaped the political opportunities for those confronting the disappearances during three distinct historical periods.

Governance, Disappearance, and Mobilization Prior to 2006

Governance and Disappearances Under the PRI

Mexico under the rule of the Partido Revolucionario Institucional (PRI), from 1929 to 2000, was famously coined the "perfect dictatorship" by Mario Vargas Llosa. The label stuck, with this "perfection" referring to its apparent ability to hold violence and unrest at bay while promoting moderate prosperity, through its corporatist structure that balanced a diverse and powerful coalition of labor, peasant, popular, and military interests (Scott 1964; Verba

1965; Hellman 1978; Huntington and Moore 1970). Mexico under the PRI actively cultivated this image internationally, accepting exiles from those fleeing the dictatorships of Central and South America, and paying international public relations firms to make sure this image was successful (Fox and Hernández 1992). Many scholars attributed this "peace" in part to a strong presidency,[6] pointing to the limited power of governors, all of whom depended on the federal government for funding, did not have their own armed forces, and could be removed by the president at will.[7] More recent scholarship (Gillingham and Smith 2014; Hernández 2008) , however, has shown that governors and other state-level officials actually had considerable autonomy during this period: as long as governors maintained political stability and order within their territory, they would usually be left alone by the president.

Local stability during the PRI era was largely achieved through city- or town-level negotiations between local strongmen, called *caudillistas* or *caciques*, and politicians, creating a dynamic in which power was disaggregated, "personal, informal, to a degree reciprocal, and resistant to formal laws and regulations" (Knight and Pansters 2005, 3). State and local institutions were consistently atrophied. At no time under the PRI were local institutions— the police, courts, or legislatures—invested with any real power to regulate contentious social or economic relations. Local judiciaries usually develop through mediating local conflicts. But in Mexico, local *caciques* provided the conflict resolution, leaving local institutions as little more than shells through the early 2000s.

When these local dynamics failed to provide the peace the federal government desired, the military was called on to restore order. The military was brought in to repress labor unions in the 1940s and 1950s, students in the 1960s, and other regional rebellions and strongman threats to state power throughout its rein (Pansters 2012, 15). Importantly, even during the heyday of the PRI's rule, control over the military was disputed. While

---

[6] By the 1980s, "it had become a standard view" among social scientists "that the Mexican state—or in naively personalized form, the Mexican president—enjoyed pervasive and untrammeled power" (Knight 2012, 212). Dresser (2003) and Beer (2012) refer to the PRI during this period as a hyper-presidentialist regime "in which presidents used unwritten norms to control the legislature, the judiciary, and state and local governments" (Beer 2012). Scholars have also referred to these unwritten norms as "meta-constitutional powers" (Dresser 2002); and the *"presidencia imperial"* (Krauze et al. 1977), or "imperial presidency."

[7] Presidents often exercised this power: between 1946 and 2000, Mexican presidents removed 70 out of 252, or around a quarter, of governors after the governors had displeased them. See Hernández 2008.

the federal forces were formally controlled by the president, they were in practice controlled by local squadrons, which operated largely according to the commands and interests of the aforementioned local coalitions of power (Migdal 1988; Rath 2013). These local coalitions also controlled illicit markets, which often brought significant funds to those involved in trafficking drugs, local officials, and members of the military. Drug traffickers were, at this time, mostly linked to the state of Sinaloa, and their business was legally tolerated, if not encouraged, by the local officials who profited from their trade (Shirk 2011). The role of the military became more visible to Mexicans and the world following the repression of student protests at the 1968 Olympics in Mexico City, the Tlateloco massacre[8] and the ensuing state-sponsored terror of the Dirty War.[9]

While the military was active in repressing internal dissent during this time, its power was also beginning to erode as drug trafficking organizations (DTOs) grew stronger. In the late 1980s, a shift began in the dynamics that had enabled the tacit alliances and comparatively peaceful and mutually beneficial relationships between DTOs and state officials. US demand for drugs began to rise with the counter-culture movement of the 1960s, spurring the success and profitability of Colombian DTOs in the 1970s and 1980s. As transit routes were disrupted in Colombia and the Caribbean by US-led drug eradication and interdiction efforts in the name of the War on Drugs in the 1990s, however, drug routes shifted to land. This made Mexico the principal transit route between drug-producing countries in Latin America and the lucrative US market—and spelled huge profits for Mexican DTOs. By the early 1990s, Mexican cartels were supplying about a third of the heroin and marijuana coming into the United States and a significant amount of cocaine as well (Astorga and Shirk 2010; Gerth 1988; Miller 1991). Struggles for control of ballooning drug profits led to increased local violence in the form of political assassinations and unpunished killings of anyone who interfered with the increasingly powerful DTOs (Pansters 2012).

[8] The human toll of this massacre remains disputed: the government claimed that 49 people were killed; others insist that nearly 400 unarmed protesting students were gunned down by the military. See Witherspoon (2008) for a narrative of the massacre.

[9] There has been some pushback among scholars (Calveiro 2019) regarding the use of the term "Dirty War." De Vecchi (2018, 15) writes that "this term responds to a logic in which two armies regarded as equivalent parts are in confrontation, and some 'dirty' tactics are used by one side to defeat the other. It is a term that corresponds to the way in which the state has explained the events: there was a war and all the available resources had to be used to protect the nation." Despite these very valid concerns, I use "Dirty War" because for most readers, the term rightly links the illegal practices used by many Latin American dictatorships between the 1960s and 1980s.

As DTO power grew, the Mexican state and the political stranglehold of the PRI were weakening. The Mexican miracle—an era of economic diversification and prosperity—was over, and in the early 1980s Mexico faced the first of several serious economic crises as world oil prices collapsed, forcing Mexico to turn to the international community for loans and accept the austerity measures required to receive international capital. On the heels of this economic crisis, the Mexican government displayed ostentatious incompetence and corruption in the aftermath of the deadly 1985 Mexico City earthquake. Presidents Salinas de Gortari (1988–1994) and Zedillo (1994–2000) doubled down on neoliberalism and oversaw an even greater widening of inequality; a rebellion led by the Chiapas-based Zapatistas:[10] and the devaluation of the Mexican peso. As the PRI became more desperate to hold onto power, they increasingly resorted to fraud and repression. Under Salinas de Gortari, an elite squad of the Federal Judicial Police became particularly well known for their lawless tactics, including disappearances, murder, and torture, in the name of the "war on drugs" (Lutz 1990). The rise in Mexican DTO power, paired with the first real contestation for the presidency in 1988 and the first PRI electoral defeat at the gubernatorial level in 1989, made the cracks in PRI-controlled federal power visible to all Mexicans. As the PRI's power eroded, DTOs took full advantage of the long-standing institutionalized corruption between drug traffickers and government officials at all levels to facilitate the distribution, transit, and protection of their ever-more-valuable commodities (Shirk 2011, 9).

In 2000, the PRI lost the presidency of Mexico for the first time in 71 years. Vicente Fox, a former Coca-Cola executive, won running under the center-right PAN (Partido de Acción Nacional), and expectations were high: Mexicans hoped they would see the benefits of democracy for which so many had struggled for so long. Fox, however, had an unremarkable administration. He deepened the neoliberal policies of his predecessors and failed to meaningfully address the waning power of the federal government and the growing power of DTOs. While he wielded considerable authority over the armed forces and judicial system (see Trejo and Ley 2020), he made minimal use of this power.

---

[10] The Zapatistas, formally known as the Ejército Zapatista de Liberación Nacional (EZLN), the Zapatista Army of National Liberation, are a largely Indigenous guerrilla group based in Chiapas who launched an armed insurrection for autonomy on January 1, 1994—the day the North American Free Trade Agreement (NAFTA) was implemented. While the armed threat they posed rather quickly subsided, they have remained a powerful voice in Mexican politics advocating on behalf of Indigenous and poor Mexicans.

Mexicans were unimpressed: democracy didn't seem to be delivering on its promise of equality, participation, and change. In the 2006 elections, only the second in which democracy and fair elections seemed probable, voter participation fell. Voters reported that they were unenthusiastic about Felipe Calderón's campaign platform stressing public security and the rule of law. Overall, there was little sense of the impending security crisis that would come to dominate governance and civil society mobilization in Mexico for the next 15 years.

Mobilization Before Democratization: Activism Around the Disappeared

Family members of the disappeared who became activists during Latin America's military dictatorships of the 1960s through the 1990s were in a very different position from that of the family members of those disappeared in Mexico after 2006. The people being disappeared were largely part of leftist organizations, and they were targeted because of their beliefs and challenges to ruling regimes. In the wake of their disappearances, the activist organizations they were part of made and mobilized international human rights norms to condemn states that tortured, incarcerated, and disappeared their perceived political enemies throughout the region. In some ways, these victims were isolated and criminalized: the revolutionary groups were blamed for what happened to their members, and regimes throughout the region sought to downplay the significance of their disappearances. At the same time, the victims and their families were, by their nature, part of national and international social and political networks that gave them access to common repertoires of contention. In response to disappearances throughout the region, there were hunger strikes, demonstrations outside government offices, and large Mother's Day mobilizations.

The practice of enforced disappearances in Mexico is understood to have begun in 1969 when a teacher with revolutionary politics named Epifanio Avilés Rojas was taken from his home in the state of Guerrero by military police (De Vecchi 2018). The Fox administration—at first eager to distance itself from Mexico's authoritarian past—commissioned a report of what had happened and who was responsible for the atrocities committed by the Mexican state during the Dirty War. After the Fox administration reportedly deemed the report too politically explosive to release, part of the contents were leaked and the key findings were summarized by the *New York Times*:

> The Mexican military carried out a "genocide plan" of kidnapping, tor-
> turing and killing hundreds of suspected subversives in the southern state
> of Guerrero during the Dirty War. . . . In those towns, soldiers rounded up
> all the men and boys, executed some on the spot and detained others, and
> then used violence, including rape, to drive the rest of the people away. . . .
> Most of those detained suffered severe torture, including beatings, electric
> shock, and being forced to drink gasoline, at military installations that were
> operated like concentration camps." (Thompson 2006)

According to the official report eventually issued by the Mexican government (Office of Special Prosecutor 2016), this campaign resulted in a total
of 645 disappearances—most of which were in Guerrero; 99 extrajudicial
executions; and more than 2,000 cases of torture—though civil society cites
higher numbers, claiming that up to 1,300 people disappeared (De Vecchi
2018).[11] The report laid responsibility for these atrocities firmly at the feet of
the federal forces, including the president.[12] This failure to engage in a reckoning with what scholars recognize as "state specialists in violence" (Trejo
et al. 2018) has had far-reaching consequences, as it failed to reset the rules of
how Mexican state agents control and coerce their own citizens.

Early organizing in response to state violence in Mexico brought to-
gether victims of different state-perpetrated crimes. In 1977, Rosario
Ibarra's[13] search for her son led her to found Comité pro Defensa de Presos,
Perseguidos, Desaparecidos y Exiliados Políticos de Monterrey (Monterrey's

---

[11] The numbers in the Special Prosecutor's report are slightly different from those in the Comisión Nacional de Derechos Humanos CNDH, National Human Rights Commission, Special Report, which claims there were 532 cases of enforced disappearances in the late 1970s and early 1980s, with 332 of these cases in Guerrero. The Asociación de Familiares de Detenidos Desaparecidos en México, AFADEM, believes there were approximately 1,300 disappearances during this time. For further details of civil society's understanding of the Dirty War, see De Vecchi (2018). For a more detailed account of how and when these disappearances occurred, including the role of the Brigada Blanca in enforced disappearances, see Lutz 1990.

[12] According to the report: "With this [the Dirty War suppression] operation, a state policy was established in which all the authorities connected to the army—the president, ministers of state, the presidential guard, commanders of the military regions in Guerrero, and officers and troops in their command—participated in the violations of human rights with the justification of pursuing a bad actor. . . . Such an open counter-guerrilla strategy could not have been possible without the explicit consent and approval of the president."

[13] Ibarra's son Jesús Piedra Ibarra was a medical student and activist with the Communist League; he was disappeared by judicial police in 1975.

Committee for Political Prisoners, Persecuted, Disappeared and Exiled), which would soon extend its scope nationally and in 1984 be renamed the Eureka Committee of the Disappeared.[14] This organization secured an important early win: in 1978, President Lopez Portillo signed an Amnesty Law[15] that eventually led to the liberation of 1,500 political prisoners (De Vecchi 2018, 103) and enabled political exiles to return to Mexico. This victory, however, did not extend to investigatory progress in the cases of the disappeared, and these early cases of disappearances remain unsolved.

Eureka became the country's most prominent organization of family members of those who were forcibly disappeared because of their beliefs during the 1980s and 1990s.[16] Ibarra also brought the issue of disappearances to the world stage, forming relationships with Amnesty International and different UN agencies, and leading Eureka to participate in the formation of FEDEFAM, the Federación Latinoamericana de Asociaciones de Familiares de Detenidos-Desaparecidos (Latin American Federation of Associations for Relatives of the Detained-Disappeared), an organization founded in 1981 to bring family members of the disappeared together from all countries in Latin America. FEDEFAM also played a central role in drafting the UN Convention on Enforced Disappearance.[17]

Eureka initially attempted to negotiate with the federal government, despite believing it was responsible for their loved ones' disappearances. Members met with each presidential administration privately beginning in the 1970s. According to De Vecchi (2018, 117), "During the late 1980s and early 1990s, the federal and local governments' responses in private meetings [with Comité Eureka] indicated that they would set the disappeared free,

---

[14] Eureka means "I have found it!" in Greek, and Eureka changed its name to this after the release of the political prisoners. Monterrey's Committee then formed the Comité Nacional pro Defensa de Presos, Perseguidos, Desaparecidos y Exiliados Políticos de México (National Committee for the Defense of Political Prisoners, Persecuted, Disappeared and Exiles of Mexico). The committee had member from Chihuahua, Jalisco, Mexico City, Mexico State, Puebla, Guerrero, Oaxaca, San Luis Potosí, and Sinaloa (De Vecchi 2018, citing Castellanos 2007, 284, and Maier 2001). Ibarra and the Comités, together with leftist party Partido Revolucionario de los Trabajadores (PRN), founded the Frente Nacional Contra la Represión, por la Solidaridad y las Libertades Democráticas (FNCR) (National Front Against Repression, for Solidarity and Democratic Liberty), which provided links to the party system and was a jumping off point for Ibarra's political career. See Fox and Hernández (1992) and Alfaro et al. (2016).

[15] See Amnesty International Annual Report 1979 (67–69) for specifics of the Amnesty Law.

[16] There was a lesser-known organization of mothers of disappeared children in Chihuahua as well as a Mothers' Committee. See De Vecchi (2018) for further detail.

[17] See Rice (2018). Member organizations of FEDEFAM are from the following countries: Argentina, Bolivia, Brazil, Colombia, Chile, Ecuador, El Salvador, Guatemala, Honduras, México, Nicaragua, Paraguay, Perú, Uruguay.

implying that they were kept—alive—in clandestine prisons." When this didn't happen, activists had little choice but to continue to pressure the government and to look internationally for solidarity. These early and failed attempts at advocacy confirmed their activist strategies and outlook. Eureka subsequently supported leftist political projects within Mexico, including the 1994 Zapatista uprising in Chiapas.[18] Ibarra herself ran as a Senate candidate with the Workers Revolutionary Party and eventually served in the Senate as a Partido Revolucionario Democrático, PRD, Revolutionary Democratic Party legislator.

H.I.J.O.S., Hijos por la Identidad y la Justicia contra el Olvido y el Silencio, "Children for Identity and Justice against Oblivion and Silence," made up largely of the offspring of Eureka members, was from its inception in 2000 focused on denouncing the state for its role in the commission of enforced disappearances.[19] H.I.J.O.S., whose stated goals are memory, identity and justice, is a branch of the international organization by the same name, which originated in Argentina. H.I.J.O.S. has participated in domestic political solidarity, including the Zapatistas' 2005 Otra Campaña, and helped to link Eureka and victims of the Dirty War to newer human rights organizations and victims collectives. Its members understand the impunity of post-2006 disappearances as a through line from the failure of the state to address the disappearances of the past and have played a key role in bringing an understanding of the struggles of the 1970s and 1980s to Mexico's current context.

The Guerrero-based Asociación de Familiares de Detenidos Desaparecidos en México (AFADEM), the Association of Families of the Disappeared Detained, also focused on denouncing state violence from the time of its inception in 1997 (though its roots go back to the late 1970s as well). As discussed in the previous section, Guerrero was the focus of Dirty War efforts. It was Mexico's poorest state during the 1960s, which contributed to the rise of two armed insurgency groups, including the Partido de los Pobres (Party of the Poor), led by Lucio Cabañas.[20] The Mexican state launched a large, repressive campaign as the PRI struggled to maintain power—which was explained as "draining the water to kill the fish"—in Guerrero, and families affected by enforced disappearance and state repression came together

---

[18] The Zapatistas likewise saw their struggle as linked with Eureka and organized events to honor their struggle (Rice 2018, 97).

[19] "Hijos" means "children" in Spanish. See De Vecchi (2018) for extensive discussion of H.I.J.O.S.

[20] Cabañas, still a well-known reference for activists in Mexico, is a graduate of the Ayotzinapa Rural Teachers College—the same institution from which 43 students were disappeared in 2014.

to form AFADEM. They did not join forces with political parties and from the beginning did not negotiate with the state. It was within this context that Rosendo Radilla, an activist folk singer, was forcibly disappeared in 1974. The activists who later formed AFADEM took on Radilla's case and succeeded in bringing it before the Inter-American Court of Human Rights (IACtHR).

Mobilization: Civil Society and Human Rights

It is telling that these disappearance-focused organizations were fairly isolated, at least in their early stages. A linchpin strategy of the PRI was the systematic fragmentation and co-optation of civil society groups that could organize to challenge the government's power (trade unions, farmers' organizations, business organizations). For the families of the disappeared, this meant that in the 1970s and early 1980s there were no established human rights NGOs or ACs to turn to in their early stages of organizing. In the early 1980s, the organizations that did exist were divided among those devoted to providing social services, many of which were affiliated with the Catholic church, and those focused on electoral rights.[21]

The 1985 earthquake in Mexico City, however, would prove to be an unexpected turning point for Mexican human rights organizations. The earthquake, which destroyed most of downtown Mexico City and killed more than 10,000 people, was a watershed moment for the growth of civil society organizations in Mexico as it had been in other countries previously.[22] The unprecedented demonstration of state incompetence and corruption, paired with the comparative competence shown by international and domestic NGOs as they worked in the hardest-hit communities to rebuild and aid those most affected, transformed the imagined possibilities of non-state political action (Keck and Sikkink 1998, 112; Cantú interview 2013[23]). The contested 1988 elections provided another boon in civil society energy. As it became clearer that the PRI's grasp on power was dwindling, civil society channeled this energy and poured resources into promoting free and fair elections. Alianza

[21] See Fox and Hernández (1992) for further discussion of early Mexican human rights organizations.

[22] Most notably, the 1972 earthquake in Nicaragua was the beginning of the end for the Somoza regime in Nicaragua.

[23] Jesús Cantú, interview with author, Nuevo León, Mexico: February 2013. Cantú is a longtime journalist, political analyst, and currently a professor in the School of Government at the Tec de Monterrey University in Monterrey, Mexico.

Cívica, a coalition of electoral observation organizations formed prior to the 1994 elections, coordinated tens of thousands of volunteers, successfully pushing through transparency measures that played a significant, if not decisive, role in the ousting of the PRI in 2000.

The growth of Mexican civil society in the 1980s seeded the nascent Mexican human rights community. In 1984, there were only four human rights NGOs. By 1991, there were 60, and by 1993, 200 (Fox and Hernandez 1992; Keck and Sikkink 1998). The groups that would come to dominate Mexico's human rights community were born following the earthquake: the CMDPDH, Comisión Mexicana de Defensa y Promoción de los Derechos Humanos A.C. (Mexican Commission for the Promotion and Defense of Human Rights) was founded in 1989 and would serve as a bridge between academia, the state, and international institutions.[24] Organizations explicitly linked to Jesuit thinking and liberation theology were also established, and their politics were more explicitly critical of the state. Arguably the leading human rights NGO in Mexico was founded during this time: the Centro ProDH, Centro por los Derechos Humanos Miguel Agustin Pro Juárez[25] (Center for Human Rights Miguel Agustin Pro Juárez), was founded in 1988 by the Society of Jesuits.[26] Outside of Mexico City, organizations formed to address the human rights concerns of Indigenous Mexican communities, with prominent and enduring organizations in Guerrero and Chiapas. Unsurprisingly, nearly all of these activist human rights organizations formed in states with direct experiences of federally sanctioned violence and repression.

[24] The leading figures from this organization and its precursor later took up positions within international institutions, rotating between bodies like the UN, OAS, international foundations, and leading human rights posts within the Vicente Fox and Calderón administrations. Mariclaire Acosta, the lead figure in both the Mexican Academy and CMDPDH, would be later join the Fox administration as the sub-secretary of Human Rights and Democracy. Later, Juan Carlos Gutierrez, a Colombian-born lawyer who also led CMDPDH, would be instrumental in crafting the legislation establishing the accusatory justice system, and he would later join the Calderón administration within the Secretary of the Interior (SEGOB), as the head of the Unit for Promotion and Defense of Human Rights.

[25] The center is named for José Ramón Miguel Agustín Pro Juárez (1891–1927), a Mexican Jesuit priest who was executed by President Calles. He was beatified by Pope John Paul II in 1988.

[26] Other Jesuit-affiliated human rights organizations founded around this time include the Centro Fray Francisco de Vitoría, founded by Father Miguel Concha in 1984 in Mexico City. In 1989, Samuel Ruiz, the Catholic Bishop of Chiapas, founded the Frayba, El Centro de Derechos Humanos Fray Bartolomé de Las Casas, A. C. (Fray Bartolomé de las Casas Center for Human Rights) in Chiapas, and in 1994 Abel Barrera Hernández, a Guerrero-based anthropologist, founded the Centro de Derechos Humanos de la Montaña "Tlachinollan" (the Tlachinollan Mountain Human Rights Center).

By 1989, in the post-earthquake civil society organization boom, these organizations were numerous enough to form a coordinating organization which they called the RedTDT, la Red de Todos los Derechos para Todos (the Network of All Rights for All People).[27] The member organizations shared a commitment to human rights and holding the state responsible for their violation; overwhelmingly, they embraced an activist approach to negotiating with the state.[28] One of the Red's first collective projects was to independently document state-perpetrated abuses committed during the Dirty War, and it quickly published the names of approximately 1,200 people who had been disappeared in the 1970s and early 1980s. Despite being the largest network of human rights organizations in Mexico, however, it had less visibility than other human rights networks in the region.[29]

These early human rights organizations—specifically CMDPDH, Centro ProDH, Tlachinollan, and FrayBa—have come to be seen as "gatekeeper organizations," defined by Bob and Frey as organizations with the "power to certify new human rights claims" (Bob 2010; Frey 2015). Their gatekeeper status is made clear in various ways: most have consultative status with the United Nations;[30] they receive the majority of international funding targeted toward improving human rights in Mexico, principally from the Ford and MacArthur Foundations; and they are seen by the international community, including the US government, as the go-to organizations to articulate the

---

[27] The RedTDT currently has 74 member organizations in 20 states. It was initially housed with the offices of Centro ProDH and is now housed within the offices of another important support organization, Servicios y Asesoría para la Paz, or as it is commonly known, SeraPaz. SeraPaz grew out of CONAI, the Comisión Nacional de Intermediación, which is closely linked to FrayBa and best known for its work facilitating the San Andrés Accords of 1996 between the EZLN and the Mexican government. These accords outlined the rights of indigenous people in Mexico and were agreed to by these communities; they are largely viewed as having been violated by the Zedillo administration. As I discuss in the next session, SeraPaz plays a facilitative role with many human rights organizations, including the Movimiento por Nuestros Desaparecidos, and was the physical location of the MPJD plenary sessions from its founding through 2013.

[28] There is regional variation among the member organizations mainly along the lines of whether groups focus on civil and political rights or social, economic, and cultural rights. With the AIDS epidemic, the rise of LGBTQ and environmental movements, the rights foci of the member groups of the RedTDT expanded to include these new social concerns.

[29] This was due largely to the Mexican state's success in promoting its image abroad as favorable to human rights (Keck and Sikkink 1998; Jesús Cantú, interview with author, Nuevo León, Mexico: February 2013).

[30] Centro ProDH, Tlachinollan, la Red TDT, and the CMDPDH all have consultative status with the United Nations.

human rights situation in Mexico.[31] I argue that their status as gatekeepers would become problematic after 2006, as the locus of violence shifted away from federal perpetrators and toward the more diffuse local actors.

2006–2012: The War on Drugs and the Explosion of Disappearances

Calderón, Institutional Reform, and the Militarization of Mexico

Despite the relative calm that most Mexicans perceived in 2006, President Felipe Calderón inherited a Mexican state that he perceived as critically threatened by DTOs[32] (Beittel 2009, 6; Bailey 2014, 1). He knew that DTOs had grown to be a significant economic force: the estimates of Mexico's profits from the drug trade ranged from $10 to $30 billion per year in 2006 (Rizzo 2019) (which at its upper range would constitute 3 to 4 percent of Mexican GDP), and the drug trade was thought to employ more than half a million people (Shirk 2011). DTOs were building power, and in some places they had flipped the script on their public sector allies. Instead of paying local officials a share of their profits in exchange for their protection, they were increasingly challenging their authority. DTOs' booming profits enabled them to more fully co-opt government officials, confront police, procure sophisticated weapons to defend their economic interests, and absorb significant economic and security setbacks (Bailey 2014).

In the meantime, Calderón had barely scraped together his narrow electoral victory, defeating PRD candidate Andrés Manuel López Obrador (the current president of Mexico) by less than 1 percent. This left him with a legitimacy deficit. He addressed this, in part, by seeking to redirect the public's attention away from the contested election and toward the country's growing security crisis (Trejo and Ley 2020). This not only had the benefit of uniting

---

[31] In a Wikileaks cable from September 24, 2009, entitled "Embassy Engages Civil Society on Human Rights Presaging Future Partnership," the US Embassy called together "representatives from Mexico's leading human rights non-governmental organizations (NGOs)" including Tlachinollan, FUNDAR, CMDPDH, RedTDT, FrayBa, Fray Vitoria and ProDH.

[32] As Calderón discusses in his book *Los Retos que Enfrentamos* (2014), his campaign platform did not clearly indicate the levels of militarization he was contemplating, focusing on (1) preventive policy and strengthening the rights of victims, and (2) public policy against crime, focused on improving the justice system.

the country behind the armed forces, but it also enabled Calderón to use the limited power he had to do *something*. He did not have an effective governing coalition in Congress, which limited his abilities to legislate effectively; he had few international political issues that could be used to mobilize legislative or popular support; and his own leadership team regarded the police and intelligence services to be corrupt. Calderón inherited institutions that struggled to perform their most basic duties, with the police in perhaps the direst situation. Writing in 2010, Shirk noted that "ten years after Mexico's first democratic transfer of power between opposing political parties, its police agencies continue to suffer from dangerous and deplorable working conditions, low professional standards, and severely limited resources. Police themselves believe that rampant corruption is institutionally predetermined and attributable to high-level infiltration by organized crime and inadequate internal investigations" (2010, 11).

In response to the weakness in the police and judicial sector, there were ambitious, broad-reaching institutional reforms initiated under Calderón. In 2008, a package of legislative and constitutional reforms set Mexico on a path to transition to an oral / adversarial system of justice from a written / [modified]inquisitorial system: for the first time, judges (in certain cases) would issue their verdicts after hearing arguments from the accused and the prosecutor—instead of reading a case file under an antiquated system that was known for relying on evidence acquired by illicit means, including bribery and torture. This transition to the new system was to be fully implemented by 2016. The judicial reform also included provisions for alternative sentencing and alternative dispute resolution (ADR), due process and the presumption of innocence for the accused, and a constitutional amendment to allow *arraigo*, detaining a suspect prior to criminal charges being brought, in cases of serious crimes.[33]

In November 2009, the Inter-American Court on Human Rights ruled against Mexico for failing to exercise due diligence in the investigation of Rosendo Radilla's disappearance (discussed earlier in this chapter) and for giving a military tribunal jurisdiction in a criminal case in which the victim was a civilian.[34] Largely as a result of this ruling, in June 2011, Mexico passed a constitutional amendment that gave prominence to international human

---

[33] Parts of this section are excerpted from the chapter "Critical Disconnects: Progressive Jurisprudence and Tenacious Impunity in Mexico," by Gallagher and J. Contesse, forthcoming in Botero et al., *The Limits of Judicialization: Progress and Backlash in Latin American Politics*.

[34] *Radilla Pacheco*, Inter-Am. Ct. H.R. (ser. C) No. 209.

rights treaties in domestic law. According to the Mexican government, this amendment was "the most important reform since 1917,"[35] and "changed the relationship between state and society."[36] As part of a process that started more than two decades earlier in other parts of Latin America,[37] Mexico too decided to give human rights treaties an enhanced place within the domestic legal system.[38] The constitutional reform effectively placed human rights treaties at the same level as the national constitution, codifying what is known in other jurisdictions as the "block of constitutionality" doctrine, that is, an understanding that individuals are protected not only by domestic guarantees (such as a bill of rights) but also—and directly—by international norms. With the constitutional amendment, Mexico signaled its unequivocal commitment to a *legalized* protection of human rights: those whose rights were violated could seek redress through claims based on both domestic and international law.

These institutional reforms, however, would take a long time to implement—and in the case of the 2008 reforms, corruption, a lack of funds, and a failure to implement key parts of the reform (training to police to conduct investigations; involving the National Guard in investigations; continued weak forensic ability) have largely undermined its intent to overhaul and improve the provision of justice in Mexico,[39] though Magaloni and Rodríguez (2020) find convincing and promising evidence that the reforms have meaningfully deterred torture as a means to extract confessions. While these important institutions were in flux, the federal armed forces were one of the few significant political forces under Calderón's control. He declared war on Mexican drug cartels soon after being sworn in in December 2006, sending the army into his own territory with the mission to recapture the state from the DTOs. Between 2006 and 2009, with the financial support of the US-backed Mérida Initiative,[40] he deployed approximately 45,000

[35] Gobierno de México, Secretaría de la Gobernación. January 12, 2016.

[36] Gobierno de México, Secretaría de la Gobernación. June 9, 2017.

[37] Decreto por el que se modifica la denominación del Capítulo I del Título Primero y reforma diversos artículos de la Constitución Política de los Estados Unidos Mexicanos [Decree that amends the name of Chapter I, Title I, and amends several articles of the Constitution of the United Mexican States, June 10, 2011, Diario Oficial, Primera Sección, p. 2.

[38] Cases include the Brazilian Constitution of 1988, the Chilean constitutional amendment of 1989, the Colombian Constitution of 1991, the Peruvian Constitution of 1993, and the Argentinean constitutional reform of 1994.

[39] See Hinojosa and Meyer (2019) for an overview of challenges in implementing the adversarial system. See justiceinmexico.org working papers for ongoing monitoring of judicial reform impact.

[40] The US Congress allocated $2.4 billion to the Mérida Initiative between 2008 and 2014. This aid has been overwhelmingly focused on financing the training and equipping of Mexico's security forces (Beittel 2015).

military and 5,000 federal police throughout Mexico (Felbab-Brown 2009). He employed a strategy known as a kingpin or *descabezando* (decapitating) strategy, in which the army targeted the heads of different drug cartels (Kristlik 2013). After top cartel leadership was removed, lower-ranked captains of that cartel often engaged in bloody struggles for control of the cartel. Weakened cartels often attracted the attention of rival DTOs as well, who would also engage in violent battles to wrest territory from the leaderless or feuding cartel. Trejo and Ley (2020) divide Calderón's strategy into two phases: the initial descabezando phase, and the proximate "managing violence" phase, in which the government was forced to respond to the historic, destabilizing violent backlash the initial strategy had caused. Trejo and Ley wrote, "President Calderón and his team were no longer Weberian state officials trying to establish the monopoly of coercion within a given territory, but opportunistic politicians trying to adopt a new strategy of damage control" (185).

Disappearances Under Calderón: Unclear Perpetrators and Victims

Felipe Calderón's militarization strategy led to a higher level of violence in Mexico, which has continued under Peña Nieto and into the beginning of Lopez Obrador's presidency. Between December 2006 and December 2012, more than 70,000[41] violent deaths and an additional 26,000[42] people were reported as disappeared. The rise in violence in the context of the drug war presented new legal challenges and, as discussed in the next section, upended the founding principles and strategies of the Mexican human rights community.

As violence exploded in Mexico, so too did the understanding of who was committing violence and who was being victimized. Perpetrators of disappearances under the PRI had been understood by the human rights community to be state agents (usually federal). Under Calderón, the material authors of disappearances became much less clear, and more often than not the best guess of who was responsible included a tangled mix of local, state,

---

[41] These numbers are disputed and have been revised many times; 70,000 homicides is the estimate from Peña Nieto's attorney general, released in 2013 (El Comercio 2012).

[42] The government figure, as of February 2013, was 26,122 (BBC News 2013).

and federal forces and their DTO collaborators. Local government-DTO coalitions, which had controlled localities during PRI rule, were already destabilized by the simultaneous ballooning of DTO profits and unraveling of PRI control between 2000 and 2006. With Calderón's intervention, however, many of these coalitions fractured completely and began to vie for power with neighboring local coalitions. The breaking apart of these fragile local coalitions unleashed lethal violence.

The lack of clarity around the perpetrators' identities made their legal standing unclear, since state-perpetrated violence is classified differently from criminal violence under both domestic and international law. A 2011 report from the UN Working Group on Enforced or Involuntary Disappearances describes the blurry lines between *enforced* disappearance (which is by definition state-perpetrated) and disappearances *perpetrated by individuals*:

> Many cases of abduction and offenses similar to enforced disappearances are committed by organized criminal groups. However, apparently, not all disappeared persons were abducted by independent organized criminal groups; the State is also involved in enforced disappearances in Mexico. The Working Group received specific, detailed and reliable information on enforced disappearances carried out by public authorities, criminal groups or individuals with direct or indirect support from public officials. Due to the prevailing impunity, many cases which could come under the scope of the offense of enforced disappearance are reported and investigated as different offenses, or are not even considered to be offenses. (UN 2012, December 20)

This shift also muddied the waters for human rights activists: violence perpetrated by DTOs had never been considered a human rights violation. With the increase in lethal violence perpetrated by a mix of state and DTO personnel, the human rights community at first failed to react and adapt their strategies in the face of this unprecedented assault on the right to physical integrity and the corresponding shift in civil society concerns. Joy Olson, then executive director of the Washington Office on Latin America (WOLA), a key ally of many of the Mexican human rights groups, wrote in 2012:

> This kind of violence doesn't fit the traditional human rights framework. . . . The work of human rights groups is based in international human rights law. That law, originating in the Universal Declaration of Human

Rights, is focused on the responsibility of the state. . . . Killings, torture, and disappearances carried out by the state are violations of human rights. On the other hand, killings, torture and disappearances carried out by the Zetas and other criminal organizations are crimes.

The identity of victims of violence was also more complex after 2006. As Ansolabehere, Frey, and Payne (2021) explain, in order for the state to get away with either perpetrating or failing to investigate disappearances, "an active process of creating official myths about the disappeared begins to justify the violence against them" (6). The "official myth" was to blame the victim by claiming that they *estaban en algo*—roughly translated, the victim must have been involved in criminal activity, which not only explains their disappearance but implicitly absolves the state of the responsibility to investigate.

This theory was often voiced to victims directly: in the case of Iván Baruch Núñez Mendieta, documented in a 2013 Human Rights Watch report, judicial police told his family, "It's because he was selling drugs. Don't look for him" (40). The mother of another missing young man was asked by an investigator "if her son had any 'vices.' When his mother said his only vice was smoking cigarettes, the investigator told her that 'one vice leads to another' and that her son had probably been a drug addict, which had led to his disappearance" (HRW 2013, 41). In a 2013 interview, a spokesman for the mayor's office in Monterrey[43] told me the story of his disappeared nephew, a young man whom he had never known to be in trouble. When he had disappeared several months before, the spokesman used his contacts in the attorney general's office to look for him. He explained to me in a knowing tone that he stopped looking when he found out his nephew was a regular at the local casino—gamblers, he said, were known to be involved in criminal activity. This guilt-by-association thinking convinced this state official that it was not only fruitless to look for his own nephew but that he didn't *deserve* to be looked for.

While it was clear to many that the state's criminalization of victims was unjustified, the looming question remained: why *were* they being disappeared? As Durán-Martinez (2018) argues, there are certain political incentives for criminal organizations and state actors to make violence less visible. If the

---

[43] State government spokesperson (name withheld at their request), interview with author, Nuevo León, Mexico: March 2013.

threat of getting caught or prosecuted for committing homicides increases, the incentives to disappear people, rather than murdering them, also increases. Ansolabehere, Frey, and Payne (2021) argue that in violent "post-transition" democracies, "perpetrators face more monitoring mechanisms, institutional checks, accountability systems, and barriers to freedom of speech that could expose and halt disappearances. International legal instruments. . . . further pressure states to align their domestic legislation and institutional practices with human rights standards" (92). While these perspectives help us understand why a perpetrator might disappear someone (rather than murder the individual), the answer to the fundamental question of why apolitical victims are being targeted remains disputed.

While many cling to the criminalization narrative, others point to the seeming randomness of many disappearances, where many innocent people have been caught in the wrong place at the wrong time and have become victims of perpetrators who place little value on human life. In a rare interview with a Mexican *sicario* (assassin), the *New York Times* (Ahmed and Villegas 2019) reported that a DTO hitman "had grown numb to killing, hunting for targets with a mechanical indifference. Life mattered even less to him, his own included." This indifference toward the lives of others may help explain the inexplicable horror of disappearances. When killings and disappearances are not random, they often affect upstanding citizens, including the targeting of "legal professionals, police officers, potential witnesses to crimes and any civilians who dared check the ambitions of a multitude of criminal organizations and their political accomplices" (International Crisis Group 2017).

Since most lethal violence and disappearances are generally not investigated, it is difficult to rigorously empirically interrogate the causes of disappearances. A key and implicit part of the advocacy frame for victims is that regardless of whether the disappeared person was involved in criminal activity, their case deserves to be investigated, and the disappeared person is deserving of justice. Calderón, for his part, did appear to shift his understanding of disappearances by the end of his administration. He took the first steps to establish a national database of people disappeared in Mexico, though he did not make the information public. After the database was leaked to the *Washington Post* by officials who feared the information would be lost as Calderón left office, it revealed something that thousands of families and nascent organizations suspected: more than 25,000 people had disappeared since 2006.

Mobilization Under Calderón: Activist/Advocate Divide

The increase in violence under Calderón shook Mexican society to its core. Mobilization shifted its focus toward demands for security and justice, and an increasingly diverse group of societal actors demanded that the Mexican state answer for violent crimes committed by its own agents and also that it stop the wave of violence it had been instrumental in creating. These diverse societal actors, however, did not agree on the very nature of the state nor on the most effective mobilizing strategies to confront violence and impunity.

Some regarded the state as criminal, seeing Calderón and his governing allies as clearly responsible for the overwhelming violence in the country. At worst, he was seen as colluding with DTOs and seeking to benefit financially through the War on Drugs. Others saw the state as merely flawed, arguing that the violence plaguing Mexico was the unfortunate result of criminal activity, and while there were undoubtedly some bad apples within the state, the Mexican government should be regarded as having the best interests of the Mexican people at heart. Mobilized groups, even those who saw the state similarly, diverged on organizing strategies. A sub-set of human rights organizations, most often those who had experienced firsthand repression at the hands of the federal government, saw the post-2006 Mexican state as fundamentally anti-democratic and incapable of reform. For these activists, legal reforms or victories in specific judicial cases were bandages at best. The strategy was to avoid the state and not allow them to dictate victories—a position reminiscent of the "against the law" perspective. Pedro Faro, an organizer and lawyer at FrayBa, the prominent Chiapas-based human rights organization and member of the network of pro-Zapatista NGOs, articulated this position in a March 2011 interview. He told me:

> Our goal is not to win cases. Our goal is to prevent the state from hurting social movement leaders, because this causes a weakening of the movement. . . . We try to get the leaders out of jail, and to have a strong political presence so that nobody interferes with us. But we consider this a political, not judicial, intervention. . . .
>
> Of course, the judicial statistics will improve a little with the coming [judicial] reforms, but this is because capitalism needs certain demonstrations like this—but nothing will change. We do not want to make our successes

dependent in any way on the state. We want to strengthen the autonomy of the communities.[44]

For FrayBa, then, strengthening the provision of justice was not a priority and was seen as perhaps undermining the political prospects of social movements. Fray Juan de Larios and FUUNDEC, organizations advocating on behalf of disappeared people in Coahuila, and in Mexico City–based Comité Cerezo, had similar perspectives.[45] Fray Juan de Larios, a Jesuit-sponsored accompaniment organization, was led by a community organizer trained at FrayBa. And while they did hold participatory investigations with the state, they did not expect "favorable results." Juan López, a Fray Juan de Larios lawyer and organizer at the time, told me, their goal was actually "to establish that the justice system still doesn't work." He saw judicial reforms as the government's "demonstration" of its commitment to rights but not a substantive way to uphold them. Rather, such demonstrations serve to uphold capitalist interests[46].

Most organizations of the RedTDT, the national association of Mexican human rights organizations, tended to view the Mexican state as flawed but reformable under Calderón. A cohort of young lawyers working at Centro ProDH in the early 2000s, who later fanned out to run the legal arm of many regional NGOs and international organizations,[47] became convinced that they could accomplish what lawmakers hadn't been able to through litigation. These lawyers articulated two separate but related strategies: *defensa integral*, integrated defense, and *litigio estratégico*, strategic litigation. Integrated defense refers to the practice of exhausting litigation options (beginning in domestic courts and continuing on to international courts) while at the same time applying political pressure for a positive judicial outcome primarily through media strategies, including close and extensive collaboration with international actors. Strategic litigation refers to choosing cases to litigate that would establish important legal precedent if won—also referred to as paradigmatic cases. Integrated defense and strategic litigation became

---

[44] Pedro Faro, interview with the author, Chiapas, Mexico: March 2011.

[45] Comité Cerezo, a small human rights group founded by brothers and their allies who had been held as political prisoners and tortured in 2001, focuses on revealing the true nature of the Mexican state through publicly documenting state-perpetrated human rights abuses.

[46] Juan López, interview with author, Mexico City, Mexico: May 2012.

[47] These organizations include Tlachinollan in Guerrero, *Indignación* in the Yucatán peninsula, as well as important international funding agencies and the offices of the UN High Commissioner for Human Rights.

the predominant strategies among these reform-minded organizations during the 2000s.

Litigating within the IACtHR has been a particularly important strategy for these organizations despite the lengthy requirements for getting a case admitted. This approach has resulted in several significant judicial victories, with 14 decisions and judgments on 11 cases—with eight of these decisions being issued during the Calderón administration. The Inter-American Court's finding in the case of the enforced disappearance of Rosendo Radilla in 1974 has, arguably, been the most legally significant (and is discussed further in Chapter 6). It is also illustrative of the possibilities and limitations of strategic litigation in international courts. While the Radilla case yielded a landmark ruling in international law, spurring Mexico's constitutional court to both elevate the importance of international law within Mexico and to strengthen jurisprudence around disappearances, achieving this ruling took 35 years. While the gatekeeper human rights groups see the Radilla case and other international legal victories as part of a long-term strategy to establish legal precedents in line with international human rights standards, smaller organizations, especially those that operate in states with pressing security concerns and scarce resources, have found strategic litigation frustrating. The head of a small state-based NGO who wished to remain anonymous reported to me in March 2011 that "for us, strategic litigation has been a disaster. There is simply not the space for success, because there is total impunity [within the state courts]." The human rights organizations discussed in this section would largely continue this slow, lawyer-intensive, and selective model of human rights advocacy during the Calderón administration. This strategy, however, made it impossible for them to accept the thousands of new cases of disappearances and homicides that emerged after 2007. They simply did not have the resources to adopt more than a few new cases.

Even before the violence of the Calderón administration, conservative groups sponsored by coalitions of businesspeople or a single wealthy person pushed a law-and-order agenda. These groups[48] focus blame for violence on criminal groups—and explicitly reject a systemic critique of state collusion with DTOs. Under Calderón, most worked in favor of the 2008 and

---

[48] The most prominent of these groups are Renace, or Reborn, founded in 1994 in Monterrey, and México Unido Contra la Delincuencia, MUCD, Mexico United Against Delinquency, founded in 1998, best known for its role in planning a large 2004 national protest that called for judicial reform and security. Renace advises victims of their rights but does not provide continuous support. Rather, it sees its role as lobbying for changes in national legislation.

2011 legislative and constitutional reforms. While concerned about justice, these groups do not accept individual cases or advocate on their behalf. Two leaders from among these groups, Alejandro Martí and Isabel Miranda de Wallace, became well known after suffering personal tragedy.[49] Calderón repeatedly called upon them when he wanted to counter-balance the more critical voices of both the human rights community and legitimate policies and legislation. For example, both Martí and Wallace were featured guests at press conferences announcing the Victims' Monument, a project widely criticized as meaningless by victims organizations and the human rights community.

Prior to 2011, state-based human rights organizations (as opposed to Mexico City–based gatekeeper organizations) in the north of Mexico and in other areas affected by violence experienced a dramatic increase in demands for assistance. These organizations, mainly small human rights and Christian-affiliated centers that had formed to serve the human rights needs of local populations throughout Mexico in the mid-1990s, were suddenly the primary civil society resources for the ballooning number of people affected by violence. Many began using the type of crime a victim had suffered as the criterion for selecting which victims they would serve, with some organizations serving families of female victims of violence; state violence; homicides and/or disappearances. They generally focused on (1) providing psycho-social support for family members of victims, which refers broadly to the psychological and social support that victims of violence need; and (2) pursuing justice and encouraging the state to investigate crimes. Their small staffs, limited budgets, and outsider political status, however, limited their impact and confined them to activist roles. With the notable exception of Chihuahua (whose local organizations had organized extensively and powerfully in response to femicides in the late 1990s and early 2000s), these groups did not have regular access to state officials, and hence could not play an effective advocacy role. In several states, most of which didn't have any human rights organization, small organizations led by people missing a

---

[49] Fernando Martí, the 14-year-old son of well-known CEO Alejandro Martí, was kidnapped and killed in July 2008 with the apparent involvement of federal police. Martí would go on to found the organization México SOS, which focuses on citizen security, giving security tips to citizens as to how to stay safe when traveling. Isabel Miranda de Wallace's son was kidnapped in 2005. Wallace founded the organization Alto al Secuestro (Stop Kidnapping) and worked to draft and pass anti-kidnapping legislation. She has since been accused of giving false statements and falsifying evidence in her son's case.

family member began to organize and meet informally. They too were unable to meaningfully negotiate with state officials.

Despite these organizations' best efforts, most simply didn't have the capacity or political access to effectively advocate on behalf of the growing number of family members affected by violence. Meanwhile, the Calderón administration continued to claim that only *los malitos*, bad people (see Villarreal 2021), were being affected by the country's increasingly bloody struggle to combat DTOs—a position that was at odds with the experience of the growing number of families whose loved ones were missing or killed. In the spring of 2011, the senseless killing of Juan Francisco Sicilia by DTO members after a barroom disagreement struck a nerve. Juan Francisco was a paradigmatically "good" young man: an upper-middle-class, light-skinned medical student, clean-cut athlete, and son of prominent poet and journalist Javier Sicilia. Javier began to walk to Mexico City with a handful of others with the rallying cry of *estamos hasta la madre*—roughly, "we've had it—and by the time he got to Mexico's main square several days later, tens of thousands of people had joined him.

This mobilization led to the formation of the Movement for Peace with Justice and Dignity (MPJD). Sicilia, an established political columnist and ally of the left, appealed to a cross-section of Mexican society: human rights organizations, established social movements,[50] and perhaps most important, the growing number of people affected by the escalating violence but who, until the MPJD, had not mobilized. Sicilia and the MPJD connected these diverse constituencies, or in social movement terms, brokered scale shift, between these previously disconnected or, in many cases barely articulated, groups.[51] They sought to contradict the state's narrative blaming victims and downplaying the impact of violence by centering victims' testimonies and shining a national spotlight on the cities and towns throughout Mexico being affected by violence. To these ends, the MPJD physically traversed the country in two nationwide caravans. Making more than 35 stops, they traveled from Mexico City to the northern border at Ciudad Juarez in June of

---

[50] The MPJD formed important alliances with the NGOs SeraPaz and the Centro Nacional de Comunicación Social (CENCOS). These organizations commonly hosted press conferences and provided meeting space for the MPJD.

[51] In social movement literature, scale shift is defined as "the number and level of coordinated contentious action leading to broader contention involving a wider range of actors and bridging their claims and identities" (McAdam et al. 2001, 331). *Brokering* is defined as "information transfers that depend on the linking of two or more previously unconnected social sites" (9). This brokering is done with the goal of building a bigger, stronger movement.

2011, and worked their way south to Tapachula on the Guatemalan border in September of 2011. The caravans were composed of nearly 20 buses and other vehicles carrying more than 700 people, including two dedicated buses each for family members of those killed or disappeared, and members of the national press. At each stop, caravan participants set up a stage where family members active in the MPJD gave their testimony and invited local people affected by the violence to give theirs. My first contact with the MPJD was as a participant in the September 2011 southern caravan, and I was especially struck by the new and somewhat unlikely coalitions that organized to meet us, feed us, and house us in each city: local human rights organizations and social movements came out—but so too did local business associations, unions, and families. Perhaps most important, many families affected by violence met at these large rallies and subsequently continued to work together in new victims' collectives, often with names that signaled their link to the MPJD (i.e., Xalapa por la Paz, in Veracruz; Zacatecanos por la Paz in Zacatecas; and Acapulco por la Paz and Hasta la Madre in Guerrero). These visits would be definitive organizing moments in many places, spurring the creation and/or consolidation of victims' collectives.

Apart from its role connecting citizens, organizations, and movements, the MPJD also presented a very different model of interacting with the state from its inception. Javier Sicilia became well known for his practice of *besos y abrazos*—embracing all those he met with, including President Calderón. Sicilia was not naïve in his view of the state, writing and speaking frequently of systemic corruption and incompetence, but he cited pacifist leaders such as Gandhi and Martin Luther King Jr. as inspiring his position of peace and reconciliation. In his eyes, cooperating with state officials and negotiating in good faith was not only consonant with his Christian beliefs but was also the strategy most likely to result in affecting government policy and practice. This approach resonated with many of the new victims' collectives.

2012–2018: Peña Nieto and the Deepening Crisis

A Return to the PRI, Not to Peace

In the 2012 presidential election, 38 percent of Mexicans voted for PRI-backed Enrique Peña Nieto in a three-candidate field, as Peña Nieto promised to return Mexico to its comparatively peaceful recent past. With this underwhelming plurality, Peña Nieto assumed the presidency. Despite guaranteeing a change in strategy and a reduction in violence, his administration largely continued Calderón's militarized response to the security challenges facing Mexico. As shown in Figure 3.2, while homicides and disappearances dipped in the first years of his administration, by the final two years, violence had once again exploded—exceeding the peak and total violence of the Calderón years.

Peña Neto did not substantively address the root causes of violence and impunity under the previous administration, and he failed to examine and address the underlying ties between state security forces and organized crime. He re-branded and reorganized the National Police, launching the now-defunct gendarmerie (which was rolled into the National Guard in 2019), adding another chapter to the "alphabet soup of new and subsequently dismantled police agencies from the 1980s through the present" (Shirk 2011, 11). Perhaps the best-known debacle of his presidency illustrated the depth of collaboration between state and DTO forces. After Joaquin "El Chapo" Guzmán was captured (for the second time) to great national and international fanfare in 2014, he escaped from prison less than a year later, presumably with extensive help from corrupt government officials. Accusations of corruption associated with energy privatization; campaign donations and bribes from Odebrecht, the infamous Brazilian construction firm linked to bribes and corruption throughout the region; and credible accounts of the president's cronies tapping oil pipelines for their own financial benefit plagued his administration, sinking his poll numbers and eroding even further confidence in Mexico's government.

It wasn't expected that Peña Nieto would be a champion for human rights. As governor of the Estado de México before his presidency, he had presided over the 2006 brutal crackdown on protests in the small town of San Salvador Atenco. After 40 flower vendors were evicted from their stalls sparking local discontent, Peña Nieto sent in 3,500 state police. They killed two people and threw scores of people in jail, including many women who subsequently reported being tortured and raped. Eleven of these women brought their cases before the IACtHR. When confronted by students during a university visit during his presidential campaign about his handling of Atenco, Peña Nieto doubled down on the state's repression, saying, "It was a decision that I made personally to re-establish order and peace, and I made it with the legitimate use of force that corresponds to the state" (Goldman 2017). He then accused the assembled students of being paid agitators. This spawned

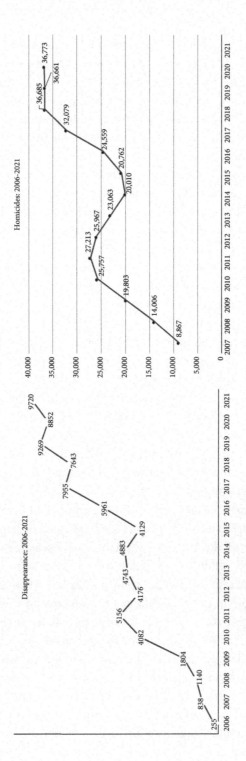

Figure 3.2 Homicides and disappearances in Mexico

Source: Homicide data from INEGI (National Institute of Statistics and Geography; disappearances data from Registro Nacional de Personas Desaparecidas y No Localizadas

a wave of anti–Peña Nieto organizing led by the students themselves: 131 of the students from the university made a video testifying to their presence at the event, and the hashtag and slogan #YoSoy132, I am the 132nd [student], went viral (see Alcántara 2017).

Unsurprisingly, Peña Nieto did not rigorously pursue the implementation of the 2008 judicial reforms designed to make a dent in the struggle against impunity. While the administration allocated significant resources for the implementation of the reforms, which required retro-fitting courtrooms and investing significant time and resources into training government officials, there was little positive result. According to a 2016 report by the Washington Office on Latin America (WOLA), "In practice, the allocation of these resources has been disorganized and the training unequal, which has diminished the functionality and effectiveness of the new system in the short term" (Meyer and Suárez-Enríquez 2016, 4).

The 2011 constitutional court amendments were supposed to strengthen the legal status of human rights in Mexico, and in particular to improve the legal accountability of the military. The strength of these reforms would be tested throughout Peña Nieto's term. In June of 2014, 22 civilians were executed by the military in the town of Tlatlaya. The soldiers reportedly assumed they were cartel members and shot them after they had surrendered. Seven soldiers were acquitted in the killings, and only one was convicted—for the crime of disobedience. Attacks against journalists also reached historic highs, making Mexico the most dangerous country in Latin America for journalists (Ureste 2019), with more than 2,000 attacks and 47 murders of journalists occurring during Peña Nieto's administration. More than 40 percent of these attacks, according to NGO Article 19, were perpetrated by government officials. As the implementation of Mexico's justice system limped along, forces that sought to undermine public security seemed to presume that these reforms wouldn't lead to meaningful change and accountability.

Family members of victims of disappearance know that they face dauntingly bleak prospects in finding their loved ones, much less pursuing justice. When victims mobilize in Mexico, they may receive threats to their safety. While these are fairly common, assassinations remain fairly rare, though there have been several high-profile assassinations of victim activists that remain unsolved. Nepomuceno Moreno Nuñez was an MPJD activist whose son was disappeared in his home state of Sonora (see CNN 2011; Herrera 2011). Don Nepo was known for wearing an envelope around his neck at all times; it contained the key evidence he had assembled—evidence he believed pointed to the state police as responsible for his son's disappearance. He had presented the case file personally and publicly to President Calderón six weeks before he was gunned down during the middle of the day on November 28, 2011, in Sonora. His murder served as a clear warning from the protection racket of DTOs and state officials that not even those who have brought their cause to the halls of power are safe. Similarly, the 2017 murder of Tamaulipas victim activist Miriam Elizabeth Rodríguez showed the limits of what was possible for victims pursuing justice (see Amnesty International 2017; Villegas 2017). Rodríguez was killed in her home on Mothers' Day after she had publicly called for the imprisonment of cartel members who, she alleged, had disappeared and then killed her daughter. While these killings are far from the norm, they continue to serve as warnings to other victim activists of the dangers involved in organizing. In both of these cases, no perpetrators have been prosecuted.

Disappearances Under Peña Nieto: Participatory Investigations, Ayotzinapa and the Turn to *Búsqueda*

Peña Nieto did not take meaningful steps toward addressing the unsolved disappearance cases of the previous administration, and his security policies would lead to more than 38,000 new cases of disappearances during his term, including more than 7,000 per year during the final two years of his administration. Despite meeting with the MPJD during his candidacy[52] and signing the Victims' Law[53] at the beginning of his time in office, he largely avoided meeting with victims' collectives and international human rights advocates

[52] On May 27, 2012, a month before Mexico's presidential elections, the MPJD brought together the four presidential candidates at Chapultepec Castle in Mexico City. Their goal was to place the drug war, the violence it had generated, and the lack of justice for victims at the center of the electoral agenda, and to ask the candidates to commit to end the violence if they were elected. Sicilia, together with family members of people killed or disappeared during Calderón's administration, national press, and each candidate and their staff sat together and for 90 minutes spoke of the way forward for Mexico. See Animal Político (2012) for an excellent brief summary of the MPJD's presentation to each candidate, which includes the full transcript of each candidate's response. Peña Nieto famously quoted Gandhi's saying "there is no road to peace—peace is the road." This would be proved to be anathema to his approach to security as president.

[53] The Ley de Víctimas, Victims' Law, signed into law on January 9, 2013, by Enrique Peña Nieto, obligates the government to create a reliable registry of the murdered and disappeared, mandates the financial compensation of family members of victims of violence, and lays out victims' rights as they seek protection from the government. It was written by a coalition of academic and civil society groups who came together at the MPJD's request following their 2011 meetings with President Calderón. This coalition was able to present it to Mexico's Congress by April 2012.

during his term, preferring to delegate the issue to his attorney general and interior minister. Confusion continued around who and how many people disappeared—with little progress toward the long-promised database of the disappeared.

While the national crisis of disappearances worsened, the victims' collectives spurred by the MPJD flourished and matured. Increasingly, victim-led collectives were able to effectively engage in both activism and advocacy. Prior to the MPJD's emergence in 2011 victims of violence had been limited to the activist strategies of protesting and criticizing the state (or, depending on where they were located, they could join more established and professionalized activist organizations); during the Peña Nieto administration, many realized that much more than their established and institutionalized allies, they were willing and able to play the roles of both activists and advocates. They leveraged their political legitimacy as people directly affected by the tragedy of disappearance—and the visibility and access facilitated by their own growing political visibility as part of a nationwide movement—to alternately protest and publicly critique state officials, and also to engage in ongoing participatory investigations with the state. While some of these collectives partnered with and benefited from the experience and perspective of small local human rights organizations, many collectives emerged in places where these organizations were scarce or non-existent.

Participatory investigations became a common strategy both for advocacy organizations and for victims' collectives during Peña Nieto's term as a way of having dialogue with state judicial officials. However, belief in their possibility to facilitate justice began to erode. Rather than hoping that sitting down with state officials would itself lead to locating the disappeared person, participatory investigations became widely regarded by victims' groups as a necessary first step in the process of unlocking investigations into disappearances, but as insufficient to guarantee meaningful progress in cases of disappearance. These meetings do guarantee that cases analyzed in the participatory investigation meetings escape the fate of the majority of disappearances in Mexico: falling into the black hole of unsolved cases where reports of disappearances are never again touched or investigated, and where no responsible party is ever identified. However, these investigations most often do not locate the victim or result in charges against anyone involved. While victims and their representatives come up with new leads, state investigators most often do only the minimum: they attend the sometimes exhaustively long meetings and take the limited set of actions necessary to follow up on leads generated by the victims themselves. But that is where it ends. They fail to generate new leads themselves; and as several lawyers who work with victims told me, they don't generate a working hypothesis of the events of the disappearance.

While participatory investigations may be regarded by the state as, essentially, cheap talk because the risk of exposing state agents and their DTO allies to prosecution is minimal, it is worth noting that I heard from many victims, especially when the participatory investigations were first established, what a huge difference it made to be treated with respect and listened to by state authorities. As one mobilized victim whose husband had been disappeared in Guerrero recounted in a 2013 interview:

> Before I joined the [collective], I went alone to the attorney general's office, but how the attorney general himself treated made me feel worse. . . . [H]e said things like: "Madam, we know that wives also order their husbands to be killed." I was very afraid that he would invent a crime to charge me with. Maybe he wanted to scare us and he achieved this. I was panicking. (Placencia 2017, 92)

The change in treatment from hostility, criminalization, and threats to being treated respectfully and promptly by members of the state bureaucracy feels like a significant victory for many.

Even as it became increasingly clear that under Peña Nieto, Mexico's commitment to impunity and militarized approaches to security would leave the disappearances of the past unresolved, new cases continued to pile up. In early 2014, victims who had grown frustrated with the meager results of participatory investigations gave rise to citizen-led efforts to use forensic science to find their loved ones. Victims' organizations were already performing many investigative activities as part of the participatory investigations, including finding and interviewing witnesses, researching the circumstances of the disappearance, and obtaining cell phone records. They were now determined to do something about the failure of the state to systematically gather family members' DNA and compare it to unidentified remains. Researchers from the United Kingdom, for example, introduced what they called Ciencia Forense Ciudadana, CfC, Citizen-led Forensic Science, a project that aimed to create a national registry of the disappeared.[54] Each

---

[54] The national database was called the Registro Nacional Ciudadano de Personas Desaparecidas, or RNCPD. CfC aimed to "bring the public back to the forensic sciences, to put the relatives of

of the people I profile in this book initially participated in CfC. Indeed, the initiative initially brought together most leaders of disappeared collectives in 2014. They held their first meeting in early September 2014.

They had no idea that by the end of the month, the ground would shift beneath them. On the night of September 26, 2014, the most high-profile enforced disappearances in Mexico's history occurred: 43 young men, all first-year teaching students from poor, rural families in the state of Guerrero, were disappeared from the Ayotzinapa Rural Teachers College, while an additional six people were killed. Indisputably, the local municipal police were involved: they had surrounded buses that the students had commandeered, and later forced the students into police vehicles. None of those students were ever seen again. As others fled the attack and sought to help some of the 20 wounded students, they were forcibly removed from a private hospital by soldiers. These soldiers were members of the 27th Infantry Battalion and were stationed less than two miles away from where the disappearances took place. Apart from their actions at the hospital, however, they did not intercede.[55]

The disappearance of the 43 Ayotzinapa students re-figured the political and legal landscape around the issue of disappearances. As shown in Figure 3.4, it sparked a massive wave of protests in Mexico,[56] which brought together a wide and diverse swath of civil society: students, human rights activists, and even a *contingente carriola*, a brigade of moms pushing strollers, at the

disappeared people at the center of forensic science, not only as a victim but as experts who can make the right to the truth a reality." They also aimed to create a DNA biobank containing biological samples of the families of the disappeared in Mexico for the purpose of serving as a reference for identification of the family members looking for their loved ones; the biobank would be "governed, administered and designed for and by the family members of the disappeared in Mexico." The project, registered in Mexico under the name "Forensic Citizenship Governance A.C.," comprised a group of young academics and Mexican students and was headed by Professor Ernesto Schwartz-Marin (Schwartz-Marin and Cruz-Santiago 2018).

[55] There is additional evidence that points to the army's involvement: for example, there is evidence that the cell phone of Julio César Mondragón Fontes, the Ayotzinapa student who was murdered and later found mutilated on the night of the attack, was used for months after the attack, and that it pinged off cell phone towers near the military installation. These facts have been documented extensively in books, articles, and within Interdisciplinary Group of Independent Experts (GIEI) reports. See Gibler 2017.

[56] My research team documented 38 protests and marches in the year after the disappearances—21 in Mexico City, and 17 in the Mexican state of Guerrero. By sourcing from the three national and three local newspapers, we determined that participants in these protests rose to a high of about 75,000 in Mexico City in November, 2014—nearly two months after the disappearance of the students. By May 2015, monthly protests in Mexico City fell to a low of about 250 people. Notably, on the one year anniversary of the disappearances, the protests again swelled to 35,000 people.

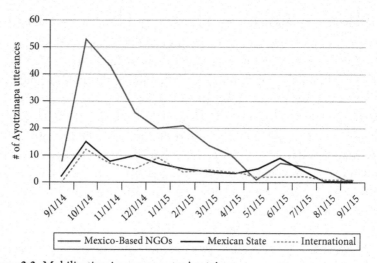

Figure 3.3 Mobilization in response to Ayotzinapa

Source: Based on author's analysis, originally published by NACLA: https://nacla.org/news/2016/09/27/human-rights-crossroads-24-months-after-ayotzinapa

zócalo protests. Ayotzinapa put the issue of human rights, and specifically enforced disappearances, on the map both within Mexico and internationally, with the major international bodies, including the United Nations and Organization of American States, calling for a rigorous investigation into the events of that night (see Figure 3.3).[57] Jan Jarab, the representative for the UN High Commission on Human Rights (UNHCHR) told me in the fall of 2020 that "in 2014, Ayotzinapa really changed everything. . . . [Since then] I would say disappearances have become the leading issue for us [the UNHCHR]."[58] Ayotzinapa also caught the attention of international funders concerned with Mexico's worsening human rights crisis.

For many who had been involved in the MPJD, who had lost their loved ones prior to 2014, or who had been involved in the struggle for human rights in Mexico, Ayotzinapa felt like a turning point. Surely now—with the eyes of the world and the calls from the street all pressuring the Mexican government

---

[57] My research team coded the "utterances"—each time an organization made a public pronouncement including the term "Ayotzinapa"—of 14 relevant state and 17 non-state actors (12 of whom were international). The Ayotzinapa disappearances prompted Mexico-based NGOs, different Mexican state entities and international actors like the UNHCHR, the Inter-American Commission on Human Rights (IACHR) and Human Rights Watch (HRW) to publicly call for accountability.

[58] Jan Jarab, interview by author, via Zoom: September 2019.

to punish those responsible and address the issue of disappearances—
something had to give.

And for a brief moment, it seemed that things would change. The Peña
Nieto administration took the unprecedented step of asking the IACHR
for technical expertise and assistance in investigating this case. This led to
the establishment of the Interdisciplinary Group of Independent Experts
(GIEI), a group given a mandate to monitor and assess the investigations by
Mexican authorities of the student disappearances, and which was convened
with the participation and advice of civil society. It included highly respected
academics, prosecutors, and forensic experts from around the world.

Apart from responses specifically to the Ayotzinapa disappearances, civil
society mobilized to promote other institutional changes. Most important,
in 2017 the General Law on Disappearances was passed, which defined and
criminalized "enforced disappearance" and "disappearance by non-state actors" throughout Mexico's 32 states and required the immediate investigation and coordination of information needed to search for the missing. The
Law on Enforced Disappearance spawned the creation of a special investigatory unit within the Attorney General's Office in 2018 and also created the
National Search Commission. I discuss these institutional changes, and their
results, more extensively in Chapter 6.

While legislation, constitutional changes, and new judicial bureaucracies
became more responsive to the issue of disappearances under Peña Nieto, it
bears repeating that more than 38,000 people were disappeared between 2012
and 2018, with more than 15,000 of those occurring during the final two years
of his administration. Ayotzinapa brought Mexico's crisis of disappearances
to the attention of its own citizens and the world—but the resulting political
fallout and mobilization failed to head off the tragic deepening of the crisis.

Disappearance plus Enforced Disappearance
Post- Ayotzinapa

Ayotzinapa did, however, break down much of the disconnect between the
human rights community and victims' organizations, and in many ways it
united the old and the new guard of human rights advocacy and activism
in Mexico. Those who had been mobilizing around the Dirty War of the
1970s and 1980s saw in Ayotzinapa the state engaging in ostentatious attacks
against these leftist students. But the attack on the students was also similar

in many ways to the cases that had been ignored, for all intents and purposes, by the larger Mexican human rights community: these were disappearances carried out for no clear reason against a large number of civilians; and the perpetrators were likely a mix of state authorities at all different levels and criminal organizations. The students were more politicized than most post-2006 victims of violence and disappearances, but there are no indications that they were targeted individually for their activism.

These dynamics rippled through Mexico's human rights organizations. The changes at Mexico's arguably most important human rights organization, Centro ProDH, are instructive. Prior to 2014, ProDH, like other human rights organizations, focused on cases where the state was the clear perpetrator of human rights abuses and primarily focused on litigation of a small number of cases in domestic and international courts.[59] It stayed away from cases in which the material author of the crime was unclear. The three cases I document in this book, for example, would not have been good candidates to be taken on by Centro ProDH prior to 2014; state agents were likely involved in some way in each of these disappearances, and the material author is probably a mix of DTO and state forces. After Ayotzinapa, there was a reckoning within the organization. It began to move away from a strict model of strategic litigation, and in 2016, ProDH decided to take on the case of Juan Carlos's four disappeared brothers. Members of the organization explained to me that in some ways they were doing what they had always done—accompanying the cases according to the wishes of those affected by the crime. This meant they would be operating in several different spheres: they would be doing the legal work relevant to the disappearance of the four Trujillo-Herrera brothers, but they would also be accompanying the other victims' collectives who joined the Herreras in the organizations they were involved with, including the National Citizens' Search Brigades. When the Brigades focused on Veracruz, for example, they arranged for the renowned Argentine Forensic Team to provide them with training and also hosted their press conference and send-off of the activists who would accompany the search brigade.[60]

---

[59] For example, ProDH litigated the cases of two Indigenous women raped by members of the army, and another concerning the false accusation of a Central American man on organized crime charges.

[60] The divides between the victims' collectives and the traditional human rights community are not, of course, completely gone. iDHeas, for example, a Mexico City-based NGO, which specializes in strategic litigation, has repeatedly gone to Veracruz, searching specifically for cases of enforced disappearance. According to one person who accompanies different collectives in the state, this has led to divisions and jealousy, since cases that have legal accompaniment are understood to have a better chance of yielding results and advances.

Ayotzinapa also led directly to a shift in tactics by victims' collectives. Following the disappearance of the students, there were unprecedented efforts to scour the surrounding countryside looking for the students. While the students' remains were not found,[61] hundreds of other bodies were. This led to the formation of a new victims' collective which called themselves Los Otros Desaparecidos, the Other Disappeared, made up of more than 200 families from Guerrero whose loved ones had also disappeared. Los Otros Desaparecidos pioneered a new strategy: since the state was not searching for the remains of their loved ones, they would do so themselves. With few resources, Los Otros Desaparecidos pioneered not only gathering the DNA of the families of the disappeared but also searching for the remains of the disappeared. Their idea was remarkably simple: they would collect and identify the remains that were being discovered and try to match these remains with family members because the state wouldn't or couldn't. This idea of citizen-led search for the remains of the disappeared soon spread throughout Mexico. By 2016, 66 different collectives joined together to form "Red de Enlaces Nacionales," a network of collectives from all over Mexico who have come together five times to search for their loved ones in clandestine graves. Juan Carlos Trujillo Herrera, profiled extensively in Chapters 2 and 4, played a leading role in establishing this network, and in promoting citizen-led searching.

As tactics on the ground shifted toward searching, participatory investigations also adapted. Instead of focusing exclusively on pursuing a criminal investigation, participatory investigation meetings were used to focus on searching for the victim—in many cases, to the exclusion of seeking to prosecute those responsible for the disappearance. We see evidence of the shift to searching in Figure 3.4: there are several differences from the previous notes (see Figure 1.4), which indicate that this meeting may be oriented toward searching for the remains of the victim rather than pursuing justice, a distinction I talk about extensively in Chapter 5. In the Guerrero meeting minutes shown in Figure 3.4, there are no *investigatory* officials present, nor investigatory tasks discussed. Rather, members of the state and national

---

[61] Remains of the students were not found by searching the mass graves in the Guerrero countryside. However, the remains of three students have been found and identified. The remains of Alexander Mora were identified in December 2014 after being found in a nearby river by Tomás Zerón; at that time he was the lead investigator and is currently a fugitive from justice due to his possible collusion in the disappearance of the students. The remains of Jhosivani Guerrero de la Cruz were identified in 2015, and those of Christian Alfonso Rodríguez Telumbre in 2020.

Figure 3.4 Participatory investigation meeting notes: *Búsqueda* (searching)

Source: Information provided by the Comisión de los Derechos Humanos del Estado de Guerrero in response to information request to Guerrero State Government

human rights commissions and security forces are represented. The purpose of this meeting is explicitly to "locate the six disappeared members" of the same family, and strikingly, to make a plan to carry out a search the day after this meeting with the accompaniment of 100 members of the army and 20 members each of local ministerial police, state police, and federal police to ensure they are complying with the UN's order that they provide "precautionary safety measures" to the collectives and family members. This stands in stark difference to the notes in Figure 1.4—which show evidence of significant involvement by the State Attorney General's Office, or PGJE (the meeting notes are on its letterhead, the PGJE is mentioned in the agreements, and at least one member of the PGJE signs the meeting notes).

Conclusion and Reflection

This chapter contextualizes how the family members of victims of disappearance in Mexico's current wave of violence (2006–present) went from political and social isolation and marginalization to politically powerful protagonists. Widely ignored and then criminalized by the Calderón administration (2006–2012), by 2019 the UN High Commission on Human Rights considered disappearances "the leading [human rights] issue" in Mexico,[62] and presidential candidates vied for the support of victims' collectives.

How do we explain the growing power and independence of victims of violence? In this chapter I reviewed three time periods: Prior to 2006; 2006–2012; and 2013–2018. In each time period, I focused on significant developments in governance and illicit markets; examined the dynamics around the commission of and reaction to disappearances; and finally turned to larger civil society mobilization in order to understand how disappearance around mobilization merged (or diverged) from larger mobilization trends. Prior to 2006, the Mexican government had forcibly disappeared a comparatively small number of political activists as part of its brutal campaign against internal dissent. These victims organized early social movements and made international ties—but the targeted nature of the repression and of the PRI-controlled Mexican state made advocacy impossible, and limited these groups' ability to challenge impunity.

After 2006, a new wave of disappearances began as a result of the growing power of Mexican DTOs and the Calderón administration's militarized response. Victims of disappearances were no longer limited to politicized activists: instead, apolitical young people began disappearing in shockingly large numbers. At first, this change in victim identity left victims of violence in a political and organizational no-man's-land, with social movements steeped in the practice and ideology of human rights unsure of what to do in cases where the identity of the perpetrator of violence was unclear, as were the motives of the disappearance. As the scale of the tragedy became clear, however, social movement organizations, both new and old, began to take up the cause of disappearances. Some of these organizations formed working relationships and participatory investigations with state actors—engaging in advocacy impossible prior to democratization—to attempt to move forward on investigations; while other activist organizations built on the work of both human rights organizations and organizations of the families of the disappeared from the time of the Dirty War to make impunity politically costly, and to reframe victims as rights-worthy.

[62] Jan Jarab, interview by author, via Zoom: September 2019.

Under President Peña Nieto, and especially after the 2014 disappearances of the Ayotzinapa students, disappearances became a dominant and undeniably grave human rights crisis in Mexico. The seriousness of the crisis, together with the cumulative efforts of activists who had challenged the state's criminalization of victims of disappearances, legitimized the family members of the disappeared as political protagonists. At the same time, victims' collectives, many of which had been seeded by the 2011 MPJD mobilization, were maturing, and by 2014 many had the experience and contacts to work independently from their civil society allies in established organizations. These increasingly organized and independent victims' collectives were able to leverage their legitimacy with the state to shift fluidly between advocacy and activism, and also to work with human rights organizations that had begun to embrace the cause of disappearances—regardless of the perpetrator—as their own. They used this legitimacy to push through the 2017 Law on Disappearances, as well as to conduct coordinated searches for the remains of the disappeared—something the state had refused to do.

This chapter frames the journey of the family members of disappearance from obscurity to political power in the current era in the larger national political, security, and movement context. This, however, is only half of the story. In Chapter 4, I return to Nancy, Lucía and Alfonso, and Juan Carlos to help us understand how previously apolitical families become protagonists in their own cases and in the victims' movement. By looking at both piece of this puzzle—at the larger context, and the journey of individuals—we begin to gain a deeper understanding of how people become rights-claiming and, ultimately, rights-bearing citizens.

4

The Evolution of Legal Consciousness

Gaining Voice and Grappling with the Law

Nancy: When I arrived, I couldn't speak, I only knew how to cry . . . [but when I started] going back and forth to the Movement for Peace, I tell you that I learned to know myself because I saw that I could—I had that potential, that is, I realized that I could speak, I realized all that I could do.

Lucía: What am I proud of or surprised by? Before, I couldn't speak. The pain . . . I just couldn't . . .but you know what? These miserable people— they thought we were like crystal, but we have been forged like iron after being beat down so many times.

Juan Carlos: At first, I didn't understand what "agendas" were . . . [nor] what do they even mean by "dynamics," "systematize the evidence" . . . All words that I completely didn't understand. I didn't go to high school. For me it was triple the work to understand everything. . . . So, at first I felt like an idiot. But little by little I figured out what they were talking about. . . . Seeing the different messaging, I dared to start talking a little more.

For Juan Carlos, Lucía and Alfonso, and Nancy, the disappearance of their family member marked a turning point in their lives. The nature of this devastating and disruptive event would refigure nearly everything about their lives: how they make a living; how they spend their days; and their most intimate relationships. It would also fundamentally shift the way each one thought about their own voice and agency in relation to the law, legality, and the state.

In Chapter 2, we learned about the early lives of each of these families, as well as the tragedy and immediate aftermath of the disappearances of their loved ones. In Chapter 3, I discussed the context and practice of disappearances in Mexico—and explored how victims of Mexico's current wave of violence went from atomized and isolated at the political margins to protagonists at its center in the past decade. In this chapter, I pick up threads from both of these chapters, following each family as they react to the disappearance of their loved one. We see them come face to face with institutional

Bootstrap Justice. Janice k. Gallagher, Oxford University Press. © Oxford University Press 2023.
DOI: 10.1093/oso/9780197649978.003.0004

incompetence and atrophy as well as the nascent social movements and victim-led organizations described in Chapter 3—and we witness them confronting the barriers, continuing to mobilize, and asserting agency within this context. We see how the particular nature of disappearance as a grievance compels them to action, and witness the importance of biographical availability and social movement exposure in shaping their response. Finally, we see how the way they think about themselves in relationship to legality and the law—their legal consciousness—is transformed, and in turn transforms their actions.

In what follows, I posit that dramatic life events can rapidly and fundamentally shift how people think about themselves in relation to the law, which in turn reconfigures what they imagine is possible and how they assert agency. Juan Carlos, a door-to-door gold seller, met with several presidents and helped to found two organizations dedicated to searching for the disappeared. Lucía, who hadn't worked outside of the home and thought of herself as a "submissive" person, deftly navigated state bureaucracies, figuring out how to access state officials and arrange for drones to remotely search narco-controlled territory. Nancy emerged from a deep depression and economic hardship to found her own organization and play a central role in getting the PGR[1], the attorney general's office, to adopt key reforms.

After the Disappearance: A Theory of Sustained Mobilization

In this chapter, I argue that we can understand these dramatic changes only by looking closely at how the disappearance event destabilized the way each thought about themselves, the law, and the state. As I argued in Chapter 1, disappearances upend the lives of their loved ones—dramatically and quickly changing what they do, who they know, and, in time, how they think about their ability to effect change and assert agency in their interactions with the state and the legal system.

Studies of legal consciousness tend to interpret legal consciousness as resulting largely from macro-political, sociological, and economic

---

[1] PGR, the Procuraduría General de la República, the Federal Attorney General, was rebranded the FGR, Fiscalía General de la República, by a 2014 constitutional reform. In 2019 the name of the PGR was officially changed to FGR (and, on paper, a host of reforms to promote transparency, impartiality, and effectiveness accompanied this change in name). Throughout this book I refer to the PGR (not FGR) because at the time of these interviews, the PGR was the name of this federal bureaucracy.

structures.[2] Much of this literature situates the state's actions centrally, asking, for example, how ineffective laws, clumsy regulations, and unresponsive state actors shape the legal consciousness of laborers seeking workplace protections (Gallagher, M. 2006, 2017), state workers seeking family and medical leave (Albiston 2010), and employees seeking redress for sexual harassment (Marshall 2005a, 2005b). Other scholars of legal mobilization[3] centrally situate how activists use the law as a tool for social change—for example, they use international human rights language as an organizing tool in the case of Burmese LGBT activists (Chua 2015, 2018), to expand the protection for differently abled people (Vanhala 2011; Heyer 2015), and to mobilize women in the fight for equal pay (McCann 1994).

These works centrally consider (1) how people's experience with movements shape their legal consciousness; and (2) how people's understandings of the law—often learned in the mobilization process—are employed to achieve social movement goals. In this chapter, I complement and expand these approaches in four significant ways. First, I centrally situate the *nature of the grievance* itself, and look closely at how the experience of disappearance and the legal labyrinth of the state that must be navigated to address them has shaped legal consciousness.[4] Second, I look more holistically at legal consciousness, linking and acknowledging people's experiences both in *movements* and *individually*, and discuss the tensions that arise between individual and movement understandings, goals, and strategies. Third, I think about the *dynamism* of legal consciousness in the wake of trauma and explore the pathways through which these three families, situated in different worlds before the disappearance of their loved one, come to think, act, and mobilize in parallel and sometimes overlapping ways following disappearance. Fourth, I trace how legal knowledge and evolving legal consciousness ripples through the actions and decisions of these family members.

I argue in this chapter that a shift toward the "with the law" perspective in legal consciousness—that is, the strategic understanding that the law is made

[2] For example, Chua and Engel (2019) divide legal consciousness scholarship into three schools: the identity school, which centers on how people's multiple identities and positionalities shape their relationship to the law and worldview; the hegemony school, which views law as a "pervasive and powerful instrument of state control;" and the mobilization school, which studies legal consciousness "to understand law's potential for transforming society, particularly by deploying rights that are intended to achieve justice or protect disadvantaged populations."

[3] I adopt Vanhala's (2011) definition of legal mobilization as "any type of process by which an individual or collective actors invoke legal norms, discourse, or symbols to influence policy or behavior."

[4] This again echoes Simmons's (2016) call to think more deeply about the nature of the grievance that people mobilize around.

up of an array of different people with different organizational incentives—results from engaging in ongoing mobilization in Mexico. For those who previously viewed themselves as "before the law," engaging in ongoing mobilization and negotiation with the state shatters any idea of the omnipotence and grandeur of the law. In the day-to-day struggle to find their loved one, a fragmented state emerges with individual actors exerting decisive influence in how justice is—or is not—meted out. For those who viewed themselves as "against the law," mobilization entails confronting the state—and when the state yields in certain ways, granting meetings, agreeing to take particular investigative actions—this defies an understanding of a coherent set of actors aligned against them. For those who saw themselves as "with the law," their understanding of legality as a game with strategic actors is more compatible with their experience of mobilization and negotiation. They home in on the motivations of different state agencies and officials and are poised to deftly navigate the political and judicial bureaucracy. In sum, the experience of activism and advocacy in the context of uneven state terrain pulls people toward a "with the law" perspective. This pulling creates a reenforcing cycle: once people see state officials reacting to political incentives and treating the search for their loved ones as a strategic negotiation, they are both incentivized to continue to act in this manner and to understand legality through this lens. This spiral generates momentum in reconfiguring the way they think about the law and in adjusting their own actions to conform with this continually evolving perspective.

While this shift to a "with the law" perspective is, I argue, a cognitive adaptation that facilitates sustained mobilization, it is not sufficient. Individuals deciding to mobilize make ongoing decisions regarding the costs, benefits (material and non-material) of organizing, and especially the security risks involved in mobilizing—and regardless of how they think about the law, in order to engage in sustained mobilization they must constantly decide that the benefits and satisfaction of organizing outweigh the costs and risks. These benefits, as will be demonstrated in this chapter, vary greatly from person to person; they may be spiritual, ethical, or reputational, or they may hinge on the individual's particular understanding of what "justice" is and whether they believe they are progressing toward it.

Relatedly, individuals who mobilize are continually evaluating their resources: do their life circumstances afford them the time and financial resources to engage in mobilization? As I will show, this question of biographical availability is dynamic and contingent. As they transform their understandings of the law and what it requires of them to continue to search for their loved ones, they also transform their life circumstances. This ability to transform, and to become full-time activists and advocates, is contingent on the financial and emotional support of others. Finally, as family members connect with others who have also experienced the same tragedy, their social networks are transformed. While almost none of the hundreds of family members I interviewed had ever thought of engaging in any contentious political action prior to the disappearance of their loved one, in this chapter I follow Nancy, Lucía and Alfonso, and Juan Carlos as they are immersed within organizations and organizing spaces filled with family members who are also searching for their loved ones. These relationships and experiences transform their socio-spatial positioning and in so doing reshape their claim-making behavior and available repertoires of contention.

In this chapter, and as illustrated in Figure 4.1, I posit that these constitutive concepts explain the sustained mobilization of individuals. I argue that the energy and motivation for sustained mobilization stem from the nature of the grievance. In cases in which the nature of the grievance is ongoing and highly disruptive to core aspects of people's lives, like the disappearance of a loved one, there is tremendous impetus to mobilize. Those who do, however, must determine that there is a net benefit in mobilization—for example, that the pleasure in agency (Wood 2003) they experience together with the slim hope they have of a positive outcome outweigh the financial costs and professional and personal disruptions that ongoing mobilization requires. They

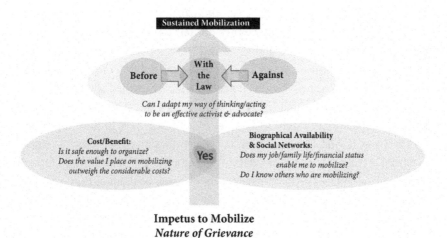

Figure 4.1 A theory of sustained mobilization

must also have life circumstances and exposure to people, movements, and networks in which mobilization is rendered an option. These considerations are ongoing and may be shifted by changes in external or internal conditions at any time. Even if they are determined to persevere despite the risks and costs, are biographically available, and are enmeshed in social networks that facilitate mobilization, however, those who engage in such ongoing action must be willing and able to conceive of themselves and the law strategically.

This chapter focuses on the mechanisms and processes through which the disappearance of a loved one spurs shifts in legal consciousness and inspires convergence among affected family members to see themselves as "with the law." In line with Taylor (2020) and Kruks-Wisner (2018), I argue that the density of exposure is key: as people gain more experience interacting with a variety of state agents—from local policemen, to state investigators, to high-level politicians, and with other people from diverse backgrounds who are also struggling to find their loved ones—they transform their socio-spatial exposure. If they are sufficiently cognitively flexible to learn from the lessons of these interactions, they will be channeled into a mode of thinking in which, both as individuals and collectives, they are strategically navigating the different state agencies and the bureaucrats within them. This transformation lands them firmly "within the law."

Early Investigation: Existing Perspectives Enacted

Chapter 2 followed Nancy, Lucía and Alfonso, and Juan Carlos from before to immediately after the disappearance of their loved one. Before the disappearance, Nancy worked to actively avoid the oppressive forces of the law, while Lucía and Alfonso operated within its bounds in order to have peaceful and prosperous lives. Juan Carlos, however, always regarded law as "a hustle." This chapter will show that for Nancy, and Lucía and Alfonso, responding to the disappearance of their loved ones made prior ways of thinking about and relating to the law and their social world untenable, even as these perspectives shaped their mobilization trajectories; for Juan Carlos, it forced him to deepen his strategic thinking. I follow each of them as they begin to think increasingly strategically about what they need from the legal system, and learn to navigate a complex labyrinth of actors in order to achieve the goal of finding their loved ones. Their stories illustrate how the trauma of the disappearance and the necessity of investigation pushed each of them to shift how they regard themselves. Over the 10 years since the disappearance of their loved one, their relationship to the law has become much more similar to the "with the law" perspective. This consciousness, in turn, has facilitated changes in their activism and advocacy, life circumstances, and social networks, which make it possible for them to continue to mobilize.

Here, we pick up chronologically where we left off, with each family taking the first steps that will result in their engaging in sustained mobilization.

Nancy

After Nancy went to the police on January 5, 2011, less than a week after her son Elvis's disappearance, she hoped that her interaction with them would be different from her experiences in the past. When she initially called to file the complaint, the person on the other end of the line agreed that the blame for Elvis's disappearance lay with Fernando, the director of the drug addiction clinic where Elvis had been in residential treatment for the previous six months. Fernando's culpability seemed straightforward at first: he had been in charge of Elvis and failed to take care of him. Nancy gave her version of events over the phone and was then told to come to the police station to *ratificar* (certify) her report. This meant the police would type up her account, and she would make an official complaint by signing it. When she went back a week later, they couldn't find the complaint. So she told her story again, and again returned to the police station a week later to ratify the complaint. Again, it was missing. Finally, after a month of trying, she was told that her complaint had been registered. She hoped they would finally start to investigate.

For the month following Elvis's disappearance, Nancy was desperate. In addition to the difficulty of reporting the disappearance, Nancy also believed that Fernando knew more than he would admit. Fernando at first appeared to sincerely apologize and look for her son, then quickly shifted to blaming Elvis for his own disappearance. Fernando accused Elvis of stealing his truck and running away so that he and other two boys he left with could party and steal. He told Nancy that he had received a profane text from the three boys saying they were out partying, though he refused to show the text to Nancy. Though Nancy thought Fernando was lying, the more she learned about him, the more she understood why Elvis might have run away. She heard stories that other patients had escaped from the clinic and that Fernando had threatened the life of another patient over an alleged affair with his wife. She also learned that Fernando always carried a gun—something a treatment clinic director shouldn't need to do. All of this made her hope: perhaps her son was out there, hiding from Fernando, and scared of being arrested. And he would at some point come home to her.

With the state's reluctance to register, much less investigate, Elvis's disappearance confirming her belief that they would not help her, Nancy and the families of the two other missing boys hired a private investigator her sister recommended. The investigator, who turned out to be a *ministerio público* (MP, public prosecutor) from the state attorney general's office, charged each family 15,000 pesos (about US$750). Nancy had to borrow the money from her family but didn't hesitate—she thought this might be her best hope to find Elvis. The investigator persuaded the other two families to report their sons missing, something they had resisted because they also at least partially believed Fernando's story that the boys were off committing crimes. They feared that if they reported them "missing," this would make it more likely that they would be arrested, which seemed like a real possibility since all three boys had been addicts and had previously engaged in petty theft. By the time they too reported their sons' disappearances, six weeks had passed.

At about the same time, the ministerial police searched Fernando's clinic for the missing boys. During the search, employees of Fernando's later told Nancy, Fernando told the investigators that they would not be able to access certain parts of the clinic, explaining that he had sick people in certain places. At the time, Nancy thought that maybe he was allowed to do this, since it was his property. Later, she saw it differently: "I know now that an inspection by the ministerial police is an official inspection, and that even if he said no they needed to enter by force."

After this flawed raid by the ministerial police, the families tried to follow up with the private investigator. He had told them that he had pulled the cell phone records of the boys and had scheduled a meeting with Fernando. After the raid, however, he wouldn't return their calls. He kept their money and any evidence he had gathered. Had he told Fernando the police were coming? Taken money from him to hide evidence? They would never know but suspected the worst.

Nancy was deeply frustrated but also relatively disengaged in the face of these setbacks. As we would expect of someone who sees themselves as against the law, Nancy did not contact those responsible for conducting the investigation to complain that it was problematic; she did not go to the media to publicly denounce Fernando, the corrupt PI, nor the ineffective police. She had always seen the law as against her, and several months after the disappearance of her son, her perceptions had largely been confirmed.

Lucía and Alfonso

After returning to Mexico City from Monterrey following their son's disappearance on January 27, 2011, Lucía and Alfonso continued to work their network. A friend of a friend worked for the federal government in a ministry that regulates telecommunications, and through them the families were able get Alejandro's phone records. The nephew of another friend was a snack food distributor in northern Mexico; delivering soft drinks and potato chips, he regularly traveled along the route that Alejandro would have taken on his way to Texas. Through him, they learned that there were ranches throughout northern Nuevo León and Tamaulipas controlled by cartels, each holding more than 50 of the cartel's prisoners. The snack distributor managed to circulate a picture of Alejandro at two of these ranches near Nuevo Laredo—and learned that Alejandro wasn't being held at either. They also heard the name El Chabelo—a local leader of the brutal Zeta cartel who controlled these ranches and who they came to believe was key for their case.

By March 2011, Alfonso had arranged for a federal policeman, a *ministerio público,* and the director of anti-kidnapping from Mexico City to accompany him to Nuevo León to continue the investigation. On that trip, they learned that they had done all they could on their first trip in terms of contacting state institutions. They were encouraged to see some signs of their investigation: they had circulated a picture of Alejandro to the federal police in January, and when they arrived at a federal police office they hadn't previously been to, they saw Alejandro's picture posted on the wall.

For Lucía and Alfonso, there was now nothing left to do except to wait. Their "before the law" perspective led them to believe things would work out: they had taken all the advised actions with state agencies. Their son was innocent of any wrongdoing, but if something had happened to him, they had taken the appropriate steps to activate the state's investigatory bureaucracy. And so they waited.

Juan Carlos

After the disappearance of his first two brothers in 2008, Juan Carlos was able to make contact with local, state, and national officials quickly. He sat down with the Guerrero state attorney general four days after their disappearance; and with the president of Mexico within six months. Not that this was easily achieved: Juan Carlos remembers sleeping outside the offices of state officials in order to get them to meet with him. But eventually, he and his brother did meet with nearly everyone they had wanted to. Juan Carlos and his brother Rafael returned to the site of the disappearances in Atoyac, Guerrero, many times, personally interviewing the last people who had seen their brothers: the bartender and Raúl's girlfriend, the dancer.

After the disappearance of two more brothers, Gustavo and Luis Armando in 2010, Juan Carlos and his brother Rafael had learned hard lessons from their previous experiences. They decided that pursuing redress with the state was not an option:

> Rafael and I decided, in the first moments, that we would search in *el campo* (in the field/on location) so we could try to figure out what happened. . . . Since we knew Veracruz was a complicated state, with important investments from the Zetas in the Gulf region, with the information we had we decided not to go to any governmental institution. Instead, we would try to negotiate; we had all we needed to go and talk to the criminals directly. If we opened up space for the Attorney General of Guerrero to come in, they weren't going to send anyone . . . because it's tough to get there, and because they're afraid.

In order to gain access to the Zetas, who were known for being secretive and difficult to access, Juan Carlos took it upon himself to, essentially, disguise himself and go undercover in the town where the brothers had disappeared. He got to know the local drug users, and through one of them, finally was able to set up a meeting with the *jefe de plaza*, the cartel leader in charge of the local drug routes and drug trafficking. Juan Carlos was taken to meet with the *jefe* blindfolded in the back of a truck and asked for the return of his brothers. He offered money and his trucks in return. The *jefe* rebuffed him—refusing to answer questions about the whereabouts of his brothers. After one of the *jefe*'s men threatened him with a gun against his temple, Juan Carlos was dropped outside of town and told never to come back.

For Juan Carlos, accessing powerful state officials, interviewing witnesses, and seeking out drug cartel leadership were the strategic responses he saw to a fragmented political landscape in which the responsibility for, and therefore the ability to meaningfully address, the disappearance of his brothers was shared among differently situated people. Unlike Nancy or Lucía and Alfonso, and in line with his "with the law" perspective, he did not impute a coherence to the state or its agents—whether benign or aggressive. Instead, he focused on learning and strategically responding to the political calculations of these different actors.

Early Contact with Social Movements

Each family, in the initial stages of their investigations, hewed close to their pre-established ways of thinking about the law, the state, and legality. These trajectories, however, would soon be meaningfully altered due in large part to the people they met in the course of their search. While we know that as socio-spatial positioning shifts individuals' ways of thinking and decisions about whether to mobilize also change, how exactly does this happen? In other words, how do social movements shape people's ability and desire to mobilize?

Nancy: "I Need You to Help Me Yell Louder"

Nancy's experience of corrupt institutions designed to work against her was initially confirmed by her early experiences with social movements. In February 2011, Nancy searched online for who might be able to help her. She found a local organization called Asociación de Niños Robados y Desparecidos, the Association of Stolen and Disappeared Children. When she arrived at the organization's office, they asked her for 500 pesos (about US$25) to cover the costs of the paperwork and snacks provided to participants in the organization. When Nancy couldn't pay this amount, the director covered her, though as she would realize later, there were strings attached. This organization helped Nancy get Elvis's picture in local and national newspapers and on major news stations; also, the director introduced Nancy to investigators from SEIDO.[5]

---

[5] SEIDO, the Subprocuraduría Especializada en Investigación de Delincuencia Organizada, Attorney General's Special Office on Organized Crime Investigation, is the branch of PGR dedicated

In June 2011, the director asked Nancy to speak about her case at an event to be attended by hundreds of state officials from all over Mexico. Nancy was hesitant to accept. She still couldn't talk about what had happened without tearfully breaking down. But she was determined: she recognized this as an opportunity, and she wasn't going to let it pass her by. "So, I armed myself in courage, and I didn't cry. I saw all those authorities sitting there, and I told my story." Afterward, she opened another case file in SEIDO, and even started to attend meetings at SEIDO together with three other families involved with the Asociación de Niños Robados y Desparecidos. The head of the organization, after witnessing the power of Nancy's testimony, asked her to start giving talks at schools. She offered Nancy a stipend for doing so—but Nancy declined, asking only that the organization cover the cost of her transportation. Nancy's gut told her that something was off with the organization, and she began to distance herself. When other members told her that the director had asked them to clean her house—to mop, clean the kitchen, prepare food—in return for the assistance they were receiving, Nancy decided she no longer wanted to work with the organization.

At the same time Nancy was working with this organization, her uncle suggested she contact an acquaintance of his, a local reporter named Jorge Garralda who had covered other cases of disappearance. After the report aired, Nancy got a call from the State Prosecutor of Mexico State (EdoMex):

> Right after the spot appeared on television . . . at that moment, the Attorney General of EdoMex called me. I asked him for an appointment for us. And yes—he finally gave it to us. But when we went, they treated us really harshly. At that meeting, the prosecutor still told us that we were not going to get what we wanted from [the reporter] Jorge Garralda. Because Jorge was involved in "yellow journalism," not that I understood what that meant. He told us lots of bad things about the television program and this man. And we were shocked into agreeing: we said "Oh, that's ugly, isn't it?"

The attorney general then assigned two ministerial policemen from special affairs to the case. It was agreed that they would speak with Fernando. In what was becoming a pattern, after they arranged to meet with Fernando, Nancy never heard from them again. Frustrated, she stopped talking with the parents of the other two boys: "what need was there to be talking to each

to investigating organized crime.

other if we had nothing to report? I mean, they didn't have any news. I didn't have any information. What need was there for us to meet?" For Nancy, even though she had begun to meet others involved in looking for their loved ones, this was a moment when she decreased her social connections with others engaged in struggle.

In the six months following Elvis's disappearance, a lot had happened: Nancy had quit her job to dedicate herself to searching for Elvis, had gone to the police, had hired and been deceived by a private investigator, had given interviews to countless news organizations, had joined a civic organization dedicated to searching for the disappeared and left after being disenchanted with their practices, and had met with state and federal judicial officials. Despite this, she believed she was no closer to finding her son. This frustration was compounded because she held herself responsible for his disappearance: she was the one who had insisted he go to rehab, and she had trusted Fernando. "I kept remembering what I had said to my son when they took him—'it's for your own good, my dear son. You're going to be fine and this will save your life.'"

This guilt and frustration weighed heavily on Nancy, and she began to have panic attacks. "We'd go somewhere and suddenly I'd have a crisis: I'd start screaming, and I would even scare my husband because he'd be driving and suddenly I'd be sitting up very straight and I'd start screaming until my throat burned." Nancy entered a deep depression, barely leaving the house until the end of the year. In July 2011 and January 2012 Nancy attempted to take her own life by intentionally overdosing on medication. Both times, a neighbor knocked on her door, saving her life. Nancy's suicide note read that she would only know where her son was when she joined him in heaven.

The day after her suicide attempt in January 2012, just over a year after Elvis's disappearance, Nancy turned on the news, something she rarely did. The first thing she saw was a report about a presentation called Ponte En los Zapatos del Otro, roughly "Put Yourself in Someone Else's Shoes," happening at the Teatro de la Ciudad, and co-sponsored by the MPJD. Nancy decided to go. When she told the organizers what had happened to her son, they found her a seat in the front of the theater, near to Javier Sicilia, the leader of the MPJD (see Animal Político 2012b for photo of Nancy directly behind and to the right of Javier). Nancy couldn't believe it, but told herself, "For some reason God has put me right here right now, and I have to say something!" After a moment of silence for those who had disappeared, Nancy tapped Javier on the shoulder and said, "I've come here only to speak with you. My son has been disappeared, and I need you to help me yell louder." Javier promised to support Nancy in any way he could and connected her with organizations involved in the MPJD's work. I met Nancy three days later, when she arrived to CENCOS, one of the two MPJD support organizations. Together with another advocate, I took her testimony. I remember her as being panicked and near tears as she recounted in minute detail all that had happened.

Nancy soon joined the activities of the MPJD: caravans, meeting with authorities, public marches and protests, and more meetings. Her immediate goal was to get her son's face into the public eye as much as possible. She learned from other victims how to give her testimony, and she was invited to help with the logistics of several small protests. She was handed the microphone at one of them by one of the directors of SeraPaz, and for the first time since the summer, she spoke in public about what had happened to her son. The experience was instrumental in revitalizing Nancy's energies to search for her son. "When I arrived, I couldn't speak, I only knew how to cry," she told me years later. "As I started to realize that I wasn't the only person that this had happened to . . . I learned during this time with the MPJD that, yes! I could speak! . . . that I was the only person defending the dignity of my son. If my son couldn't talk because he wasn't here," she concluded, then, "he had a *pinche* mother that would speak for him."

Nancy's involvement with MPJD soon led her to become more independent. In the first six months after the disappearance of her son, her uncles had driven her to and from meetings with authorities. After they needed to return to work, Nancy learned to navigate public transportation to get to her many meetings. This, however, was a time-consuming option, as she lived in a poorer part of town not easily accessible by the metro, and her husband urged her to get her driver's license. "I had never had one and always just depended on my husband, who had a motorcycle," she said. She was also scared to drive, so as an incentive, her husband surprised her one day with the keys to a new car he had bought her, and told her "now—learn to drive it!" She did, and the car dramatically shifted what Nancy was able to accomplish. Since she had stopped working the moment her son was disappeared, her husband's salary from his job as a manager at the gas station allowed her to devote herself to searching for Elvis full-time. He also bought her a laptop when Nancy noticed that other family members of victims were using the internet as a resource, and he paid for them to have internet at home so Nancy wouldn't need to frequent the local internet café. Nancy soon learned to use Facebook, Twitter, Instagram, and YouTube as tools in her search. Even her neighbor, the one who had knocked on her door just in time to frustrate her suicide attempt, played a key role: she knew Nancy used to work as a seamstress, and she started giving Nancy clothes to mend. Whenever Nancy was too depressed to get up and open the blinds, the neighbor would knock on the door—insisting she needed her clothes back, and in the process making sure Nancy was safe.

These early experiences with social movements began to pry loose Nancy's belief that avoidance was the best tactic to deal with the institutions she felt were aligned against her. As she got a glimmer of the power of her testimony, she began to fight rather than resign herself to mistreatment. While she became disillusioned with the Asociación de los Niños Robados, she recognized that her affiliation with them had managed to secure for her meetings with powerful people; this hadn't been possible before, and realizing this propelled her to seek out other social movements. Nancy's biographical availability also shifted soon after she became involved in the MPJD: the support of her husband, family, and community enabled her to actively and independently engage in the search for her son and to participate in the MPJD's mobilization efforts.

Lucía and Alfonso

Alejandro had disappeared just a couple of months before the emergence of the MPJD. When Lucía and Alfonso came to Mexico City after the chaos of the first several days post-disappearance, they tried to think of who else might be able to help them. Watching the news, Lucía saw a report that representatives from the UN had been in Coahuila talking about enforced disappearances. Alfonso remembered that Lucía had seen a United Nations office in Polanco, the wealthiest neighborhood in Mexico City. She and Alfonso went there and were re-directed downtown to the main office of the UN High Commissioner for Human Rights. They were told that while the United Nations did not do their own investigations, they knew of a human rights organization in Monterrey that might be able to help them—CADHAC.

The next time Lucía and Alfonso were in Monterrey, they went to CADHAC and met with Hermana Consuelo Morales, a nun who had run a small human rights NGO in Monterrey since the mid-1990s. She told them to come back the following Wednesday when they could meet with other families who also had a disappeared loved one. This opened up the door to the world of social movements confronting violence in Mexico for Lucía and Alfonso. When the MPJD emerged in March of 2011, they heard from CADHAC about the march from Cuernavaca to Mexico City. While they didn't join the three-day march, they decided to go to the *zócalo*, Mexico's enormous central plaza, for the final gathering. The MPJD opened up the stage to any family members of victims in the crowd of more than 100,000—and Lucía, with Alfonso's encouragement, decided to give her testimony. It was the first time she had publicly spoken about Alejandro's disappearance, and she remembers it as a surreal and almost out-of-body experience.

Participating in a social movement didn't come easily to them. Lucía and Alfonso were quite used to having the resources to operate according to their own timelines and priorities. When Hermana Consuelo asked them to come to the weekly meeting in Monterrey, this entailed flying from Mexico City to Monterrey (about the distance between Boston and Richmond, Virginia). They had the resources to do this, but it was disruptive to their lives. When the MPJD's northern caravan reached Monterrey and it was decided that the attorney general would engage in participatory investigations with the assembled family members, Lucía and Alfonso weren't there—they were in Mexico City. When they asked Hermana Consuelo if they could join these meetings, she had serious misgivings: she told them since they hadn't attended the march, they would not be included in the meetings. Lucía, however, didn't accept that answer: she learned from other attendees when the meeting would be and arrived with Alfonso before the first meeting started. The couple waited at the attorney general's office and managed to persuade Consuelo that they deserved a seat at the table. When it came time for them to discuss their case, the amount of investigating they had done impressed state officials, and their presence at these participatory investigations was cemented.

During several of the early meetings that Lucía and Alfonso had in Monterrey, I observed a natural division of labor taking shape: Lucía managed the politics and dynamics of the relationships with the other victims' families, with CADHAC, and with the investigators; while Alfonso homed in on the details of the investigation. For Lucía, like Nancy, her first experiences with social movements marked a shift in her relationship with authorities, voice, and power as well as in her own marriage. Lucía's early experience giving her testimony and then fighting for a place at the meeting with authorities, which CADHAC and the MPJD had arranged, showed both Lucía and Alfonso her vital role and competence in searching for Alejandro, marking a departure from the traditional roles she had assumed in most aspects of their lives previously. Lucía saw it as her role to get them in front of as many state agents as she could so her husband could run down investigatory leads, keep track of the details of who had been interviewed, and monitor any pending investigatory actions. Lucía's role was not submissive nor subservient—and in time, her role expanded. Alfonso continued to run his business during this time—though he had the prerogative to take significant time away. Lucía's biographical ability and Alfonso's continued financial support meant she was available to devote her time to mobilization activities.

Juan Carlos: "This Is My Space. It Is Worth It, and Yes, I Am Going to Struggle"

Following the disappearance of two more of his brothers from Veracruz in 2010, Juan Carlos was exhausted. In 2011, he remembers deciding to give up. "I didn't want to participate in anything," he told me. "I didn't want anything to do with searching anymore." When Juan Carlos heard that his mother and some other family members and neighbors from Pajacuarán, his hometown, were going to a march in spring 2011, he wasn't interested. By that time, between 17 and 20 people had disappeared from his town, and his mother, María, started bringing people with her to MPJD meetings. "I said, 'Well, I hope it goes well for you,' but that was it," Juan Carlos told me.

María learned of the June 2011 MPJD caravan from a family member, who had heard about it on television. Neither María nor her son had ever participated in any type of mobilization before, but the MPJD's message that *estamos hasta la madre* (roughly, we have had it) appealed to her. She traveled to Mexico City and joined the MPJD's first caravan, which was made up of around 800 people, including several hundred whose family members had been disappeared. Together they traveled to cities beset by violence throughout the north of the country. For María, the experience was a turning point. She had felt isolated and alone in her search, and the MPJD gave her a sense of belonging.

When she came back from the caravan, her family members started accompanying her to weekly meetings in Mexico City, a more than six-hour trip from her home. She would tell her son *"Voy a mi movimiento,"* I'm going to my movement, recounted Juan Carlos. "I noted something different about my mom. She didn't have such a sad gaze." Before she joined the caravan, "my mom had spent two or three months just looking at documents [relating to the case], but she wasn't eating or sleeping. But then she goes, she goes to the caravan and comes back. And I looked at her face—looked in her eyes, and there was something that inspired me.... Something happened. So, I came to Mexico [City] with her."

Before coming to the movement, Juan Carlos had also felt isolated in his search. He'd experienced people distancing from him when he tried to share his family's story. "Many people pushed us away," he said. "So when I arrive to Mexico, to CENCOS, [in the summer of 2011] and everyone was saying to my mom 'Ay, Doña Mari,' and hugging her and lifting her up like a ball, up and down, because they cared about her so much," he was moved. After Mari introduced him to the group, another member of the group grabbed his hands and hugged him. "It was one of the first hugs I felt strongly—a legitimate hug, full of hope, love, strength.... I was feeling the strength of the people." Juan Carlos went to the bathroom and began to cry. "I cried because I had so much resentment, so much anger for everyone who promised help but in the end only used you. If you didn't help advance their interest, you weren't worth anything."

His experience at the meeting changed him. "I said, 'This is my space. It is worth it, and yes, I am going to struggle. And yes, I am going to search for my brothers.' I think this is an important point that defines today who I am, an important part of my life." Moved not only by his desire to find his own brothers but by the stories of others who had also lost loved ones, Juan Carlos began to mobilize. He saw himself and his mother changing from "orphan victims" to people with a "path and hope," and he understood that this path would be easier in a group than alone: "Simply and basically, in order to find my brothers, I knew we need[ed] collective strength so that amongst all of us, we're looking."

While these fundamentals of organizing resonated immediately for him, the ways in which seasoned organizers spoke and thought about mobilizing tactics, messaging, and interacting with state officials were quite foreign:

At first, I didn't understand what "agendas" were . . . [nor] what do they even mean by "dynamics," "systematize the evidence." . . . All words that I completely didn't understand. I didn't go to high school. For me it was triple the work to understand everything. . . . So, at first I felt like an idiot. But little by little I figured out what they [social movement leaders] were talking about. . . . Seeing the different messaging, I dared to start talking a little more, and I took that feeling and said "it's time to see my country from another perspective."

From the time of the first disappearances of his brothers in 2008, Juan Carlos's "with the law" mindset had guided him to intuitively negotiate with the state, form relationships with particular officials, and attempt to extract justice from a broken system. But doing this by himself was exhausting, and he saw its futility. Once his socio-spatial exposure shifted and he met others in his position who were also mobilizing, it changed his life and path.

The importance of collective support and strength not only resonated for Juan Carlos personally—but it is also the central guiding principal in his strategic action. Luis, Juan Carlos's Centro ProDH lawyer, summed up Juan Carlos's mindset in a 2020 interview: "For Juan Carlos, the question is always how do we turn this [particular action on my brothers' case] into changes in public policy; how do we make it so that this is something which benefits everyone? For him, it's like the tortilla line: if you're at the end of the line, the important thing isn't that you go to the front of the line—but that everyone gets a tortilla, until the last person." Juan Carlos intuitively recognizes the importance of knowing and working with others who share the experience of a disappeared loved one—and this realization continues to guide his actions.

* * *

In the wake of their loved ones' disappearances, each family took further steps toward sustained mobilization when they connected with social movements. However, the mechanisms and processes through which social movements enabled and encouraged mobilization worked differently for each family—in part because of their initially divergent legal consciousness. Nancy's "against the law" perspective began to shift when she connected with MPJD activists who impressed her with the access to power that collective action afforded (while the support of her family enabled her to become "biographically available" and to continue to mobilize). Lucía and Alfonso realized that they needed to challenge the state and coordinate among different state and non-state actors in order to move forward the investigation into their son's disappearance, challenging their previous assumptions about the orderliness of the law. They also realized that a local human rights organization could be important in giving them access to state actors. Juan Carlos, worn down by the arduous work of investigating alone the disappearance of four brothers—and the repeated disappointment of high-level officials' broken promises—was revitalized by meeting others who were mobilizing. The solace of working with others re-energized him, changing him from someone who had given up on mobilization to someone who would become a sustained mobilizer. As we will see take shape more fully in the next section, contact with social movements and exposure to a multitude of state officials knitted together to transform each person's understanding of themselves and their own agency in relation to the state.

With the State: Strategies that Enable Sustained Activism and Advocacy

Returning to the theoretical framework of the chapter, then, where are we? Each family was propelled to mobilize by the disappearance of their loved one. After their initial contact with the state and social movements, each family member had encountered significant costs of mobilization—including mental anguish and exhaustion, concerns for their safety, and economic hardship brought on by the costs associated with looking for their loved ones and changes to their ability to work. Despite these costs, each decided to continue to mobilize. Those with significant barriers to biographical availability had transformed their circumstances (or would soon do so, in the case of Juan Carlos) to allow them to continue to mobilize. And each had met other people who were searching for their disappeared loved ones, something that proved important in distinct ways for each of them. Despite these affirmations, however, this did not mean that they would necessarily continue to mobilize. At any point, their life circumstances or considerations of whether to mobilize could change. And even if they decided to continue their search—their sustained mobilization was not assured.

Their continued mobilization was in part contingent on a convergence in their thinking and action. As they engaged and grappled with the state in their search for their loved ones, reified understandings of the legality as natural law (*before the law*), or alternately, unidirectionally aligned against them (*against the law*), were shaken loose by their experience. In their place, more nuanced understandings of the law and the state emerged. In the course of the struggle, then, they evolved to have "a vision of legality as engagement and conflict, resource and process" (Ewick and Silbey 1998, 131)—perspectives constitutive of the "with the law" perspective.

In this section, I talk about five activist and advocacy strategies that each of the families pursued in their own way: (1) confronting the state with contentious action, (2) partnering with social movements to access state officials, (3) strategically navigating the state's judicial bureaucracy, (4) locating allies within the state, and (5) participating in independent searches for their loved ones. Whenever possible, I trace how each person came to pursue this strategy. These strategies constitute the central elements of the repertoire of contention for the loved ones of the disappeared. In this section, we can see how these families contributed to innovating on existing strategies, and gain insight into how and why they chose to participate in these strategies—which lie at the core of what make a sustained mobilization a threat to collusive impunity.

While Nancy, Lucía and Alfonso, and Juan Carlos employ these strategies in distinct ways, it is striking that each of these very differently situated family members engages in these same strategic repertoires of contention. In this convergence, I argue that we see evidence of the importance of social movements and networks, and also the magnetism of the "with the law" perspective. As the density of contact between state officials and individuals grows, victim activists are drawn toward this perspective, and a certain set of actions naturally follows from this transformation in consciousness. Alternately, those who are committed to a "before the law" or "against the law" orientation are repelled from mobilization and often choose to exit: the actions of state actors and the progress (or lack thereof) of the investigation make clear that their previous worldviews are not productive, sustainable, or tenable. This provokes a relatively quick and fundamental change in perspective, which has implications for how we understand legal consciousness and mobilization more generally.

Confronting the State with Contentious Action

I have seen Nancy, Lucía and Alfonso, and Juan Carlos march together, go on hunger strikes or support those who are doing so, and fiercely confront state officials. While this looks different for each of them, partly due to their lives and ways of thinking prior to their loved ones' disappearances, each has decided to engage in contentious action despite never having done so prior to their loved one's disappearance. What types of contentious action does each engage in, and how do they think about its role in their mobilization?

* * *

Even before Nancy linked up with the MPJD, she understood that she needed to do something beyond negotiating with the state. In 2011, she organized a *caminata* (small march), with the mothers of the other two boys who disappeared with Elvis. It had little effect and didn't make the news. After meeting Javier Sicilia in early 2012, Nancy met other victims from the State of Mexico through the MPJD network. At the time there were no victims' organizations in her state, so five mothers whose children were all disappeared decided to come together to form EdoMex's first victims' collective. All the women held the common goal of publicizing their children's photographs with the thought that if they were being hidden or had been detained, perhaps someone would recognize them—or perhaps their children would realize their families were looking for them.

In the summer of 2012, they decided to organize a march in the center of EdoMex, something that, besides the *caminata*, none of them had done before. Nancy went through her contacts—collected in notebooks and on business cards stuffed hastily into her pocket—to bring together the names and contact information of everyone she had met who was also looking for a loved one in EdoMex; she called, visited, and emailed them to come out to their march. She didn't know anything about organizing a march or whether they needed a permit, and she nearly canceled it the night before, convinced no one would show up or they would get in trouble for holding the event. But the march was a success: all major press outlets from EdoMex showed up to interview and feature the more than 30 family members of victims who assembled.

Nancy was at the same time deepening her involvement with the MPJD. "Sometimes we didn't know what the event we were going to was even about, but we would show up to support the others, and also to take advantage of the fact that we knew the media would be there." As the MPJD victims escalated their actions from marches and meetings to more direct action in 2012, Nancy decided to join the three mothers she had met in the MPJD who were on a hunger strike. For seven days, the mothers lived in a makeshift camp—sleeping in tents, cooking on camp stoves, and sitting on crates—all in the center of Mexico City, right in front of SEGOB, the Ministry of the Interior closely aligned with the president. This hunger strike opened the doors to participatory investigations (see Mendoza Aguilar 2012), which I discuss elsewhere in this chapter. In May 2013, after progress at these participatory investigations stalled, Nancy decided it was time to do a second hunger strike: "I didn't really think it would work, but I figured we had to try. I stopped and said—well, f**k it. Let's go. We have to do it."

Nancy was one of the leaders of this second hunger strike. She recruited participants and formed bonds with the other victims on hunger strike, one of whom began to teach Nancy and her fellow EdoMex victims about what it means to be a human rights defender. She reflected on the highs and lows of participating:

> It made me depressed to be outside—it feels horrible to be in the street, in the cold, and it was raining a lot and our tents flooded. But there were so many people that supported us—it motivated me so much that so many young people came to support us. They would come read us books, just sit and talk with us. There were two brothers who came, who I am still in touch with, who would come and pray with us.

Nancy, as someone who had regarded herself as against the law, gravitated toward contentious action. Since her understanding of her relationship to legality had always been oppositional, organizing marches and going on hunger strike came fairly naturally. The shift in her way of thinking and acting, however, came in not avoiding the state but engaging with it, and using contentious action for the clear goal of changing the state's actions. She also made connections—with other family members of the disappeared as well as people who accompanied their actions. These connections not only were important social supports, but surrounded her with people who were engaging with state actors in different ways. She would draw on their experiences in thinking through how to approach the state strategically.

* * *

Lucía and Alfonso have taken great pains to build relationships with state actors and have engaged in most contentious actions of the larger movement with one toe in the water: on the US Caravan, they came to half of it and stayed in hotels while most others stayed in church basements and other donated shelter. While Lucía spoke at the 2011 mass mobilization in the *zócalo*, she marched for only a short portion at the end. Despite some reluctance to participate fully in confrontational collective actions, Lucía and Alfonso have sought out ways to support others taking contentious actions. While Lucía didn't go on hunger strike herself, she was part of the support team who attended to the people who did. I once made sandwiches with

Lucía for the families in Monterrey who needed food to take with them as they prepped for a day of marching, standing, waiting, and confronting the attorney general. They have also often donated money to cover the transportation and meal costs of others to attend advocacy actions and meetings with state officials.

Lucía and Alfonso have engaged in direct, contentious action most often when it related directly to their case. After Lucía and Alfonso had a falling out with CADHAC and were excluded from their participatory investigatory meetings,[6] they asked for meetings with the Nuevo León Attorney General's Office for them and five other MPJD cases. While the attorney general at the time agreed, with the change in gubernatorial administration in 2015, the new attorney general took steps to "demote" their participatory investigation: he told them he wouldn't personally attend, and that the meetings would be held in a satellite location. Lucía, representing the MPJD cases, told the new attorney general—"Look, we are trying to live out our rights. There were agreements made, from the time of the caravan.[7] It was agreed that these *mesas* [participatory investigation meetings] would continue until there were results." He didn't yield—and Lucía and a handful of other victims, on the day they were supposed to meet with assistant attorney general in the distant office, showed up instead at the headquarters and demanded to be let in, staging a *plantón*, a stationary march/sit-in. While they didn't get in that day, their next meeting was scheduled at the attorney general's headquarters, and was presided over by the attorney general himself.

While Lucía and Alfonso have tended to be less confrontational in public, once seated with investigators they do not hesitate to clash with state officials. After an MP in Mexico City made what Lucía and Alfonso saw as little effort to advance their investigations, I witnessed Lucía appeal to the MP's human side—shaming the investigator for not doing more, asking whether she would stand for similar treatment if it was her child who was missing. When that was met with steely indifference, she unrelentingly upbraided the investigator with a raised voice through tears. This resolve also came out when she was told by a state official to move out of seats reserved for other victims

---

[6] CADHAC committed to bringing only those cases of family members of victims who attended their weekly meetings, something that was logistically almost impossible for the family members from Mexico to do. This led to the separation of many of the people whose loved ones were disappeared in Nuevo León but who live outside of the state from CADHAC.

[7] "Caravan" here refers to the Northern Caravan, called the *Caravana de Consuelo*. the Consoling Caravan, which was organized by the MPJD in June 2011.

during the 2013 ceremony at which President Peña Nieto signed the Victims' Law. Lucía remembers telling the official, "I'm not moving from this spot." And she didn't. When the meeting ended, and Sicilia was speaking with the president, Lucía thought about the photo that would inevitably be above the fold in the paper the next day: she looked at where the photographers were positioned, and angled the photo of her son just right. She told those around her to do the same. And the next day "the banner [headline in the newspaper] was just right, the picture too. *Padrísimo, padrísimo* [just perfect] *sí*."

* * *

Juan Carlos understood early that he would do whatever it took to gain access to state officials and that this would include contentious action. When he joined the MPJD, marching and protesting became part of his day-to-day activities. But he was also aware of the limitations of mobilization alone. In August 2012 Juan Carlos participated in a month-long caravan organized by the MPJD in the United States with 125 other people from Mexico, most of whom were also family members of people who had been disappeared. On this caravan, people marched daily, confronted US officials, and engaged in direct non-violent action. For example, in order to bring attention to the issue of the easy availability of weapons and the gun show loophole, Juan Carlos was part of a caravan delegation that bought a gun at a gun show without showing any identification, and then destroyed the weapon at a press conference.

Juan Carlos reflected on what he had learned on the caravan:

The caravan was really useful for me in the US. . . . I really learned that in order to change what was happening, this had to be from the outside [of the system; outside of the country]. I wanted to do deeper *incidencia* [advocacy work] - because for me—they would call me and say "Let's do this march, let's do this," and what was next? Nothing came of that—so I thought, from what I had seen, you have to go after the root of the problem.

* * *

For Nancy, contentious action has been a go-to strategy when she is frustrated with state inaction. Lucía and Alfonso recognize it as part of movement activity and do not distance themselves from it but reserve their own contentious mobilization for particular state officials. Juan Carlos is an experienced protester, but he doubts the power of protest alone as a mobilization tactic. In their approaches to contentious actions, we see the through lines from their legal consciousness—and also the beginning of convergence.

Partnering with Social Movements to Access State Officials

Perhaps the most common concrete demand articulated during collective, contentious action is to gain a meeting with a certain state official—as we saw in the last section. All three of the families have been able to establish meetings with officials—from the president of Mexico through local prosecutors—due to both their individual initiative and their involvement in social movements. What has this looked like for each of them?

* * *

When I asked Lucía how, exactly, she had learned to be an effective activist and advocate, she flashed me a smile, and snipped: "You mean, besides the fact that I'm charming?" And she is right: Lucía has an ingratiating manner, which I had assumed she came by naturally and which I have seen facilitate access to state officials. When I asked her about this, she answered:

> We have learned the channels through which we have to go, where to apply pressure—and as Francisco[8] has told us: "You have an ability." But this is not a natural ability I was born with. It's something I have given myself to. Over and over. Even Alfonso has admired what I've been capable of—and it scares him a little bit (laughs). And I admire myself too—though not too much, because I know where that strength comes from—the strength of a mother is incalculable.

The most central tool in Lucía and Alfonso's contentious repertoire has been accessing state officials either through their own efforts or together with other family members or organizations,[9] and then building relationships

---

[8] Francisco Romero is a volunteer movement lawyer they work with, and together with psychologist Atala Chávez, is a *co-adyuvante* (private prosecutor) on Alejandro's case.

[9] Their first contact was with CADHAC, the smaller organization headquartered in Monterrey, and they have since participated in several regional organizations: FUNDEC and FUNDENL, which I discuss more in Chapter 5, are headquartered in Coahuila and Nuevo León, respectively, and utilize more confrontational mobilization tactics. Lucía and Alfonso were early members of the MPJD as well, and served as treasurers of the movement from 2012 – 2017, as well as founding members of CfC, the citizen-led forensic organization. They were also early members of the "victims' platform" within the MPJD.

with them. After the MPJD held dialogues with each of the presidential candidates in 2012, for example, Lucía approached the assistant to the PAN presidential candidate, Josefina Vasquez Mota. Another MPJD member had marched up to candidate Vasquez following the forum and demanded that she help her look for her daughter. As her assistant began to take this woman's contact information, Lucía jumped in:

> "Also write me down. . . I was at the [meeting] table too, write me down." I mean, I was there too. . . . So he said to me, "Tomorrow on the [presidential grounds] there is a private meeting, there's not going to be any media or anything—and she [candidate Vasquez] wants to talk to you." And we went. So—she [candidate Vasquez] asks Alfonso, what do we want? And he says: I need a meeting with the [Mexican federal] Attorney General. So, she picked up the phone and called Marisela.[10] After that, we had ongoing participatory meetings with her [Marisela] and [several other victims].

For Lucía, *llevando muchas camisetas* (wearing many different jerseys belonging to many different organizations depending on what's effective at the time) is part of her strategy. When she is trying to get a meeting, she'll often say immediately that she is part of FUNDEM. Or of the Victims' Platform of the MPJD. Or simply of "the movement." By doing that, she gains access that "if I go as the nice daughter of the neighbor, this is not going to happen," and she understands that "because you're part of an organization, they give you a little more attention." But in other circumstances, when she already has secured access to a certain office, she won't hesitate to flip this and re-focus the officials on what they should be concerned with: she will snap back at an official who asks what organization she is with: "Look, before I tell you [what organization] I belong to—I am Alejandro's mother. Do not call me *Señora* [from x organization]. Know that I am a mother."

* * *

Nancy likewise is acutely aware of the importance of partnering with social movements to access state officials, especially after the first officials she came in contact with refused to register her case. After the 2012 hunger strike, the head of SEGOB agreed to facilitate meetings with their respective governors

---

[10] Marisela Morales was the top judicial official in Mexico from April to November, 2011. She served under President Calderón.

for the 45 family members of victims who were present. Nancy parlayed this into a chance to meet with the governor of EdoMex. In that meeting, Nancy and the other families established that they would have ongoing participatory investigation meetings with the state.

Within EdoMex, Nancy has evolved into an important leader among the families of the disappeared. She talked about how she uses her access to state officials to also facilitate access for others:

> I knock on the door [of state investigatory officials], I open it—and if they [state officials] only want to open the door for me, no—*no manches,* you've got to be kidding me—We'll throw it wide open and all march in. And if something is stuck and they [the other families] think I might be able to help, I'll look for the way to move things forward. I also help others see if something is really necessary: I help them think through whether a proposed state action is useful or just creating paperwork.

* * *

For Juan Carlos, when he finally came into contact with the MPJD and other social movements, he was convinced that participating in social movements was the way forward—they had motivated him to search for his brothers and had brought both him and his mother back to life in many ways. Accessing state officials, however, was something he had to figure out by himself back in 2008 after the disappearance of his first two brothers, and together with other family members, he did so remarkably effectively. With his participation in the MPJD, he realized that the access he had fought hard for alone had also been achieved by the MPJD, and that by participating with victims' organizations he would be able to have regular contact with top officials.

When he achieved this regular contact, however, he was frustrated over the inability of publicity and meetings with elites to translate into advances in his case:

> When I returned from the United States [caravan], I went to review my case [file] like usual. I saw [that there were still just] a few pages, nothing more. And then—What am I supposed to do—I would say what? To I don't know who? What good are microphones, television, international advocacy, the movement . . . when the most important thing is still a throwaway; forgotten? It doesn't matter if you sit down with the highest official in

Mexico, that you sit with the pope, with The Man—that you go to the White House, to talk with US Congressman, all that you did as a spokesperson for victims—it doesn't matter what you do. So, when I saw the empty case file, I said—"We're doing it wrong."

Juan Carlos was left wondering if there was a better way to take advantage of these investigatory spaces. When he eventually went on to found his own organization, discussed later in this chapter, he wanted to harness their collective power but was cautious about some of the drawbacks that he had seen in social movement organizations. He had observed previously how accompaniment organizations could hijack or divide their members, and he wanted to concentrate on working with groups of family members, who had each found their own way to search for their loved ones: "Minimizing the capacity of the people on the part of the organizations has been a mistake. As families, we do things that put us at risk. . . . In this moment, because of this same paternalistic system, each of us has to figure out the mechanism which will activate the person who is going to help you within the state's institutions."

Strategically Navigating the State's Judicial Bureaucracy

Partnering with social movements and taking contentious action are largely meant to secure access to state officials and generally to spur state action on their cases. What have they done with this space once they have secured it? In Chapter 3 I discussed participatory investigations as a more general phenomena. In this section, we get a sense of how each person processed experiences with state actors—leading them all to develop fine-grained analyses, theories, and strategies of state motivation and action over the course of hundreds of meetings with state officials.

Their experiences include seemingly extraordinary elements: doing raids with state agents; using drones to try to locate their loved ones; meeting with presidents and governors; going unofficially "under cover" to negotiate with cartel leaders. And these elements may indeed be different from the ones used by average mobilized family member.[11] These families are among the

---

[11] It is worth noting that I don't believe I know how unusual their experiences are: besides the high-level meetings, I didn't know about the more "extreme" actions they had taken until I conducted life history interviews, despite knowing each of the respondents well over the course of a decade. In my field notes and in other interviews I had, this phenomenon—of "average" people whose loved

more visible family members of the disappeared due to their children's being disappeared earlier than many others; the subsequent participation of these individuals in the MPJD and other social movements has given them regular access to state officials, garnered several job offers, and overall given them a relatively high profile. However, their quotidian experiences with the state are nearly universal. Nearly all families struggle for a meeting with state officials, often succeed in getting ongoing meetings, forum shop among state judicial agencies, and are subsequently and repeatedly frustrated by the results. While it may seem remarkable that all of them have met with governors and presidents—this is also common throughout Mexico.

What follows are Nancy's, Lucía and Alfonso's, and Juan Carlos's experiences navigating the state's judicial bureaucracy.

* * *

Several things shifted for Nancy following the 2012 hunger strike. First, she saw that once victims gained a critical voice, there was what she understood as an effort to co-opt, or buy off, that person and sew dissent among the victims themselves. She felt this pressure during the hunger strike, as she and others were offered everything from blankets, to resources for their investigations, to guarantees that their case would move forward if they would just break the strike and publicly accept and praise the government's response. Nancy saw that for the mothers on hunger strike—who were sleeping outside in the cold, hungry, and exhausted—these divisive tactics were quite effective, and they spawned internal disputes. These internal fights upset Nancy deeply, so when she was offered a job in the Unidad de Búsqueda (the Federal Search Unit created in response to the 2017 Disappearances Law) and then also in SEGOB, she quickly declined. Not only did she understand that accepting a job might be controversial for the movement—but she knew she wanted complete freedom to look for her son and didn't want to balance the demands and compromises she would have to make if she worked for the state: "I never want there to be a moment in which [they say to me] Nancy—don't speak; Nancy shut up. Nancy—don't go; don't say; no. So—I want to be free. For me, nobody can stop me, because the most important thing is my son."

ones were disappeared engaging in remarkable mobilization activities—also recurred and included a couple who worked with the Marines to stage a rescue operation; people who met with members of international bodies and foreign governments; and people who guided international forensic experts as they searched for bodies.

After the hunger strike and after rejecting employment with the federal government, Nancy was finally able to arrange a meeting with the governor of EdoMex. She did what she had heard others in the MPJD do: she demanded monthly meetings with the state attorney general and that investigators from his office review all the cases that the members of her collective brought before them. The state official from SEGOB had told her that the most important thing when she met with the governor was to make sure they signed a copy of whatever agreements were made—that was her official acknowledgment of what had transpired in the meeting and of the follow-up actions they agreed to. With no lawyer, no office, and no budget, Nancy produced these meeting minutes signed by the attorney general (AG) and governor herself, took a picture with her phone of each of these signed "agreements," and printed them out in a folder. Using this methodology, Nancy, in effect, became the case coordinator for these five cases. When the attorney general changed, the governor's support ensured that the meetings continued.

The dynamics of the meetings, which are ongoing as of this writing, changed over time: the AG's office began to send state-owned SUVs to pick up each member of the collective at their house, accompanied by ministerial police. Government representatives also now feed them breakfast and assemble the officials assigned to their case without a fight—including their MP, their *fiscal*, and "our police" as Nancy put it—the police working on or involved in the case. They close the meetings by speaking with the attorney general and reporting the advances in the cases. The AG, in response, "berates, sanctions, scolds [his subordinate investigators and prosecutors]—or will indicate what happens next," asking pointed questions of his staff about why certain actions have been taken, why they didn't take other actions, and how they will adjust to failed strategies.

While Nancy appreciated these steps to treat her and the other families better, she also sees this as yet another manipulation tactic.

They started feeding us *atole con el dedo*;[12] they dressed it all up; they said "Have a seat, what can I get you?" And they tried to make it all look pretty: they wrote things down, they did things; asked questions. But when it came time to show results—there was nothing.

---

[12] Literally translated: feed us *atole* (a traditional Mexican corn-based drink) with their finger. This is a colloquial saying which means to tell you what you want to hear, without actually doing anything.

So for us, it was like—they're making idiots out of all of us. SEGOB, the State of Mexico—all of them were making idiots out of us. . . . They produced a lot of paperwork. But overall, it was all false responses. It was always "We're going to do this and this and that." But what you're going to do doesn't help me. Show me what you're really doing.

In 2014, Nancy says she reached a turning point: she realized how much she had to learn if she was to effectively push back against the state's techniques:

For almost all of 2014, I soaked myself in learning. I [now] know more or less how to gather evidence; how to properly make a formal report [of a disappearance]; what tools are needed to search for someone; and to investigate. Always have a notebook and a pen, write down everything you do and everyone you meet with; what time, date, what agreements there are. . . . I have learned to get everything in writing, since words are blown away by the wind.

Nancy has learned a tremendous amount about how the state's judicial bureaucracies operate, and she made strategic calculations about which state and federal investigative bureaucracies she wanted to take the lead on Elvis's case. For example, despite the launching of the Federal Search Unit following the hunger strike, Nancy decided to keep her case within SEIDO because she understood that it had more resources than other federal investigative branches. Since cases can simultaneously be investigated at the state and federal levels, she also was putting considerable effort into working with the investigators from the "Specialized Unit" in EdoMex, where by 2013 it seemed that the case was finally going to move forward. Nancy's meetings with the governor and state attorney general seemed to be paying off: EdoMex finally replaced the police that Nancy believed were colluding with Fernando and assigned new police to the case. These new police investigators interviewed former patients, tapped Fernando's phone, and were able to hear these corrupt policemen giving Fernando information about the investigation. Nancy's newfound willingness and acquired skill in interacting with state officials was already changing the outcomes of her case.

* * *

After meeting with President Calderón as part of the MPJD delegation in 2012, Juan Carlos had the opportunity to meet one-on-one with the president: "At first, we thought when we got to the President—that would be it. He would resolve everything."[13] He quickly realized, however, that even the president was incapable of producing results in his case. At a follow-up meeting the president initiated, he told Juan Carlos and Doña Mari that he knew their story, and in Juan Carlos's words, Calderón then made a promise: He said—"I promise you as a person, and as president of this Republic, I will find your sons, and I will return them to you. . . . [W]e have also realized how much you have spent [looking for your sons], and we are going to get you on your feet again." . . . At a subsequent meeting in Guerrero, with Juan Carlos, the governor, and the president,

> [Calderón] yells at—well, he didn't yell, but really gives orders to the governor—I go over to Calderón, and I say 'Mr. President, give me five minutes, please.' And I say to him—I have never heard you have such an imposing, strong and firm voice. . . . But please let me say to you, Mr. President—your voice is less than an ant in the ears of this *cabrón*" [bastard, alluding to the governor]. And the governor turns, and he says—"No, Juan Carlos—it's that you don't know me." [And I said,] "I know him; I know both of you. And you're going to see at the end of this year—you'll see. Nothing will have been done."

Sadly, Juan Carlos would be proved largely correct. Investigation into his brothers' disappearances stalled again. And while Juan Carlos and his mother Doña Mari continued to have meetings with officials throughout the hierarchy of Mexican politics and judicial investigators, the investigation was going nowhere. This ongoing frustration—having access to state officials without results—led to profound reflection for Juan Carlos. Increasingly, he attributed this lack of progress to the complicated dynamics between state and federal officials and investigators:

> Each state has its own logic, so when we started going to the federal level, I realized that those "below" [at the state level], who really know how things work, they make things happen and they know how things happen—they pretend like they don't know anything, because they're *coludidos* [colluding] [with DTOs]. Those higher ups [in the federal government]—they make it

---

[13] Author notes of Juan Carlos's comments to a group of Central American mothers looking for their loved ones in a January 2020 meeting.

seem like they know, but they don't know anything. Up top—there's a lot of people that aren't that bad, especially compared to the people on the bottom. And when you have direct contact with them [the higher-up federal officials], the thing is that this actually generates incompetence.

Juan Carlos had learned firsthand about both the "people on the top and the bottom." The people on the top make a lot of promises but don't necessarily have anything besides hubris to back them up. He increasingly believed that political leaders were not able to deliver on their promises to find his brothers because the bureaucratic procedures and incentives for those "on the bottom" precluded investigatory advances—and left the family members constantly in a precarious state of dependency and uncertainty:

> In order for the MP to carry out actions relevant to the case [including a search], they must send an official document to the judge with supporting documentation on why they are going to do that. This is a whole procedure . . . [which leaves us waiting and wondering]. . . . And what did they say? "Yes!" And when are they going to do it? "No! Wait! Tomorrow—tomorrow doesn't work." Then you have to wait for times, that the judge grants or does not grant that you can do that action. And they decide when and how.

Despite his deepening skepticism of the possibility for judicial advances, however, there was a time when Juan Carlos saw no other options to move forward the investigation of the disappearance of his brothers in Guerrero. He had exhausted what he understood as the institutionalized forms of pressuring the state to investigate. He understood that SEIDO had the case—and hoped that Calderón would take some measures to keep his word. Juan Carlos and his mother, Doña Mari, were frustrated—but not deterred. Juan Carlos believed he was effectively navigating the state's bureaucracy. He still, however, wasn't making progress in his, or others', cases. He was convinced he needed to do something different.

* * *

Like the other two families profiled in this book, Lucía and Alfonso have gained access to high-level officials. Perhaps even more than the others, however, they have focused on, and largely succeeded in, steering the judicial progress of their case. Like Nancy and Juan Carlos, they have thought strategically about which judicial bureaucracy they want to take their case, keeping it out of the Fiscalía Especializada en Investigación de Desaparición Forzada (Special Prosecutor for Enforced Disappearances, a sub-section of thPGR), because they thought that office didn't have enough investigative resources. They have succeeded in getting several MPs they didn't like transferred off their case, and when they found an MP they liked, they persuaded the higher-ups at PGR to keep him assigned to their case even after his job was shifted to a different part of the office. This meant that each time they would review their case with their MP, he would have to travel across notoriously difficult-to-traverse Mexico City to meet them and review their case files.

Having an MP that they trust within a well-resourced area of the state investigative bureaucracy is so important, according to Lucía, because even if the attorney general, or even the president, gives stern orders to advance their case, the investigator still may not be willing or able to effectively investigate:

> Because we saw—unless there is an explicit order given, nothing happens. And even then—if the order is "search"—then it would follow that they are given the personnel and budget necessary to actually do what's necessary. They know what they need to do this. . . . and they [state officials] will do just enough to say they're doing something; to cover their backs.

While Lucía and Alfonso cultivated contacts and built relationships with state officials, like Nancy, they were careful not to permit the state to use this closeness to manipulate them or undermine their independence. After the hunger strike outside of PGR (the same one in which Nancy played a leadership role), for example, the attorney general at the time invited several victim leaders into his office. As Lucía remembers it, he said to the assembled leaders: "I just came from a meeting, and I was told to look for five families [who could join PGR to work as investigators], because who better to search [for your disappeared loved ones] than you, because you know the way." Lucía realized she was being offered a job at PGR.

> And I remember my reaction—I said, Oh, What? Am I going to be the next Wallace[14] or what? . . . and later I asked him—"[T]here are so many

---

[14] See Chapter 3. Wallace claimed that her son was kidnapped in the mid-2000s, but soon became a symbol of a thoroughly co-opted and corrupted *víctima*.

of us, why did you think of me?" And he says— "because you have taken ownership of your investigation." And I said to myself—"no, these sons [of bitches] want to be able to say later that the integrity of the search was compromised" [and to blame me]. So I told them—"no, the reality is that I really need to dedicate all of my time to looking for Alejandro. That's why I don't have my own organization. Because I really need to dedicate myself to searching for him."

While I will review the results of their case more extensively in Chapter 6, it is important to highlight the density of actions taken by the different parts of the Mexican state in their case: the documentation of their case alone consists of 14 tomes of information from their Nuevo León case files, and 43 additional tomes in PGR. Lucía and Alfonso convinced a high-level PGR official that in order to make sense of all of this information—by their estimate between 15,000 and 20,000 pages—the records needed to be digitized and analyzed. They heard that there was a computer program PGR had which they could use to help them construct a visual representation of the important people and evidence in the case. Once completed, it looks like an annotated family tree, or an organigram commonly used in many Latin American countries. The PGR assigned three people to carry out this laborious task and then assembled 20 high-ranking officials from Mexico's most important and relevant investigatory bodies, including several different areas within PGR and the federal police, to present the results to. They gathered in a conference room at PGR with more than 20 screens so that everyone could see their impressive work as well as a giant screen in the front of the room. As the three investigators laid out their theory of the case, Alfonso and Atala, a psychologist who works with their volunteer movement lawyer Francisco and the other *co-adyuvante* (co-litigator) on the case, poked holes in their analysis: they had key details wrong, undermining their understanding of the case. Nonetheless, Alfonso saw the existence of this analysis and event as a victory in and of itself.

* * *

In these stories, we see Nancy, Juan Carlos, Lucía, and Alfonso engage the state in increasingly sophisticated ways. As they succeed in gaining regular access to politicians and state investigatory officials, they strategize how— given the limitations and incentives of particular politicians and officials— they can push for action that will bring them toward their goal of combating

impunity and finding their loved ones. As they gain knowledge of the resources and inner workings of different state and federal judicial bureaucracies, they strategically select where they think they have the greatest chances
of advancing the investigation into their loved ones' disappearances, known
in the literature as "forum-shopping," and think about what to do when the
state officials they have worked so hard to access feed them, as Nancy said,
atole con el dedo. In these actions, we see clearly the ways in which evolving
legal consciousness enables each family to grapple with, contest, and confront impunity.

Locating Allies Within the State

Beyond differentiating between state and federal bureaucracies, in this section
we see all three families differentiate between specific members of the state. As
they more fully embrace a "with the state" perspective, their strategic engagement centrally includes locating allies within the state. Building relationships
with officials they understand as committed to their cases and willing to fight for
them becomes a significant part of their repertoire. The act of locating a potential
ally within government bureaucracy defies the distant and reified conceptions
of the state which characterize the "before" and "against" the law positions.
Recognizing that there are some members of the state worth partnering with
is a strategic perspective. How did these partnerships come about? How does
each family understand their importance? And what are the ways they use these
relationships strategically to combat impunity?

* * *

Building strategic relationships with different state actors has been important for Lucía and Alfonso not only at high levels but also throughout the
judicial and police bureaucracies. Lucía, for example, recounted the importance of having an ally within the federal police. After she happened to meet
a federal policeman (he was a friend of Francisco), who was also a former
prosecutor, they exchanged contact information. After that, whenever she
and Alejandro traveled to Monterrey, he arranged for the federal police to
meet them at the airport and provide them protection for the entire time they
were in Monterrey.[15]

---

[15] *Co-ayudvantes* (authorized legal representatives) Francisco and Atala believe this protection
from the federal police was actually due largely to the advocacy of another victim, whose son had

While relationships between family members and state officials are by their nature strategic, they also reflect Lucía and Alfonso's understanding of and ability to interpret the incentives and practices of state officials. When I asked Lucía to explain why it was important to have contacts like Marisela (the former attorney general of Mexico), she explained that it was because Marisela would berate whatever subordinates she was meeting with to do better. And she did this in front of Lucía and Alfonso: she would say to her subordinates, "How is it [your failure not to do more on this case] possible?!" Lucía said that in some ways it was horribly embarrassing to see these officials upbraided in front of her and Alfonso, but at the same time, she believed it was one of their only hopes for the case to advance.

Once Lucía and Alfonso have located a possible ally within the state, they analyze their political context in order to understand their incentives and possibilities. For example, when administrations change and personnel inevitably turns over, Lucía and Alfonso have developed strategies for cultivating continuity in their access to state officials. Lucía realized, for example, that while the state officials change often, their telephone numbers don't. Her first step to building relationships with new officials often entails calling their phone number, welcoming them, and requesting a meeting. Implicit in both of these strategies is a nuanced understanding of the dynamics of collusion, corruption and impunity, and how a change in administrations affects these power balances.

* * *

Forming relationships with state officials has not come easily to Nancy. When I took her testimony in 2012, she spoke of her early interactions with state agents: she told me about fighting with an MP of Asuntos Especiales (Special Cases) in EdoMex, who promised to help get Elvis's journals returned from the clinic, and then reneged. She also had found a police commander whom she felt was an ally—but who then was transferred off the case. It was not until she started working with the MPJD that she saw state officials who seemed to be on the side of the victims.

Eliana García was an early and vocal MPJD ally who participated in the 2012 US Caravan and at that time was head of the Area of Human Rights section of PGR. She came down to talk with Nancy during the 2013 hunger strike. Eliana asked her: "What do you need for your case?" She arranged

been a federal policeman and who also attended participatory investigation meetings in Monterrey.

for Nancy to meet with the attorney general, and Nancy discovered things she didn't know: that her case had been transferred (without her knowledge) from the section of PGR focusing on organ trafficking and stealing children, to the kidnapping section. Partly as a result of this transfer, the federal investigation had stalled. She also learned that a witness had come forward and said that he saw the other two boys in an auto shop, though the supposed witness turned out to be lying in a ploy to get the reward money.

After beginning to trust Eliana, she and Nancy worked together on a number of initiatives. In Nancy's words:

> She [Eliana] has taught us about so many legal things—or how do you say? Policies; what is law; what is the Senate; the Chamber of Deputies— what benefits us, what will hurt us . . . she teaches us: we have had our eyes closed, and then we ask her—"Eliana, what does all this mean? What does that mean? What about this law?" And she says: OK, come on in. And she explains: the law this and that.

Eliana taught Nancy and the other members of her collective what a "*co-adyuvante*" was and helped their collective gain this official legal recognition to participate in their cases. Eliana introduced Nancy to the head of the anti-kidnapping unit within SEIDO. This official "knew I was supported by Eliana, and since she was part of the commission for Human Rights in PGR, [this official] agreed to work with me extensively."

Eliana also worked closely with the collectives to create the Victims Law, coaching them on how to lobby effectively. In 2015, Nancy and her collective had the idea of creating a program similar to the milk carton campaign they had seen in the United States: they wanted Mexico to do more to get the faces of the disappeared out into the public. Again, Eliana connected them with one of her staffers, and they crafted the "*Has visto a* . . .",[16] the "Have you seen . . ." initiative, a program now run out of PGR that focuses on publicizing the photos of the missing by putting them on buses and billboards, and showing them in the media. Following this, they persuaded the attorney general to give rewards for information leading to finding any disappeared person whose case is in PGR rather than leaving each family member to have to advocate independently for this. Nancy led her collective to spearhead a

---

[16] "Conoce el programa ¿Has Visto A . . . ?" https://www.gob.mx/fgr/articulos/conoce-el-progr ama-has-visto-a. Accessed 3/1/20

similar program in EdoMex: many buses leaving EdoMex for other places in Mexico now display the faces of the missing and disappeared.

Nancy has used relationships with the officials she trusts in her home state to help keep her safe and to help her to get an education. After the new local police began to sincerely investigate her case, they tapped Fernando's phones. In the course of conducting this wiretap, they also stumbled on a plot to discredit Nancy. Corrupt police who would later be found to be working with Fernando wanted to coerce her to be quiet because she was "making too much noise." Because of her relationship with the newly assigned policemen and the state investigators, they were able to stop this effort before it gained any traction. And with the financial support from a scholarship which CEAV[17] recommended her for, Nancy is working to get her high school diploma, and from there, she hopes to go to university and study law.

Talking with her during our final interview in 2021, Nancy said that she understands how the way she interacts with state officials had changed over time: "I am much more strategic now. Rather than being the go-between for the families who have someone who has recently been disappeared, I now immediately connect them with the state official who will actually take their case." She also noted that she has become less combative. When an MP treated one of her friends and fellow collective members disrespectfully, rather than engaging with the MP directly, Nancy brought the issue to the attention of the Fiscal, the MP's boss, with whom Nancy has built a relationship. In front of a large group, she made clear that she wasn't going to ask for the MP's resignation; rather, she deferred to the *Fiscal* to correct his behavior.

* * *

Juan Carlos has also leveraged his relationships with certain state officials to ensure his safety. At one participatory investigation meeting between the victims' collective and the governor of Veracruz, for example, Juan Carlos lost his temper and told the notoriously corrupt and brutal governor Javier Duarte to his face that "his cabinet was full of Zetas." This violated the implicit agreement not to name the collusion between the state and DTOs— and that day Juan Carlos's vehicle was aggressively pursued after the meeting

---

[17] CEAV, the Comisión de Atención a Víctimas, Victims' Attention Commission, was created by the 2013 General Law on Victims. These victims' commissions exist both at the federal level, and in every state. They are charged with, among other things, disbursing funds to support victims' efforts to search for their loved ones.

by the Marines and state police as he attempted to return home. Juan Carlos had federal police providing him protection at the time, which was possible because of his relationships with federal officials. His protection was granted by the head of the Federal Special Operations Unit on the order of Jesús Murillo Karám, the top judicial official in the country at the time. Juan Carlos also spoke almost daily with the head of the Federal Disappearances Office, Salomon Baltazar, and while he criticized Baltazar's office for not having enough investigators, Baltazar regarded Juan Carlos as the legitimate interlocutor—not only on his case but in association with other cases in Veracruz. The result of these relationships, especially with Baltazar, Juan Carlos believes, is that the federal police protected him that day, allowing him to escape the trap the Veracruz state government and Marines had set for him.

While Juan Carlos also used his personal relationships to spur investigative actions in his and others' cases, he also increasingly saw meetings with state officials as futile. Specifically, he came to view the paradigm of investigating in order to punish those responsible as ill-suited to his priorities. He wanted to find his brothers more than anything else, and he began to accept that punishing those responsible was not a possible goal within the Mexican justice system; in fact, it might be leading them away from what they really wanted:

> We were always sitting in meetings, participatory investigations . . . and we thought things were moving forward. . . . In Mexico the impunity pacts are enormous—so they [state officials] are not going to try to track down the criminals because they will find themselves. They [state officials] are the principal criminals.
>
> But there's a more important thing: we were losing, or we lost, our families amid these dialogues. While these so-called investigations were happening, we stopped searching—because we started to train ourselves to become anthropologists, or lawyers, or human rights defenders.

As I will discuss in the next section and in Chapter 5, Juan Carlos now has a highly visible role promoting on-the-ground searches for the remains of the disappeared. He, together with other family members, was central to the creation of two different organizations in 2014 that are dedicated to locating human remains, and when possible, identifying them and linking them to the identities of disappeared people. This work initially was extra-legal: after asking the state to do this work and being rebuffed, these collectives decided to do the work themselves. They have continually sought the state's involvement to provide them protection and to assist them with the forensic analysis of any remains they find. Juan Carlos did manage to form a relationship with an MP (investigator) from PGR, Maria Lourdes Palacios, who was willing to accompany the earliest search brigades. She did so on her own time and provided her own financial resources, since what she was doing was outside the scope of work her bosses sanctioned. Her participation was invaluable in legitimating the work of the search brigades, and, in Juan Carlos's view, in deterring the state and DTO actors from stopping the searches. These officials and drug traffickers opposed the searches because they were afraid these efforts would uncover evidence that would incriminate them. Though Palacios has since passed away (of natural causes), Juan Carlos and the lawyers that work with the Citizens' Brigades have continued to work with people from her office. For the Citizens' Brigade of 2020, for example, Juan Carlos and his lawyers asked Palacios's assistant to run the forensic work on the ground. While at first his bosses didn't want him to, Juan Carlos and Doña Marí lobbied for this to happen. They spoke with the higher-ups at PGR and secured a signed guarantee, in a meeting with the bosses at PGR, that this MP could accompany the brigades as they searched for human remains. According to the lawyer Juan Carlos works with at ProDH, the relationships Juan Carlos and Doña Mari have built, together with their growing national reputations as victim leaders, have made this possible—and have made them even more powerful negotiators than ProDH at times.

* * *

Any state should, in theory, protect its citizens and investigate any harm that comes to them. Since this rarely occurs in Mexico, each family member of a disappeared person has used personal relationships with state officials to accomplish some of what the state should do as well as to reform the state from within. In this section, we saw Nancy, Juan Carlos and Lucía, and Alfonso leverage personal relationships in order to learn how to use the legal tools of the state and push for reform; compel the state to systematically gather and analyze evidence; and protect them as they conduct their own complementary work to the investigation. These actions, however, fall far short of a satisfactory response. What have these families done with their dissatisfaction?

Participating in Independent Searches for Their Loved Ones

By 2014, having exhausted what he understood as all institutional forms of redress, Juan Carlos was at a loss—what else could they do? For him, the 2014 disappearance of the students of Ayotzinapa and the innovations in mobilization this spawned—was a turning point. Juan Carlos told me that he considers the 43 disappeared students to be "angels—because they taught us how to search for our loved ones." When people—both family members of the disappeared students and others—began to search for the Ayotzinapa students, they did not find the students' remains. As discussed in Chapter 3, they did find the remains of hundreds of other people, prompting the creation of the victims' collective that called itself Los Otros Desaparecidos— the Other Disappeared. This group, which grew to 450 families by 2016, was at the forefront of a new and highly visible wave of collectives that decided to mount a coordinated *búsqueda en campo* (searching for remains) campaign.[18] With no real forensic expertise, they began to search for graves. They used tips and word of mouth to point them toward the places that community members believed bodies might be buried.

Juan Carlos heard about the work of the Otros Desaparecidos, and it clicked for him: he saw families and collectives physically searching for the remains of missing loved ones and inviting the media to accompany the searches after the state refused. This was a way to expose the vulnerability and dependency of victims on deeply unreliable state actors. Having to wait for the state to act, he told me,

> is not the same as I, Juan Carlos, and all the families that are here saying, "no" to you; to the MP, . . . [W]e say to you—the prosecutor of the state of the republic—"I am going now, to search, there—because he is my brother." He [the MP] doesn't expect me to accommodate him. . . . [H]e says "Do what you have to do." If you realize that procedures must be broken when there is something so important to accomplish, then the media, rather than the legal system, can help to argue for a better system; [they can help make the case] that the system is broken when there is so much human misfortune.

---

[18] Previous to Los Otros Desaparecidos, other collectives had also conducted search campaigns, largely in the northern states. These groups included Unidos por los Desaparecidos de Baja California, led by Fernando Ocegueda, and civil society groups in Chihuahua who organized in response to the femicides of the late 1990s and early 2000s.

And so, Juan Carlos and his brother Miguel went to Guerrero, and learned how to search alongside Los Otros Desparecidos. Mario Vergara, whose brother had been disappeared and who emerged as a leader with a natural talent for forensic work, taught them how to recognize the physical evidence, the odor, and signs that they were near human remains. They then created two organizations in 2014: (1) their own victims' collective, which they named after their mother: Familiares en Búsqueda María Herrera, Family Members Involved in Searching—María Herrera; and (2) together with family members of the disappeared whom they had started to work with in Veracruz, they formed an organization called Red de Enlaces Nacionales, the Network of National Links, which brings together victims' collectives throughout Mexico to find, identify, and return human remains to the families of disappeared people in Mexico. Juan Carlos had the idea to organize something like a caravan, like he had seen done in the United States. In this caravan, however, he would bring together family members of the disappeared to join forces and search together for the remains of the disappeared. At the time, Juan Carlos wasn't working and had to scrape together the resources to make this idea a reality: he still owned a car lot in EdoMex, and he decided to sell all the cars from that to provide the seed money for what he imagined would be a national organization dedicated to searching for the disappeared. By the end of 2014, about 25 collectives of family members of the disappeared had joined in this effort. To date, they have conducted five of these family-led search brigades, identifying over 400 remains and involving nearly 1,000 family members in the work.

Juan Carlos sees the shift to searching for loved ones rather than pursuing those responsible for the disappearances, as simultaneously being driven by necessity, and also becoming a different way of struggling—in social movement terms, a disruptive innovation in the repertoire of contention—which re-figured what was possible politically and also "gave us some of our dignity back."

What does it mean to put your hands in the earth, as a way of changing the political framing of the whole problem? What does it mean to do what the state is never going to do? To find, to save, the remains of one deceased person in order to save the life of someone who is living and who is waiting for him? . . . Pick the shovel up, put on your boots and let's search for the missing. I told them you know what that means, it's a hard political blow against all the law. What we want, what we need is to search and find—from there come the contents of social transformation, and not from legal engagement. . . . A family member who lost their loved one—what is it that he wants? to find them, and how does he find them? looking for them, and if nobody looks for them, we get lost in a lot of other things. . . . [T]he mourning and the healing process generates many things, but it doesn't generate the important core content: look for me because you lost me, find me because you're looking for me.

The slogan of the Red de Enlaces is *buscando nos encontramos*, roughly translated as "by searching we find (ourselves/each other)." For Juan Carlos, the double meaning of this slogan is important: he sees searching for the disappeared as the lynchpin of a strategy that puts the humanity of both the disappeared and the families of the disappeared at its center. "This [searching] is the way that we become human again. This is the necessity of a human: to look for and find ourselves; to look for and find others."

* * *

Lucía and Alfonso and Nancy have joined some of the search initiatives that Juan Carlos has spearheaded. All three families were part of an initiative called Ciudadana Forense, a family-led effort to collect DNA samples to then match with recovered bodies. Individually, they have also searched for their missing sons.

Lucía and Alfonso have arranged for the federal police to conduct several operations in northern Mexico, including sending drones over ranches thought to be controlled by DTOs and the possible sites of clandestine graves. They watched on a small computer screen as the drone searched in areas too dangerous for investigators to physically access in Tamaulipas, searching for evidence of shallow graves or live prisoners to no avail. They demanded and ultimately obligated the department of prisons to undertake the arduous task of photographing every inmate in 12 states where they suspected Alfonso could have been imprisoned, and to repeat this exercise bi-monthly. They have also looked for Alejandro in pictures from hospitals and morgues.

When one of their friends from the movement was working in the PGR, Lucía compelled the attorney general's office to pay for them to go to Nuevo Laredo, a border city in the state of Tamaulipas. They coordinated with members of the local human rights organization, whom they had met through their work with CADHAC in neighboring Monterrey. When they got to Nuevo Laredo, they looked at pictures of unidentified corpses to learn whether Alejandro was there. They arranged with the local human rights NGO leader to give the lead investigator a heads up—alerting him that they were movement people and to make sure they were treated well. But this time, they found only a handful of photos. When they asked why—they were told that family members had already come to claim the bodies. The local human rights defender had another explanation: the *fiscal*, prosecutor, overwhelmed with the number of corpses, was sending these unidentified bodies to a local funeral home. There, with no investigatory protocols or documentation, the bodies were being buried. In Lucía's words:

> [They were throwing bodies in] a clandestine pit, as we've seen them do. There are so, so many bodies that there are clandestine graves everywhere. The [number of bodies] overwhelmed them, and then there were even more. And they're not prepared—not at all. They want to push the horror that we are living under the rug.

Nancy continues to look for her son in a methodology referred to by movement members as *búsqueda integral*—holistic searching, or searching for people in places where they could be found alive or where their remains may be located. In July 2013, she arranged to participate in a joint operation between the state attorney general, federal police, and SEIDO to raid Fernando's clinics. She dressed in a hood, black t-shirt, boots, and dark glasses and went with the roughly 20 vehicles and 180 personnel to raid all of Fernando's clinics. She made the case that she could be useful since she had been to the clinic before. When they got to the clinics, however, they were empty, as was Fernando's house: somebody, again, had tipped Fernando off that they were coming, and he had fled.

Her collective, Deudos y Defensores por la Dignidad de Nuestros Desaparecidos, roughly translated as "the Grieving and the [Human Rights] Defenders for the Dignity of Our Disappeared," has made their own t-shirts, complete with a tree logo with branches in the shape of a heart, symbolizing both their connection to each other and their rootedness with the disappeared family members. They paid for the t-shirts themselves and wear them to their meetings with state officials. They arranged for a photo exhibition of their missing loved ones in Chapultepec Castle, passed out countless flyers with these same pictures, and marched. She has also attended workshops that Juan Carlos has helped to organize, and has learned the basics of looking for clandestine graves. Her collective joined the Red de Enlaces, the network of collectives searching for people throughout Mexico that Juan Carlos had helped to create.

Conclusion

What, then, have we learned about how and why people engage in sustained mobilization? Differently put, what do life history interviews and longitudinal ethnography have to teach us about social movements and legal consciousness?

Wendy Wolford (2006) conducted two in-depth interviews four years apart with a farmer who had participated in Brazil's landless worker movement. From these two snapshots, she draws insights about the dynamic nature of social mobilization, and the "importance of individual-group relations and the social construction of knowledge" (350). This close attention to individuals also makes space for what she calls the study of "common sense," where people are "confused, [and] life is complicated, emotional and uncertain" (Abu-Lughod 2000, 263). She continues:

> Common sense is "the simple truth of things artlessly apprehended" [Swidler 1986]. . . . The move to incorporate common sense does not mean structure, agency, and explanation should be abandoned in studies of social movements. Rather, our ability to explain movement trajectories over time depends on our ability to incorporate common sense into the analysis. (339)

Drawing on relationships I built with the respondents over 10 years, this chapter centers the common sense of people who endured a terrible tragedy and traces the evolution of their common sense. I map their early and ongoing encounters with the state and social movements onto each person's evolving legal consciousness—that is, their way of understanding *what makes sense*. As they continue to look for their loved ones and encounter the many different faces of the Mexican government, the perspectives of against or before the law cease to make sense. They are drawn to common repertoires of contention: (1) confronting the state with contentious action; (2) partnering with social movements to access state officials; (3) strategically navigating the state's judicial bureaucracy; (4) locating allies within the state; and (5) participating in independent searches for their loved ones.

At the same time, each also preserves parts of their initial approaches: Lucía and Alfonso remain focused on compelling the state to take responsibility for fulfilling their conception of what a proper state should do. Nancy continues to turn to contentious action to make inroads in the many cases she accompanies—though she fully adapts to and sees the value of negotiation as well. And Juan Carlos strategically engages with the state and its many institutions, until he decides to push the bounds of legality and look for victims of disappearances himself and with other family members.

What do we miss without the longitudinal ethnography presented in this chapter? As social movement scholars, we know that leaders emerge; repertoires are innovated upon; and people transform from laypeople to activists. Seldom do we get individual-level accounts, however, of how exactly this happens over the course of many years. The mobilization trajectories of the individuals in this chapter illustrate insights from a diverse range of literatures, and also give us new insights into the connections between trauma, legal consciousness, mobilization, and strategic action. These accounts reveal how the density of exposure to the state (Taylor 2020), changes in socio-spatial positioning (Kruks-Wisner 2018), and the evolution of common sense (Wolford 2006) shape people's actions and decisions. We also see the profound meaning and motivation that developing and asserting agency in the course of pursuing justice can generate among people who have experienced trauma and/or repression (Wood 2003). As thinking, abilities, and peer and movement networks evolve, we see a simultaneous evolution of movements themselves, along with their shared repertoires of contention. We understand what would have been hidden: how Nancy's sense of agency grows, as she shifts from someone who avoided the law to someone adept at mobilizing it; how Lucía and Alfonso evolve from people who expected the natural order of things to bring back their son or at least reveal what happened to him, to people pressing the state to coordinate its actions in concert with multiple social movements; and how Juan Carlos goes from giving up on his efforts to search for his brothers, to an organizer key to innovating on the repertoire of contention for all families of the disappeared, helping to a lead of movement of people to go beyond the state's empty promise for justice to a strategy to search for their loved ones. By drawing out the importance of biography, strategic calculations, the nature of the grievance, and the evolving nature of their thinking over 10 years—rather than focusing, for example, on two points in time—we are able to see the mechanisms that drive the evolution of these families' ways of thinking and actions. These findings point to the importance of a research approach that allows us to gain a dynamic understanding of the role of legal consciousness in mobilization—one that is generalizable beyond the case of Mexico.

5

Legal and Political Opportunities of the Uneven State

> We're asking the government to search for our loved ones, not so
> much for who is responsible [for the disappearance]: If we look for
> who's responsible, that's really another thing . . . and it would be
> asking too much. A lot of us say, "Let's not look for the guilty ones;
> we don't need to know about who took them, or who did this." The
> only thing we need to know is where are they, where are they? We
> just want them [the government] to look for our loved ones wher-
> ever they can: in prisons, in detention centers, in drug treatment
> centers . . . also in exhumations and with the SEMEFO [Forensic
> Medical Service]. . . . I'm in regular touch with the State Coordinator
> of the Search Commission, and I'm waiting today for him to call and
> tell me what new records they have.
>
> —Author interview with victim-activist from Tamaulipas,
> August 2019

Tamaulipas, the state mentioned above, is often referred to as an *hoyo negro*,
a black hole, in Mexico. It is infamous for its high levels of violence, powerful
DTOs, corrupt officials, and media repression.[1] The interviewee above is a
mother whose son was disappeared and who lives very near the US-Mexico
border. She regularly posts on Facebook video clips of gun battles, which she
can see and hear from her house. She checks social media and texts different
WhatsApp groups before she sets out to her job at a convenience store every
day: there are three different routes she can take to get to the store, and she
uses this information to analyze which one may be the safest. She and her

---

[1] As discussed in Chapter 3, Mexico is considered among the most dangerous countries in the
world for journalists. Tamaulipas tops the list of most dangerous states. See Lakhani (2020).

Bootstrap Justice. Janice k. Gallagher, Oxford University Press. © Oxford University Press 2023.
DOI: 10.1093/oso/9780197649978.003.0005

neighbors regularly witness DTOs battling with state forces (with DTOs often prevailing), and she has also observed local security forces meeting and coordinating with DTOs, which they sometimes do in the parking lot of the store where she works.

It may come as a shock to some that wanting the state to investigate the disappearance of a loved one seems like "asking too much." For those familiar with Mexico, however, it may seem even more shocking that the victim activist above is "in regular touch" with a Tamaulipas state official—whom she expects to keep her informed with updates about the search for her son.

Following the logic of Chapter 4, however, this regular contact between a victim and a state official becomes less surprising. As we followed the evolution in how Lucía and Alfonso, Nancy, and Juan Carlos thought about themselves in relation to the law, we saw their instincts become fine-tuned in terms of what was possible to achieve in any given setting: Juan Carlos decided not to turn to the state after the disappearance of his second two brothers because he understood that the state had no effective control of the *plaza* where his brothers disappeared; Nancy learned to get in writing any agreement between her and state officials since "words are blown away by the wind." And Lucía and Alfonso came to realize that to motivate a prosecutor to do their job, getting a higher-ranking official to berate them was often the most effective strategy. The victim-activist from Tamaulipas quoted above understands that holding a perpetrator legally accountable is not possible, but that searching for their disappeared loved one might be if they partner with allied state officials. In each of these examples, the victim forms an understanding of how justice (and impunity) work in a specific locale or institutional environment and formulates a corresponding strategic action that they view as most likely to advance their cause.

We can imagine how these actions, when employed by individuals, affect their ability to push the needle forward on impunity in their own cases. But these understandings were not formed by individuals in isolation, and many of the actions they inspire are undertaken collectively rather than individually. Collectives are composed of scores of people similar to the families featured in this book, each of whom has developed their own understandings of legality through struggle. As Juan Carlos explained: "Every family, every process is different, and obeys each family member's evolving understandings, development, and pain. We respect each other, and we walk together." What does "walking together" look like? How do these individual understandings scale up—and how do they explain why collectives act the way they do? How do they collectively perceive political opportunities and threats, and strategize about which rights to pursue given the configurations of power in their local context?

In this chapter, I show how victims' collectives engaged in sustained mobilization—and drawing on the shared understandings and common contentious repertoires that have evolved during the course of their mobilization—have found ways of burrowing into the walls of impunity in different, and difficult, political contexts. By taking advantage of their relationships with sympathetic state actors, moments of division both within the state and among the state and their DTO allies, and striking out on their own to search for their loved ones when the state has refused to do the work, I show how they strategically exploit opportunities to advance their right to truth, justice, and non-recurrence. I also show how certain dynamics may sideline victims' voices and initiatives while, at the same time, undermining impunity. I first briefly frame this discussion within literature which helps us understand the interactions between these different actors (state, DTOs, civil society)—but which rarely theorizes how dynamics between them shape the possibilities for the erosion of impunity. Next, I look inside the state-level justice systems to better understand the structures and incentives that confront victims as they pursue the right to justice. Finally, I unpack three different cases in which organized victims were able to make some inroads and explore the strategies they employed to confront structures of impunity.

Protective Rackets and the Production of Impunity

Scholars studying criminal governance in Latin America have helped us understand the tight yet contingent ways in which state and criminal actors are bound together. Cartels and states bargain with each other for what they value: cartels, for example, deliver lower levels of violence in exchange for less state repression and guarantees of non-prosecution (Lessing 2017); while states may permit cartels to conduct their illicit business in exchange for a cut of their profits (Snyder and Durán-Martinez 2009). These transactional relationships can produce relatively stable and mutually beneficial informal arrangements known alternately as protection rackets (Snyder and Durán-Martinez 2009), collaborative governance arrangements (Arias 2017), subnational criminal governance regimes (Trejo and Ley 2020), and transnational corruption networks (Correa-Cabrera 2017). There is an emerging consensus among these scholars that consolidated DTOs (as opposed to fragmented DTOs fighting among each other) who build relationships with similarly consolidated state actors lead to lower levels of violence (Arias 2017; Moncada 2016; Trejo and Ley 2020).[2]

What, then, disrupts these protection rackets? Trejo and Ley (2018, 2020) explore how the elections of new governors in Mexico, and the political party dynamics between those governors and the president, can lead to the disruption of protection rackets. They identify the changing of state officials as one of the key mechanisms to disrupting protection rackets.[3] For Moncada (2016) and Arias (2017), when DTOs' territorial control is challenged either by fragmented elites (both business and state elites for Moncada) or rival DTOs, this also can lead to an uptick in violence and erosion of the state-DTO protection racket. For Lessing (2017), as the state ratchets up its repression, this can likewise lead to fracture and violence. For all of these scholars, stable protection rackets spell sparse opportunities for prosecution and legal accountability. In social movement terms, this presents a "closed" political opportunity structure, with elites (i.e., decision-makers: governors, attorney generals, *jefes de plaza*) unified against the affected population, leaving little space for bridge-building, negotiation, and possibilities for meaningful collaboration between the state and domestic civil society.[4]

And yet, despite what would appear to be closed political and legal opportunity structures, organized victims have shown that advances against impunity are possible in remarkably difficult environments. Drawing on the above theories, especially Trejo and Ley (2018, 2020), I show how alternation in state officials and changes in state-level alliances open cracks in the wall of impunity. Building on what we already know about the importance of societal actors in undermining impunity (Brinks 2008; Gallagher 2017; González 2019; González-Ocantos 2016), I show the ways in which sustained mobilizers must actively intercede to turn these openings into advances against impunity.

---

[2] Durán-Martinez (2018), however, cautions that while a more consolidated state apparatus may appear to yield lower levels of violence, this is due in large part to a shift to less visible forms of violence—like disappearances, as opposed to public and visible homicides.

[3] Trejo and Ley (2018) highlight the central role of state judicial police (as opposed to municipal-level police, who are too weak to guarantee protection) as well as the state attorney general and the top prosecutorial staff in providing cover for DTOs. When a governor is elected from a new party, these authors demonstrate that replacing the state judicial police and the attorney general and their staff are consequential decisions that produce significant upheaval among DTOs. This is a departure from literature that has focused primarily on federal security forces and authorities.

[4] While it is impossible for domestic civil society to effectively advocate under these conditions, international actors may be able to play the role of advocate, as the UNHCHR was able to do in Colombia during the false positives scandal. See Gallagher 2017.

Case Selection

In order to understand how victims' strategic thinking and mobilization map onto outcomes, including the erosion of impunity, I present the cases of Tamaulipas, Veracruz, and Nuevo León in this chapter. Victims strategically evaluate the environments in which they are mobilizing in order to make decisions about the modes of contention they will employ. As illustrated in Figure 5.1, two key elements in their decision-making are (1) how they perceive the motivations of state officials and, in particular, whether they find allies who they believe are acting in solidarity with them; and (2) how they read the stability of state alliances: are there about to be elections? Has the control of the *plaza* shifted among DTOs?

To illustrate how these understandings of the local political context shape victims' mobilization, which in turn shapes impunity outcomes, I chose three contiguous states that run from the southeastern to northeastern regions of Mexico and make up the central drug trafficking corridor along Mexico's eastern coast. Traveling through these states is the quickest route from Mexico's southern to northern borders. The states were also dominated by the Zetas at some point during the past decade, as can be seen in the 2010 map (Map 5.1), and Zeta control of the Gulf coast trafficking route was strongest from 2010 to 2012 (Correa-Cabrera 2017, 42). The Zetas widely employed the use of disappearances as a means to terrorize and control their rivals and the local population. Though the DTO dynamics have shifted in different directions, with the Zetas and most cartels fracturing and subsequently reshuffling control in sub-regions within these states, by focusing on states where a significant portion of disappearances was committed by the same dominant drug cartel, I minimize the variation

Perceived Motivation of State Official(s)	State Alliances	
	Stable	Unstable
Cynical	*Impunity:* Most of Mexico	*Strategic Prosecution:* Veracruz (2016–2018)
Solidarity	*Searching:* Tamaulipas (post-2013) Veracruz (2018–)	*Erosion of Impunity:* Nuevo León (2011–2016)

Figure 5.1 Case selection

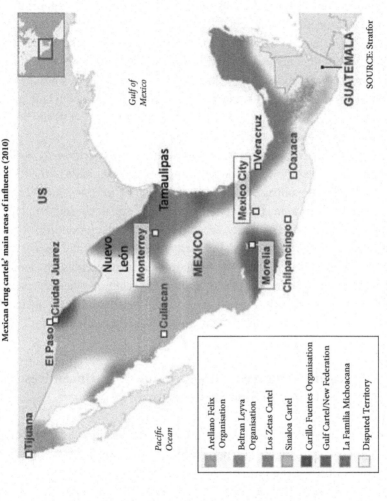

Mexican drug cartels' main areas of influence (2010)

US

*Pacific
Ocean*

Tijuana

El Paso Ciudad Juarez

Culiacan

Nuevo
León

MEXICO

Monterrey

Tamaulipas

*Gulf of
Mexico*

Mexico City Veracruz

Morelia

Chilpancingo

Oaxaca

GUATEMALA

Arellano Felix
Organisation

Beltran Leyva
Organisation

Los Zetas Cartel

Sinaloa Cartel

Carillo Fuentes Organisation

Gulf Cartel/New Federation

La Familia Michoacana

Disputed Territory

SOURCE: Stratfor

Source: https://www.bbc.com/news/world-latin-america-11174174

Map 5.1 Mexican cartels' map, 2010

in the modality of disappearances. We know, for example, that the Sinaloa Cartel did not engage in the widespread chemical disintegration of human remains, instead burying the bodies of people they disappeared and later killed. The Zetas, however, are well-known for destroying the remains of those they killed by dissolving them in acid or burning their corpses.[5] This makes identifying the remains of those murdered by the Sinaloa cartel a less complicated process than identifying people killed in those states under the control of the Zetas. This same characteristic also makes these states least likely cases: the Zetas are famous for their brutality and professionalized violence, and for their roots within the state security apparatus. If there was anywhere we would expect the repression of the DTOs and their ties to the state to prohibit both mobilization and any investigatory advances into disappearances, it would be in those states most tightly controlled by the Zetas.

In 2010, each of these states was controlled by the PRI but each voted the PRI out in the next gubernatorial election, shifting their governorship to the PAN (Veracruz 2016, Tamaulipas 2016) or an independent governor (Nuevo León 2015). If party alternation at the gubernatorial level explained shifts in political opportunities around impunity, we would expect similar results in all three states. Relatedly, if party alignment (the party of the governor and the part of the president) explained shifts in impunity, we would expect similar dynamics in 2016 when Veracruz and Tamaulipas shift to PAN control—the same party as President Calderón. This research design, then, controls for party alternation and facilitates the ability to focus on other explanatory variables.

Disappearing (Enforced) Disappearances: The Incentives of State Investigators

To understand how the victims engaged in sustained mobilization have worked to become "rights-bearing citizens" by strategically navigating the inner working of the justice system, it is important to lay out certain key aspects of this system. A central strategy of the Mexican state has been to, in effect, gaslight[6] victims by refusing to legally classify cases as *enforced* disappearances—that is, in cases in which the state is implicated as a

[5] See, for example, Claudia Solera (2015), "Ausencias que lastiman: en 2011, *Zetas* deshacían cuerpos con diesel," February 1, 2015.
[6] "Gaslighting is a tactic in which a person or entity, in order to gain more power, makes a victim question their reality" (Sarkis 2017).

Table 5.1 Disappearances/Enforced Disappearances 2006–2018

Disappearance cases (federal system)	1,121
Disappearance cases (state legal systems)	36,076
Enforced disappearances (state + federal)	1,144
	62 sentences
	* 34 sentences in Federal System
	* 28 sentences in State Judicial System
	380 complaints to National Human Rights Commission (CNDH); 20 Recommendations

Source: Mexican government, National Public Security System: https://www.gob.mx/sesnsp/accio nes-y-programas/registro-nacional-de-datos-de-personas-extraviadas-o-desaparecidas-rnped. Consulted January 13, 2020; data have since been removed.

perpetrator. Despite the well-known collusion of state forces in the commission of disappearances, a minuscule number of cases have been classified as such. For example, in January 2020 the Mexican government reported that in the over 38,000 cases of disappearances registered in the state and federal judicial bureaucracies between 2006 and 2018[7], less than 3 percent were registered as enforced disappearances, and in only 62 of those cases (0.16%) were there sentences. How has the Mexican state managed to record fewer than 1,200 cases of enforced disappearances? And what has made justice so scarce and impunity so tenacious in Mexico in the cases of enforced disappearance that the state does manage to register? While much of this explanation certainly lies at the macro level explored in Chapter 3, in this section I delineate the ways the inner workings of the judicial system incentivize inertia and hide cases in which state officials may be implicated as perpetrators.

As Durán Martinez (2018) tells us, there are many reasons that DTOs and state actors may want to make violence less visible. Visible violence unites calls for politicians to crack down on criminal actors. This is not beneficial for DTOs, that want to avoid unwanted law enforcement attention and harsher security policies; it is also not good for their state allies, who benefit from their corrupt relationship. While disappearances can be understood as

---

[7] The number of disappearances differs from the data presented earlier in this chapter in Figure 5.1. The discrepancy is due to what the figures are counting: Figure 5.1 includes *all* cases of disappearances which the government has knowledge of; Table 5.1 includes only those cases which have been *reported* to the state or federal judicial systems.

among the most invisible forms of violence, "enforced disappearances" have become quite visible thanks to international human rights norms that have filtered into domestic legal codes. Because of this, I have argued (Gallagher 2020) that states actively seek to limit the number of cases of enforced disappearances filed against them—in other words, to return disappearances to their invisible status despite the legal and, supposedly, institutional advances designed to do just the opposite.

In Mexico, the *ministerio público* (MP), or lead investigator, is immensely powerful: these individuals play the role of both lead detective and assistant district attorney (ADA); they decide how to classify cases, whether to investigate them, what portion of the resources they have at their disposal they will allocate to their investigation, and whether and when to bring a case before a judge.[8] In practice, their central role entirely removes judges from the overwhelming number of cases that never make it to trial. As Ríos-Figueroa explains, "Judges can only decide the cases that are brought to the court by someone else" (2015). While it was thought that the 2008 judicial sector reforms shifting Mexico to an adversarial system of justice from an inquisitorial system would decrease some of the MPs' power by introducing "probable cause" as the evidentiary standard for indictment (see Shirk 2011), they have nonetheless preserved nearly every aspect of their investigatory discretion, legally referred to as the principle of opportunity (*principio de oportunidad*) "which allows the prosecutor to strategically weigh his or her decision against the resource limitations and priorities facing law enforcement" (Shirk 2011, 16). The reforms also expanded the authority of the MP over police, who under the 2008 reforms report to the attorney general's office and are responsible for preserving the crime scene.

The MP's decision as to how to register the cases they receive is highly consequential. When a person reports a disappearance, for example, the MP can decide to register the case as a missing person's case, a kidnapping,[9] an illegal

[8] This almost unmitigated power in the investigatory stage has indeed been cited as part of what drives torture, forced confessions, and evidentiary mishandling in Mexico (Shirk 2011; Zepeda Lecuona 2014; Zamora et al. 2005; Naval 2006).

[9] Kidnappings, by definition, need to include a demand for ransom to be classified as such. Cases of disappearance have been dismissed because they were misclassified as kidnappings, despite the absence of a ransom note. This is what happened in the Ayotzinapa case: many of the indicted local police officers and members of organized crime have been released because they were being investigated for kidnapping, not illegal deprivation of liberty or enforced disappearance. Since there was never any ransom requested in this case, the charges filed against these officials and individuals were dismissed for lack of evidence. In the case of homicides, decision-making around registering cases is also critical in determining state accountability. While "extrajudicial execution" is not a crime on the books in Mexico, homicides can be registered as being committed by state forces.

deprivation of liberty, or an enforced disappearance. I talked to a mother in Chihuahua who said she was present when municipal police took her son from their house and forced him into their truck, never to be heard from again. When she reported the enforced disappearance of her son, the case was registered as an "illegal deprivation of liberty" (in the US justice system, legally somewhere between a missing person and an assault), despite being a textbook case of enforced disappearance. The classification of the disappearance determines whether it will be registered as a human rights violation: enforced disappearance is a human rights violation while the other ways of registering disappearances (illegal deprivation of liberty, kidnapping, missing person) are not. Human rights violations in turn trigger a series of legal consequences guaranteed by international law—which is given precedence in Mexico's constitution (see Gallagher and Contesse forthcoming). MPs also have a say in whether cases are transferred to the federal legal system from the state system—something that is done under "special circumstances," a concept that is poorly defined.

What are the institutional incentives for these powerful judicial actors? MPs are civil servants who are theoretically selected through a meritocratic process meant to insulate their jobs from political considerations. They take a series of exams, including a subject area exam, and psychological, medical, toxicology, and socioeconomic evaluations (an analysis of their finances to ensure they are not unduly indebted or inexplicably wealthy). Once hired, there is no requirement for MPs to be evaluated by their superiors or peers, a provision intended to preserve their impartiality. While this provision can make it difficult to fire an MP, they can be punished in other, equally damning ways. In conversations with several MPs I heard how, for example, when an MP is following a lead that higher-ups in the attorney general's or governor's office don't like, they can dissuade them from pursuing it by transferring them to a different office, taking cases away from them so they only have administrative, rather than investigative, tasks, or giving them an overwhelming caseload. While many MPs have indefinite contracts, when new positions are created they often have limited renewable contracts of one to three years. Not renewing a contract can be another way of sanctioning—in effect firing—an MP. In short, while certain institutional provisions seek to insulate MPs from the everyday politics of the local contexts, there are still many mechanisms through which MPs may be pressured to operate according to the political preferences of their superiors, namely, the state attorney general and the governor.

These dynamics, which make MPs vulnerable to their superiors, have been identified by the victims, and they have, in turn, developed strategies to exploit them to their advantage. For example, Lucía recounted how the victims' collectives she is involved with have noticed that near the end of a gubernatorial term for state investigators or a presidential term for federal investigators, MPs become more willing to investigate their cases. When we talked in late 2017, the year before the presidential election, she said:

> This year is critical. Because we *pongamos conciencias* [have made the MPs sensitive to/conscious of] our plight; and since they know their bosses will probably be replaced [after the election and with the change in administration]— if they have had a little of their humanity awakened, they might try to help a little bit . . . if they're good people, they're a little freer [to investigate]—without the fear of retribution. . . . Before, it was like putting a rope around their own necks, because their bosses are part of it, of course. . . . Because of the fear they have of exposing their bosses, for example—of having done it, or participated in some way—if they [investigated, they] took the risk of putting their personal security in jeopardy. [But since their bosses are probably leaving their jobs] it's not such a big risk—because now they would really only be risking their jobs.

MPs' somewhat precarious professional position influences their decision-making about classifying cases, and whether to investigate cases. As Lucía understands, we would expect there to be strong personal and systemic incentives against filing cases in ways that implicate fellow state agents and their DTO allies—since this could put their personal security at risk. While systematic evidence to support this claim is difficult to come by, a former federal judicial officer recounted to me (in a 2018 interview) that a high-ranking official within the attorney general's office under Peña Nieto had issued a directive instructing their investigatory teams to do everything possible to limit the number of cases of enforced disappearance that they were responsible for, and to send as many cases as possible back to state jurisdictions. Superiors encouraged federal investigators to question evidence that pointed to the involvement of state officials by, for example, introducing the possibility that criminals dressed as security officers might have perpetrated disappearances. The attorney general clearly saw it as in the interest of administration to decrease or even cover up evidence implying federal government responsibility. Fewer cases in the federal system, and fewer cases of enforced disappearances, help the state to claim that it is not to blame for disappearances.

Challenges to Collusive Impunity: Unstable Alliances and State Allies

Given the institutional incentives to both deny that disappearances are occurring and to preserve impunity, how have political opportunities emerged in states with active DTOs with histories of collusion with state officials? What dynamics have led to political opportunities that have allowed strategic victims to meaningfully challenge impunity?

In this section, I first summarize the relevant political context in each state, paying particular attention to (1) instability in state alliances—changes in governorships, changes in local DTO dominance, and (2) state officials who are perceived to act in solidarity with victims. Next, I discuss the corresponding strategies deployed by victims' collectives and organizations. In sum, in each state I illustrate the following:

- In Tamaulipas, cartel violence decreased slightly after 2013 following the fracturing of the Zetas, the infamously brutal DTO formed by former elite security forces trained by the United States. This decrease in violence, together with the infusion of federal officials and resources, seems to have enabled the victim advocates to search for their loved ones within a context of war, using "quiet activism."
- In Veracruz, I argue that disappearances as an issue were brought to the fore politically by activists responding to the brutality of Governor Duarte's administration (2011–2016). The next governor ran on a pro-victim, justice platform, and appointed an ambitious, controversial—and cynical—attorney general. I show how this attorney general used his office to punish his outgoing political foes, who were (rightly) accused of unspeakable violence. He engaged in strategic prosecution between 2016 and 2018 and repressed advocates' calls for overall accountability. The following administration allowed officials to act in solidarity with victims—and searching for victims became possible.
- In Nuevo León, activists and advocates were able to deploy a full range of strategic tactics after (1) a ratcheting down of DTO violence and (2) the appointment of an attorney general perceived to be motivated by

solidarity with victims' organizations. As a result, Nuevo León, between 2011 and 2016, is the most auspicious context for eroding impunity on multiple fronts profiled in the book.

In what follows, I elaborate on these processes.

Tamaulipas: Searching in the Black Hole

Tamaulipas, it bears repeating, is often called an *hoyo negro* (black hole), presumably because there is a vacuum where justice, rule of law, and any semblance of state effectiveness and institutional competence should be. Tamaulipas has been in the midst of a brutal territorial war between the Zetas and their former bosses in the Gulf Cartel since 2010, who together effectively control the state's security apparatus and whose bloody conflict has extended west through Nuevo León and Coahuila, and south to Veracruz.

> The levels of violence and terror were so intense [in Tamaulipas] that the already censored traditional media stopped reporting and the state seemed at times to have lost its monopoly on the legitimate use of force. The two crime groups [Gulf Cartel and Zetas] eventually dominated most aspects of the economy, social life, and politics. (Correa-Cabrera 2017, 187)

While the data on violence is flawed throughout Mexico, the combination of a weak state and a media vacuum makes data in Tamaulipas particularly untrustworthy.[10] Even with these data lapses, however, official figures recorded 6,131 (Alanís 2018) missing or disappeared persons between 2006 and 2018—the highest of any state in Mexico as well as the highest rates of kidnapping, organized crime, and investigations into illegal weapons in the country (Correa-Cabrera 2017).

---

[10] Because reporting on disappearances became too dangerous, most media outlets closed. In 2012, for example, after an armed attack on their offices, *El Mañana*, a daily newspaper in Nuevo Laredo, decided to cease publishing "information about violent disputes" because of the "lack of conditions for the free exercise of journalism" (Animal Político 2012c).

Stable Saturation: The War for Control of Tamaulipas

The Gulf Cartel has long made its home in the state of Tamaulipas, dating back to the 1930s and times of cross-border bootlegging,[11] and they enjoyed the loyal protection of the PRI until it finally lost the governorship in 2016. Despite an unwavering protection racket in their home state, the mid-1990s was a difficult time for the cartel. Gulf leader Juan Garcia Abregó, famous for bribing the top brass throughout the Mexican government, was arrested in 1996 and extradited to the United States on drug trafficking charges. Their protection racket was further disrupted in 1997 after their long-term PRI allies in neighboring Nuevo León lost the governorship and with that, their closest allies in the state police and prosecutors' offices (Trejo and Ley 2020).

In response to these cracks in their protection, one of the Gulf Cartel leaders vying for power made a decision that would alter the fate of thousands of people in northern Mexico: he recruited former members of Mexico's elite military forces to be the private army to protect the Gulf Cartel. This group, which would later come to be known as the Zetas, drew from the former ranks of highly trained police and military in Mexico and the region, in particular from former elite Guatemalan forces who had been trained by the United States and who participated in its genocide (Grillo 2012). From 2001 to 2006, the Gulf Cartel and their Zetas enforcers together fought a bloody battle for control over Tamaulipas against the Sinaloa Cartel, and their allies, the Beltrán Leyva Organization. This war, although no one knew this at the time, would pale in comparison to the brutality that would come when the increasingly powerful Zetas separated from the Gulf Cartel several years later.

In 2006, the Zetas formally separated from the Gulf Cartel and quickly moved to expand their control throughout much of the Mexican territory, as well as transnationally. The Zetas' modality of controlled differed from that of their predecessors: instead of turning first to extortion as a way to exert control, the Zetas ruled through terror and fear, committing savage acts of senseless brutality. This brutality most famously included the 2010 massacre of 72 migrants in San Fernando, Tamaulipas (see Aguayo 2017; Aguayo et al. 2016), and the murder of 193 people pulled from buses by the Zetas a year later (reportedly because they suspected the passengers were reinforcements for the Gulf Cartel) (Dudley 2011). Tamaulipas has been the center of the

---

[11] For history of corruption and cartels in Tamaulipas, see Padgett (2016), *Tamaulipas la casta de los narcogobernadores.*

Zetas' operations as well as ground zero for their bloody war against their former patrons, the Gulf Cartel (Correa-Cabrera 2017).

The state response to this open battle has ranged from complicit to ineffective. Former Tamaulipas governor Tomás Yarrington is now serving time for laundering money for the Gulf Cartel and Zetas during his 1999–2005 governorship (US Department of Justice 2018). From 2005 to 2010, Governor Eugenio Hernández, who was indicted in the United States for money laundering and is currently incarcerated in Mexico for the same crime, effectively ceded control over the state to these warring cartel factions. When he left power in 2010, his successor, Egidio Torre Cantú (governor 2011–2016), was not much better. Perhaps chastened by his brother's murder as he was running for governor, Cantú refused to meet with victims' collectives and presided over Tamaulipas at the height of the Zetas' power. On his watch, however, there were at least some efforts to combat state capture: half of the state police force was fired and replaced with federal forces in 2011 in an initiative to combat police collusion with DTOs.

In 2014, the federal government decided to launch a high-profile campaign that they dubbed "Plan Tamaulipas," with three goals: dismantling criminal groups, sealing illicit trafficking routes, and strengthening institutions (see Wilson and Weigand 2014). In pursuit of these goals, a large contingent of federal legal and security forces (federal prosecutors, army, navy, and marines) were brought in and divided up Tamaulipas into four sub-regions to focus on improving governance. Annual security spending in Tamaulipas reportedly averaged 3 billion pesos, about USD150 million. Perhaps unsurprisingly, given the lack of local buy-in and weak civil society, a 2017 *Reforma* headline read, "After 3 Years, Plan Tamaulipas Fails," citing increasing homicide rates, kidnappings, and an ongoing state of conflict (Reforma 2017). We see evidence of this failure in the ongoing commission of violence and the stability of legal impunity as part of the DTO protection racket. This deep and uninterrupted collusion between the state and DTOs means that even when DTO alliances realigned and battle lines were redrawn, the protection racket between the state and DTO forces remained solid and intact. The constant—the stability of the alliance structure—rested on the near-total capture of Tamaulipas state government by DTOs.

What, if anything, did Plan Tamaulipas accomplish, and why did it fail? First: while not systemic—Plan Tamaulipas did manage to bring in outside security actors, some of whom were seen as potential allies to victims, as I will discuss later in this section. Second: while Plan Tamaulipas continued efforts to purge corrupt security forces from state entities, there was not a viable plan to re-populate these entities with honest officials, nor to address the underlying dynamics that lead to corruption and collusion. This was most visible within the local police forces: in addition to the government-led purges, young people understandably viewed police work as a dangerous and highly undesirable career path. These dynamics have resulted in a severe shortage of police. PAN governor Garcia reported in 2017 that in a state in which 10,000 police officers are required, there were only 2,700.[12] Third and finally, Plan Tamaulipas failed to systematically address the deep levels of collusion between state and DTO forces and introduced new corrupt elements into this already volatile environment. In perhaps the best-known instance, 27 people were kidnapped by the navy between March and May of 2018, and 12 were later found dead (see Asmann 2020).

In 2016, the PRI finally lost its stranglehold on power in Tamaulipas. García Cabeza de Vaca, from the Partido Acción Nacional PAN, won the governorship after running on a platform promising victims of disappearances prompt, efficient redress for disappearances. Party alternation, however, has not proved significant in terms of changing what is possible for victim activists—and in fact, most reported that their prospects for justice had gotten worse. Cabeza de Vaca has been reluctant to meet with the collectives in Tamaulipas and is perceived by the collectives as trying to silence them.[13] In 2019, former head of the UN High Commissioner for Human Rights in Mexico Jan Jarab told me in an interview that the UN had stopped accompanying cases in Tamaulipas because "we didn't see the officials had the necessary openness to work with us." Charges have recently been brought against Cabeza de Vaca for corruption and involvement with organized crime.

Victims' Collectives: Advancing the Right to Truth Amid War

In this context of almost all-out war, civil society has been nearly silenced. As Paley (2011) noted, "There is a basic absence of advocacy. . . . [Tamaulipas] doesn't have a proliferation of nongovernmental advocacy, research or aid organizations devoted to assisting victims of the conflict and their family members." The systemic repression of civil society has meant that they are

---

[12] By June 2019, it would appear that significant progress had been made: Tamaulipas state officials reported that they were short *only* 2,500 police officers (as opposed to more than the 7,000 needed in 2017) to meet the minimum needed to effectively govern their territory (García 2019).

[13] Significantly, this is the only state where multiple victims asked me not to share even anonymized accounts of repression against them, expressing fear over possible reprisal.

effectively excluded from serious consideration as political allies. That is, when there was alternation in alliance structures, it was a foregone conclusion that there would be a reshuffling of allegiances—but civil society was so weak that they were a non-existent potential partner.

Where has this vacuum left civil society, and particularly the family members of the disappeared? Despite direct evidence of the inability of the state to guarantee security, combat or control violence, much less provide redress for violent crimes, more than 300 family members in Tamaulipas, have come together to form more than 30 victims' collectives[14] in the wake of their loved ones' disappearance. There is also a single human rights organization in the state, the Nuevo Laredo Human Rights Committee, headed by Raymundo Ramos. In a 2018 interview, I asked Raymundo what his greatest achievement was to date. "Surviving," he responded, without missing a beat. While this committee is a key voice for justice in Tamaulipas, it is essentially a one-man organization. This limited capacity, together with the atomized nature of the state because of the different turf wars, means that the victims' collectives are largely on their own—that is, they don't have a human rights center or NGO—to accompany them as they strategize around their political and legal responses.

As these collectives have formed, they have systematically probed the limits of safety: how hard can they push within this security environment? They sometimes march, usually in the wake of a particularly egregious disappearance or killing. But more often than not, their actions are confined to government offices and on-the-ground searching. They have pushed hard to schedule meetings with local and federal state officials, and they have taken perilous journeys within Tamaulipas and to Mexico City when federal officials have agreed to meet with them. The collectives are small and local and remain atomized despite their relatively close proximity to one another because it is dangerous to travel within the state. As the interviewee quoted at the beginning of this section stated: these collectives have asked the state to find their loved ones—and nothing else. Their analysis of the security environment, as well as what they have learned through tragedy, has taught them that there is no space for investigation leading to prosecution—so they do not ask, understanding that this would put everyone involved at risk.

---

[14] These collectives include Ciencia Forense Ciudadana, Justicia Tamaulipas, Red de Desaparecidos de Tamaulipas, Buscando a Nuestros Hijos Ausentes de Tamaulipas, Colectivo 21 de mayo, and Colectivo de Familiares y Amigos de Desparecidos. Chávez (2022) finds that there are a total of 34 victims' collectives active in Tamaulipas.

These understandings of their security environment are hard won. Most famously, Miriam Rodriguez, whose 20-year-old daughter Karen was kidnapped and murdered, personally investigated the perpetrators—and paid with her life in 2017. Like both Nancy and Juan Carlos recounted, Miriam went undercover to find information about her daughter, dressing in one instance as a government poll worker in order to access information about one of her daughter's suspected captors. After she found this information, she brought it to all the authorities she could find—until a federal policeman agreed to assist her. Her actions led to the incarceration of 10 perpetrators—and, on Mother's Day 2017, several of those perpetrators, who had recently escaped from prison, took their revenge. She was gunned down in front of her house. Miriam's story garnered a feature-length article in the *New York Times*, which also recounted the reaction of the family in a similar case in July of 2020 (Ahmed 2020). A teenage boy was kidnapped off the streets of the same town that Miriam is from. This time, however, his family had learned the limits of how hard they could push. The father of the missing boy told the *Times* reporter, "Look, we all want to do what Miriam did. . . . But look at how things ended for her. Dead." The *Times* article characterizes the attitude in town: "For the most part, residents don't speak out against organized crime. The risk is asymmetric. The police are unlikely to do anything, while the cartel almost certainly will — most often in the form of revenge." Miriam's son echoed this: "He had learned the lesson his mother's murder had been meant to impart: only push so far for justice. 'I won't make the same mistakes as my mom,' he said" (Ahmed 2020).

The security environment in Tamaulipas is not only dangerous for victims and their families. After one organization made an agreement with state forensic scientists to excavate the site of the 2011 San Fernando massacre, where the exhumation of 193 bodies makes it among the largest mass graves ever found in Mexico, it became clear that looking into violence in Tamaulipas is also dangerous and costly for outside advocates. In documents recently disclosed by order of the Mexican Supreme Court, the Mexican government revealed that three women leading the advocacy to uncover what happened in San Fernando—Ana Lorena Delgadillo, an organizer and leader involved in advocating for justice in the case of disappeared migrants in Mexico; forensic anthropologist Mercedes Doretti; and award-winning journalist Marcela Turati—were all being investigated for organized crime. That is, because these women sought to understand what had happened in San Fernando, the government opened an investigation against them, using it as an opportunity to track their phones, monitor their work, and follow their movements (see Sheridan 2021).

Given this security environment, it is perhaps unsurprisingly difficult to produce systematic evidence about the relationships between victims' collectives and state agents in Tamaulipas, as well as to document their results. In 2018, following Miriam's murder, I was asked to facilitate a meeting of members of nine different Tamaulipas victims' collectives in Mexico City. We met there, and not in Tamaulipas, precisely because we wanted a safe space to discuss strategies, experiences, and the way forward. Participants compared notes: they spoke of their pain; their deception with the justice system; their fear. But they also spoke of finding some MPs whom they met with to discuss their cases, some of whom they trusted to help them move forward with finding their loved ones. Unlike other states, I heard more of alliances with federal police officers—a remnant, I believe, of the personnel who poured into Tamaulipas during Plan Tamaulipas. Each of the collectives had a handful of positive stories: most had managed to find enough allies within the state to help them identify the remains of several people. All had located remains while searching for their loved ones. One attendee told a story of working with the marines to go to a ranch controlled by cartels—where a young man who had been disappeared was being held prisoner. He was alive and liberated.

In sum, Tamaulipas illustrates that even in a context that would appear closed to any investigatory advances as the state was under the near total control of warring DTOs, mobilized victims have managed to locate and exploit the little political space there is, discerning that both activism—vocally denouncing the state—and calling for the investigation or prosecution of those responsible are not possible goals. Instead, they have devoted themselves to engaging in under-the-radar collaboration with allies they have located within the state to search for the disappeared and when possible, to matching the DNA of those found with those missing. One organizer who works with the collectives estimated that 13 collectives have identified the remains of between 50 and 150 people. These identifications would not have happened without their courageous and unlikely mobilization. In this bleak context, this is a remarkable outcome.

Veracruz: Attorney General-led Strategic Prosecution

Veracruz has long been both blessed and cursed by its geography. A long, arm-shaped state on the Atlantic coast, it touches both Mexico's most southern state, Chiapas, and its most northern (and violent) state, Tamaulipas. It also contains one of Mexico's most important ports, which provided Spanish conquerors their entree to Mexico. While its mild climate has been conducive to growing coffee, sugar, and tobacco, it has also facilitated year-round transit and accessibility. Traveling through Veracruz provides the shortest route through Mexico from Central America to the United States, making it a natural route for migrants' northbound journeys and also for illicit goods. This has made Veracruz a strategic zone of control for cartels and, unsurprisingly, has led to violent disputes for territorial control.

State of Terror: Alliance Instability and Descent under Duarte
In the 1980s and early 1990s, several of Veracruz's governors went on to play key roles in Mexico's national security structure. Fidel Herrera Beltrán, the PRI governor from 2004 through 2010, was known for formalizing the relationships between the Zetas and the state security forces (Palacio and Olvera 2017). The Zetas, at that time still the enforcer wing of the Tamaulipas-based Gulf Cartel, had reportedly contributed to Herrera's electoral campaign, and in return he welcomed them into that state. The arrival of the Zetas into Veracruz not only meant an uptick in violence, but as the Zetas became independent and established themselves as the *jefes de plaza*, in charge of illicit trade in a certain area, they came to control not only the trafficking of people and drugs but also other crimes like robbery, extortion, and kidnapping. They "became the true local authorities, especially in the north of Veracruz" (Palacio and Olvera 2017).

Herrera's successor, Governor Javier Duarte de Ochoa, was also from the PRI, but his election in 2010 complicated the relationship between the state and the Zetas. At the beginning, it seemed that Duarte was faithful to the Zetas: "In Veracruz, the line between the Zetas and the Duarte government was blurred, with the government often deployed as little more than a mere offshoot of the crime group" (Corcoran 2017). Others, however, argue that Duarte was concerned that the Zetas had accumulated too much power and that their highly visible brutality might cost him politically. They argue that this caused him to flip his loyalty from the Zetas to Sinaloa-offshoot Jalisco New Generation (CJNG). According to Alberto Olvera, from Veracruz University, while "Herrera's time was the 'era' of the Zetas, Duarte's government 'permitted' another group to enter Veracruz to eliminate them" (as quoted in Janowitz 2018). Under this view, Duarte began to collaborate with President Calderón and federal forces, targeting Zeta leadership, and he reportedly set up two paramilitary groups, or Fuerzas de Reacción (Reaction

Forces) within the state dedicated to tracking down Zeta members and their collaborators. He also fashioned a torture center in the Xalapa Lencero Police Academy (complete with a zoo with exotic animals—reminiscent of a mix of Pinochet's use of military installations to torture dissidents and Pablo Escobar's fondness for exotic animals). At the Lencero Police Academy, a secret special unit named Los Fieles, the Loyal Ones, allegedly tortured and disappeared anyone suspected to have ties to the Zetas. By multiple accounts, these paramilitary forces and special units cast a broad net, disappearing innocent people and operating nearly entirely outside the law. In a case meticulously documented by a reporter for the *Intercept*, Hugo Marrieta, a young taxi driver who helped his mom sell tamales, lived at home, and didn't appear to have any spare income, was detained by one of the Reaction Forces, and then disappeared after being transferred to Lencero. His crime? His taxi number, for no explicable reason, appeared on the Reaction Force's list (Janowitz 2018).

As other cartels perceived an opening in Veracruz after Duarte's election in 2010, including the CJNG,[15] the Gulf Cartel, and the increasingly splintered Zetas (see Santiago 2019), the civilian population was increasingly caught in the violent crossfire. Duarte became infamous for presiding over a state with spiraling violence while he engaged in ostentatious corruption. He was charged with pocketing more than $2.6 billion in taxpayer funds allotted for combating violence (Bonello 2017; de Córdoba and Montes 2016). Meanwhile, more than 5,000 homicides were recorded between 2012 and 2016 (Molina 2018) and 2,750 disappearances.[16] Veracruz gained the dubious distinction of the most dangerous place in Mexico for journalists, with more than 17 killed and three disappeared during his administration (Bargent 2017). In 2016, 85 percent of Veracruz residents reported that they felt unsafe (Montalvo 2017), and under Duarte's rule the International Crisis Group (2017) dubbed Veracruz "Mexico's State of Terror," arguing that Duarte and his administration "governed with the intent of hiding or denying these crimes, and ensuring their culprits a free rein." Academics have written

---

[15] According to *The Intercept*, "In September 2011, 35 bodies were dumped on the road in the seaside city of Boca del Río, with a banner that announced the arrival of the CJNG. The banner reportedly stated: 'this is what's going to happen to all the Zeta shits that stay in Veracruz. It has a new owner now'" (Janowitz 2018).

[16] As extensively discussed, disappearance numbers are fraught and disputed. Duarte admitted to just over 500 disappearances during his term. Federal government sources place that number closer to 700 disappearances (see Vela 2016), with the majority reported in the state courts. Yunes's administration cited 3,600 disappearances from 2006 to 2016. As discussed elsewhere, however, disappearances are systemically under-reported.

that his administration reflected a kind of "sub-national authoritarianism" (Palacio and Olvera 2017). Duarte was ultimately indicted for embezzlement, collaboration with organized crime, and corruption, forcing him to resign from office two months early in 2016. He then fled the country, allegedly in a helicopter that his hand-picked successor, Flavino Ríos Alvarado, arranged. He was finally apprehended in Guatemala in 2017 and quickly extradited to Mexico, where he remains imprisoned today.

Cynical Attorney General

Unsurprisingly, the election following Duarte's indictment hinged on issues of corruption and security, with PAN candidate Miguel Ángel Yunes Linares ultimately elected on promises to address the crisis of disappearances, decrease violence, punish those responsible, and re-establish the rule of law. On his way out of office, however, Duarte had shepherded in one significant legal change: in 2016,[17] Veracruz passed legislation making the attorney general's office more independent.[18] Under this new law, attorneys general would serve nine-year terms instead of being appointed and removed at will by the governor. After receiving 38 of 50 votes in Veracruz's Congress, Jorge Winckler became the new attorney general (Avalos 2016). He had previously served as an attorney in private practice who had taken on high-profile cases and was a political ally of incoming governor Yunes. Winckler made it clear that he would take full advantage of the office's new independence, vowing that "the investigation will continue until everyone that participated in this illegal and clandestine policy of systematic forced disappearances are punished" (Intercept 2018).

In March 2017, Winckler announced that a mass grave had been located with more than 250 skulls inside, just outside of Veracruz city in a place called Colinas de Santa Fe (McDonnell and Sanchez 2017). He laid the blame squarely on the Duarte administration: "For many years, the drug cartels disappeared people and the authorities were complacent," Winckler said, adding that "Veracruz is an enormous mass grave. . . . It is the biggest mass

---

[17] This law was "published," or entered into public record, on November 6, 2016, just after Duarte had left office and during the very brief term of Rios Alvarado, who was in office only from October through December of 2016. As is evident in the law's introduction, however, Duarte was responsible for its drafting and for shepherding it through Congress (Ley Orgánica de la Fiscalía General del Estado de Veracruz de Ignacio de la Lllave 2016).

[18] Duarte's exact reasons for doing this are unclear and run counter to his overall governance record. One interviewee told me that Duarte sought to do something, anything, to make public gestures that he was complying with federal law, which indeed required this change.

grave in Mexico and perhaps one of the biggest in the world" (Associated Press 2017). After gathering internal documents from the police force, including notes that had been exchanged between the police and their superiors, Winckler claimed that he had evidence of the paramilitary groups alleged to be operating from within the state during Duarte's term. Based on this evidence, a judge ordered the detention of 31 police officers and other state actors for the enforced disappearance of 15 people in 2013. Those detained included Arturo Bermúdez Zurita, the former secretary of public security, who was charged with both torture and enforced disappearance, and Luis Ángel Bravo, the former Veracruz attorney general. Winckler recognized the historic nature of the detentions: in an interview with *El País*, he stated that "it is the first time in Mexico that criminal action has been established against the material actors of physical disappearances and against high-ranking officials who made enforced disappearance a systematic and institutional policy" (García 2018).

In these and other cases,[19] Winckler established that he was not afraid to go after corrupt state officials as long as they had committed brutal crimes against Veracruz's civilians—and as long as they were his political enemies. These actions, unsurprisingly, left him and his investigations exposed politically for two primary reasons. First, his political patron, Governor Yunes, had agreed to assume office for only two years (in order to align Veracruz's election calendar with the presidency). This was known when Yunes took power and made those in Winckler's gaze cognizant that his mandate could be limited; despite the law increasing his independence, he would clearly still be politically vulnerable when Yunes left power. Since he had threatened existing power structures in Veracruz, creating an untold number of enemies, this would prove decisive in ending his tenure as attorney general.

Second, Winckler operated as a lone wolf and hadn't built loyalty and capacity within the attorney general's office. When I asked a lawyer from Centro ProDH, the leading human rights organizations, whether the Veracruz government lacked the will or the capacity to carry out investigations, he summed it up well: "It's not complicated: they needed to hire more MPs, put more money into building forensic capacity. They did neither." This lack of capacity meant, among other things, that even if there had been the political

---

[19] For example, after a confrontation between what appeared to be a police vehicle and a truck carrying migrants, in which a 19-year-old woman from El Salvador was shot and killed, Winckler publicly accused the police of opening fire on the truck. An official from the federal government contradicted his version, instead laying the blame on the migrants (Sieff and Martinez 2019).

will to analyze and identify the human remains in the mass graves being un-covered throughout the state, Veracruz didn't have the forensic capacity for identifications. Because of this, Winckler invited the federal police to assist him in creating a registry of victims and recovered DNA. While this may have served as a band-aid solution, the failure to create a high-quality DNA data-base that could be used by all state authorities to systematically analyze and match found remains with the DNA of families looking for their loved ones has made further search and prosecution efforts more difficult. The manage-ment of the DNA registry was so riddled with problems that it prompted the CNDH to call for precautionary measures to be issued to ensure the proper handling of human remains (Agencia Reforma 2019). Winckler's politically driven, rapid investigations and incarcerations, in other words, had no way of becoming institutionalized; and he did not work to develop the capacity to respond to the demands by victims' collectives that remains be identi-fied. The consequences of his strategic approach quickly became clear when Yunes left power.

Strong Activists, Excluded Advocates: The Growth and Exclusion of Victim Collectives

As we will see in Monterrey, the MPJD's 2011 caravan was an important moment for the formation of victims' collectives in Veracruz. The caravan pulled into its capital city of Xalapa on the evening of September 18, 2011, Veracruz's central plaza, dominated by a towering yellow church and illu-minated by off-season Christmas lights hung from central shops. I was just beginning my fieldwork in Mexico and was on the caravan as part of my research. I wrote in my field notes, "So many people! Crowding the plaza, filling doorways—but also feels tense. People not as scared as in Acapulco—but feels volatile." While I didn't realize it then, the group that was greeting us in the main square, Xalapa por la Paz, had formed specifically to receive the caravan that day, drawing from families with loved ones who had been disappeared as well as local civic organizations.

These collectives would go on to form a small advocacy team during Duarte's administration. After marching and occupying the main throughfare in the city, they successfully pressured Duarte's administra-tion into meeting with them. In 2012, they held five participatory investi-gation meetings and then re-mobilized after the top-ranking official who had agreed to oversee the participatory investigations was a no-show at their first meeting (Villarreal Martinez 2016). In 2013, Juan Carlos and

Doña Marí turned their attention toward Veracruz—where the second set of disappearances, of brothers Gustavo and Luis Armando, had taken place in 2010. There, they joined with this group and met an undergraduate law student named Anais Palacios, who was the only person with any legal training among them. They began to organize, at first documenting a handful of cases. Fairly quickly, they received an onslaught of cases—about 1,200 in the first year of their work. By 2014, the collective—all volunteers, made up mostly of family members of victims with no established human rights center backing them up—had accompanied 23 cases, but only brought eight of those to the participatory investigation meetings.[20] The families of the disappeared were scared.

Unsurprisingly, advocacy was not possible under Duarte—though the nascent victims' collective tried. Duarte had fired the investigator who had been overseeing the stalled cases and appointed Luis Angel Bravo, a charming and hard-charging investigator, as the attorney general of the State of Veracruz. Luis Angel agreed to review the case files and come up with a detailed report of what had happened in the cases of disappearance under his jurisdiction, and to include in their case files the information the victims had discovered, an important step in affirming and legitimizing work they had done. But that was where it ended: he didn't find anyone who was disappeared nor charge anyone with crimes associated with disappearances.

As discussed above, Veracruz during this time was a difficult, and sometimes dangerous, place to organize—and Bravo and Duarte most likely participated in making sure this threat was felt by the victims. As I recounted in Chapter 4, Juan Carlos reported being pursued by state police after a meeting with Duarte when he publicly accused him of surrounding himself with Zetas. Anais, the young lawyer they had begun to work with, was also targeted by the government of Veracruz. The Veracruz attorney general's office stated publicly that she was on their payroll. She assured me in a 2020 interview that she was not, but this successfully branded her as someone who had been corrupted, and subsequently, victims' collectives in Veracruz split over those who would work with her and those who wouldn't.

As the meetings with Duarte and Bravo stalled, the victims' collective faced the choice of where they wanted to attempt to file the cases of disappearances they had documented, since most victims had not yet formally reported their

---

[20] In order to bring cases to the participatory investigations, most organizations require that family member(s) of the disappeared person must agree to attend. They may not do this for the reasons discussed at length in Chapter 4: fear, cost, biographical availability, etc.

cases to a judicial entity. In May 2013, in response to the hunger strike Nancy had played a leading role in, the PGR had launched a new investigative unit: the Search Unit for the Disappeared. When only 12 MPs were assigned to the unit, those who had been involved in the hunger strike and the organized family members of the disappeared were outraged (Martínez 2013). These 12 MPs were, in theory, responsible for investigating the more than 25,000 cases of disappearances at that time. Juan Carlos and the victims' collective, however, still wanted to try to get the bulk of these Veracruz cases transferred to this unit for two reasons. First, despite the limits of the Disappeared Unit's capacity, family members were still more hopeful that their cases would be investigated than if they stayed in Veracruz under Governor Duarte. Second, Juan Carlos had a strategic reason: he told me "my intention was to collapse this institution [the Search Unit for the Disappeared], in order to publicly debunk the idea that they were devoting all necessary public resources to search for the disappeared." With these factors in mind, the collective successfully argued that the 1,200 cases they wanted the unit to take over were linked (people disappeared in the same area at around the same time under similar circumstances) to cases the unit was already investigating. It made sense, therefore, that these cases should be investigated together.

Juan Carlos and the nascent organization of family members from Veracruz were in frequent contact with Baltazar, head of the federal search unit. Eventually, just as they had strategized, he asked them to stop sending cases. Baltazar called Juan Carlos, telling him the search unit was overwhelmed. Despite the sometimes tireless efforts of the few investigators within the unit—Juan Carlos and his allies frequently had marathon participatory investigation meetings with both SEIDO and the disappearance unit beginning in the morning and lasting until dawn—the cases stalled. In Juan Carlos's view, the investigators would make some headway in certain cases, only to realize that the perpetrator of the disappearance was linked to one of Veracruz's powerful and dangerous cartels, usually the Zetas. At that point, the investigation would be effectively abandoned.

Winckler and Yunes Linares had promised to vigorously address disappearances. Instead, their two-year term brought even more disappearances and a distancing from victims' collectives. In 2019, a victims' collective summed up the Yunes administration, claiming that even though during Duarte's term there had been 3,600 reported cases of disappearances, in the two years that Yunes Linares was governor there were more than 2,000—a figure that Winckler tried to hide due to a "systemic reluctance" to admit to the failures of his political patron (Zavaleta 2019). Victims' groups criticized Winckler both to his face and publicly for going after only high-profile political targets while ignoring the cases they had been advocating for. His response to their criticism was to close the door to all but the most politically connected groups. As one victims' collective went on record in Veracruz: "[I give] Yunes a zero because we had no progress in the search for the disappeared, the investigations were stopped, the participatory investigations were suspended, and individual appointments were stopped to follow up on the investigations" (Gómez 2014). Because of this, Winckler made more enemies than allies with the victims' collectives, alienating groups that should have been his closest allies: he was, after all, in theory going after state officials responsible for disappearing their loved ones.

End of Strategic Prosecutions; Flourishing of Searching

In 2018, Cuitlahuác García Jiménez, from the AMLO-backed MORENA party, was elected governor after running against Yunes's son. Like Yunes before him, García Jiménez ran on a platform promising to address violence, promote justice, and limit corruption. He also publicly pledged to meet monthly with the victims' collectives clamoring for justice and promised that the state would continue to search for their loved ones. This public discourse, along with new state officials who were allowed the political space to act in solidarity with victims' collectives, changed what was possible in Veracruz. The collectives, which had been repressed and partially silenced under Yunes and Winckler, emerged, and with the (sometimes reluctant) backing of federal police and investigatory officials, were able to conduct widely publicized searches for the remains of the disappeared in Veracruz's many mass graves.[21]

Despite a discourse of openness, there were quickly signs that the new governor would not be entirely on the side of victims. García Jiménez distanced himself from civil society and academia, opting to appoint former Duarte loyalists to key cabinet positions (Zavaleta 2018). Soon after, he began to go after Winckler, accusing him of generating "anger, frustration, complaints and pain amongst the victims' collectives." Despite the guarantees of a more independent attorney general who would serve in the position for nine years, García Jimenez set out to undermine Winckler early in his term. First, he

---

[21] For a list of mass graves in Veracruz and throughout Mexico, see https://data.adondevanlosde saparecidos.org/.

set out to reverse some of Winckler's high-level arrests: between the time García Jimenez took office in December 2018 and April 2019, six former Duarte officials whom Winckler had indicted were cleared of all charges and released from custody.[22] Next, despite the legislation that, on paper, guaranteed Winckler his post through 2025, he set out to get him fired. He pursued this goal mainly in the court of public opinion, regularly criticizing him in the media. In September 2019, García Jiménez obtained the necessary votes in the legislature to remove Winckler from his position as attorney general. His successor, Verónica Hernández Giadáns, is a political ally of the new governor, has no prosecutorial experience, and in 2020 admitted to being the first cousin of a prominent Zeta leader (Cortés 2020).

In sum, Veracruz illustrates the possibilities and limitations of politically led prosecutions. Victims' collectives in Veracruz succeeded in bringing the issue of enforced disappearance to the fore of politics in Veracruz. Attorney General Winckler channeled the public concern the collectives generated to legitimate his move to prosecute prominent members of the Duarte administration at a time of political change and instability among DTOs and between DTOs and state actors. The existing advocates, however, were inconvenient for him, and he worked to exclude and discredit them. Even as mass graves were found, the identification of remains was not a priority of the state. While these high-profile prosecutions appeared, at the time, to challenge Veracruz's "sub-national authoritarianism" and near total impunity, these prosecutions were largely vacated after Winckler left power. Despite Winckler's efforts to demobilize them, victims' collectives continued to organize with minimal state involvement during the period of high-profile strategic prosecution and were able to pivot back to quiet activism to continue their efforts to search for their loved ones amid a difficult political environment with the following administration.

[22] These officials included Ríos Alvarado, the short-serving governor who had arranged for Duarte's escape to Guatemala, as well as Bermúdez Zurita, who had been linked to the enforced disappearances of 15 people. Mauricio Audirac Murrillo, Duarte's former treasurer, and Francisco Valencia García, the former secretary of public works, were all released within days of the new governor's arrival, although charges are still pending. Duarte's former spokeswoman, Maria Georgina Dominguez Colio, was placed under house arrest in February 2019, and his private secretary Juan Antonio Nemi Dib was exonerated a month later (Rainsford 2019).

Nuevo León: The Road to Participatory Investigation and the Erosion of Impunity

Nuevo León, for a period of several years, seemed to present a model for making substantive advances into cases of disappearance. The most prominent local human rights NGO at the time, Citizens in Support of Human Rights (CADHAC), had registered an alarming increase in disappearances between 2009 and 2014, as is evident in Table 5.2.

CADHAC and the family members of the disappeared who organized themselves in a sister organization called AMORES would go on to hold participatory investigation meetings with state officials through 2014 and present some of the most promising results in terms of investigatory advances seen in Mexico. How did they achieve this?

Unstable State and DTO Alliances

When Nuevo León first elected a non-PRI governor in 1997, the loss of power shocked Monterrey's controlling DTO, the Gulf Cartel (see Trejo and Ley 2020, 125). The Gulf Cartel's leadership lived in Monterrey, which was seen at the time as a safe industrial hub where wealthy residents took advantage of vibrant community life and laid plans to build a riverside walkway (Villarreal 2015; 2021). Nuevo León was then and continues to be one of Mexico's wealthiest states, accounting for 7.5 percent of Mexico's GDP. Monterrey, the capital and largest city, is a commercial, social, and political hub, sometimes referred to as the "Silicon Valley of Mexico." Just 135 miles from the US border, it has been a convenient home for many international companies.

Table 5.2 Cases of Disappearances Registered by Local NGO CADHAC

Year	Number of Cases (Distinct Disappearance Events)	Number of Victims
2009	12, with 8 suggesting enforced disappearance	16
2010	10, with 5 suggesting enforced disappearance	76
2011	84, with 19 suggesting enforced disappearance	294
2012	103, with 28 suggesting enforced disappearance	621
2013	66, with 18 suggesting enforced disappearance	144
2014	63, with 10 suggesting enforced disappearance	91
		Total 1,242

Source: Original research; and also Villarreal Martínez, M. T. (2015).

Monterrey's reputation as a peaceful haven in the north of Mexico had made it an ideal location for DTO *capos* to send their wives and families for safety; it also conveniently gave Gulf Cartel leaders easy access to Tamaulipas, their de facto headquarters. In 2008, members of the Beltran Leyva Organization (BLO) saw the strategic value in Nuevo León and specifically in the upscale neighborhood of San Pedro, near Monterrey; it began to challenge the Gulf Cartel's rule. In 2009, Mauricio Fernandez Garcia, the municipal president of San Pedro, partnered with the BLO to perform paramilitary-style social cleansing, disappearing, killing, and asserting control over undesirable elements like petty criminals and vagrants (Correa-Cabrera 2017). BLO had just broken from their former patrons, the Sinaloa Cartel, and the Zetas had become newly independent from the Gulf Cartel. The Zetas, expanding rapidly at the time and eager to control new drug *plazas*, made an agreement with Beltran Leyva: while Beltran Leyva would stay in wealthy San Pedro, the Zetas would have the run of the rest of Monterrey. By all accounts, the Zetas successfully installed themselves in the city by expanding the local drug market, extorting local licit and illicit markets, and kidnapping. As of 2012, they were bringing in around $100 million per year (Dudley 2012).

This control came with high costs for the local population. Perhaps most famously, on August 25, 2011, the Zetas set fire to the Royale casino, leaving 52 dead and the city of Monterrey terrified. From 2010 to 2012, control of the *plaza* was highly contested and dynamic: while Beltran Leyva and the Zetas remained allies, the Gulf Cartel—at times together with the Sinaloa Cartel—attempted to take back lost territory from their former enforcers, a battle prompted by the Gulf Cartel's killing of a key Zeta leader in 2010. The Zetas were thrown into chaos after their top leader was killed in October 2012, leading to a descent into infighting and violence among the Zetas and a decline in their influence and acts of violence committed against civilians. This violence correlates with the number of disappearances reported to CADHAC (see Table 5.2 above).

Key State Actors: An Attorney General in Solidarity

Control of Nuevo León swung back to the PRI in 2009 with the election of Rodrigo Medina de la Cruz as governor. Returning to office, however, the PRI could not put the cat back in the bag: the splintering and militarization spawned by the alternation in power 10 years earlier had set dynamics in motion that would mark de la Cruz's term in office as a bloody one. This violence, however, was sporadic: a sharp spike in violence was preceded

and followed by relative calm. While his complicity in spawning this violence, guaranteeing impunity, and failing to prevent its escalation is debat-
able, the dramatic variation of violence during his tenure suggests that a
change in gubernatorial leadership was not the primary driver of violence
in Nuevo León. The appointment of Adrián de la Garza as state attorney
general in February 2011, on the other hand, marked a new approach in how
the Nuevo León government would handle cases of disappearances. De la
Garza, whose father served as attorney general of Nuevo León in the 1970s,
had spent the 1990s coming up through the ranks of the judicial police and
worked as a judge, a *ministerio público*, a case coordinator, and within the
state Office of Public Security. When Medina nominated de la Garza for
state attorney general, Nuevo León's Congress unanimously approved him
that same week.

De la Garza would prove to be an invaluable ally to local NGOs and civil
society groups. In early June 2011, just four months after his appointment,
the MPJD-sponsored national caravan of family members of victims of
disappearances and homicides arrived in Monterrey to protest the violence
and impunity throughout the north of Mexico. A group of these activists, led
by MPJD leaders Javier Sicilia and Emilio Álvarez Icaza, together with local
CADHAC leader Sister Consuelo Morales, departed for the state prosecutor's
office. When the group arrived, de la Garza opened the doors of the attorney
general's office, despite it being almost midnight. He agreed on the spot to
establish investigatory working groups that he would personally oversee,
and he made good on his promise: over the next four years, until his resignation in early 2015 to run for mayor, he presided over 24 meetings between
CADHAC and the MPs in his office.

While de la Garza's support for participatory investigations was the key
to establishing them, his support was not sufficient to ensure that they
made real investigatory progress. In Nuevo León during this time, all cases
of disappearances and homicides in the state were divided among four
coordinators of *averiguaciones previas* (investigation files). The quality of
investigation undertaken during these meetings depended largely on the
willingness and skills of specific MPs, and in particular, on the norms established by the case coordinator. The coordinators were MPs whom de la
Garza had chosen personally for their record and reputation of being strong
investigators. The strongest coordinator was responsible for issuing 80 percent of all indictments, and he appeared singularly unafraid to instruct the
MPs he managed to interview municipal police, incarcerated members of

organized crime, and victims' family members. The least effective case co-ordinator did not issue a single indictment, and investigatory actions were mostly limited to sending *oficios* (letters) to local hospitals, jails, and other sites asking if the missing person was there.

Civil Society: Advocacy and Activism

Following de la Garza's decision to open the attorney general's office to on-going dialogue with the MPJD in June 2011, CADHAC decided that it would not only document cases of disappearances, but it would also take advan-tage of the political opening de la Garza had given them to figure out how to support all family members of victims of disappearance who sought to meet with state officials. This decision reflected Morales's belief that these meetings could be productive and a recognition that shifting dynamics with the state were necessary to achieve judicial progress:

> I am convinced that if we truthfully do rigorous, serious work in the docu-mentation and deep study of the case files. . . sooner or later we have to get results. . . I am learning that dialogue [with the state] is a very important tool that requires the opening of both parties, and that we as civil society had previously closed this possibility. (Sister Consuelo Morales, author in-terview, Monterrey, Mexico: March 2013)

Collaboration with de la Garza's attorney general's office marked a new stage in the work of CADHAC. In the terms I set out in Chapter 3, CADHAC transitioned from an activist to an advocacy organization. The members had not engaged in advocacy previously largely because they had not had strong institutional support and had scrambled to hire lawyers and secure funding. But building on an established organizational structure and a strong leader who believed in the possibilities of collaborative work with the state, they pivoted into working with the state to pursue their goals. Apart from justice in particular cases, they partnered with De la Garza to advocate for better leg-islation and investigatory practice around enforced disappearances. Perhaps most remarkably, I watched representatives from CADHAC, the MPJD, the attorney general's office, and the UN High Commissioner on Human Rights step into an office at CADHAC over the course of several days to draft one of the first investigatory protocols in the country stating what should be done in the immediate aftermath of a disappearance. They produced an official document that took seriously the question of what it would take to guarantee non-recurrence—that is, to intervene immediately to prevent further disappearances.

CADHAC's decision to work closely with local judicial officials, however, was predictably controversial. Many members who had been protesting against the state to find their loved one were resistant to the relatively quick shift to partnering with them—especially in cases where family members believed that state forces were complicit in the disappearance. Morales saw the relationships with de la Garza and his staff as the key to having a chance at moving the investigations forward, and she viewed family members who insisted on continuing to critique the state as a threat to those relationships. Since, as I discuss in Chapter 6, a relatively small number of cases would result in finding disappeared people or prosecuting those responsible, many of the family members were left frustrated, angry at the state, and clamoring for a different outcome.

In spring 2012, a small group of family members who had previously participated in CADHAC's advocacy struck out on their own to participate in *bordando por la paz* (embroidering for peace), a national initiative under which family members of the disappeared embroider on a handkerchief the name, date, and circumstances of disappearance, and any identifying information of the victim (Ramírez Atilano 2014). Several family members sat for hours, every week, in front of the city hall in Monterrey—embroidering, and also discussing what was next. After meeting with mobilized victims from the neighboring state of Coahuila, they decided to form a local chapter of Fuerzas Unidas por Nuestros Desaparecidos en México, FUNDEM. They called their local chapter FUNDENL: United Forces for Our Disappeared in Nuevo León. FUNDENL did not directly confront the state at first; their activities included commemorating the anniversaries of those disappeared, participating in national marches, and visiting universities to discuss their cases. Soon, however, they moved to a more critical position. After one of their members doubted that the remains the state gave her were indeed those of her daughter, FUNDENL launched an online campaign with the hashtag #PruebaGenéticaNL (#GeneticProofNuevoLeón). They joined the on-the-ground searches for remains. And in early 2014, they next took over a public plaza in downtown Monterrey, adorning the existing sculptures with banners of the disappeared—and informally renamed it the Plaza de los Desaparecidos (Plaza of the Disappeared). When the municipal government cleaned out the plaza and removed the commemorations, FUNDENL issued a communique:

For them, just seeing the names [of the disappeared] is a bother. . . . It bothers them that we have decided not to rot with sadness locked in our homes; that we have decided to pressure the State and Federal Attorney General's Offices to do their job. It bothers them that we have not agreed to remain silent, it bothers them that we do not answer "Yes, Mr. Attorney General" or "Yes, Mr. Governor" each time they explain to us why they are not looking for our relatives. (FUNDENL 2014)

The presence of activists in the form of FUNDENL was an important motivation for CADHAC and members of the attorney general's office to deliver results—to prove that collaboration between civil society and state officials could result in judicial advances. As I have argued previously (Gallagher 2017), activist pressure when combined with advocacy provided an effective mix of pressure and avenues for state-society communication.

Closing of Political Space

While de la Garza left his post as attorney general in February of 2015 in order to run for mayor of Monterrey, the participatory investigations continued through the end of Governor Medina's term. While Medina did not express particularly strong interest in the investigations, several of the case coordinators by this time had established strong relations with CADHAC, and were able to continue their work. In October of 2015, immediately after independent governor Jaime Rodriguez Calderón, popularly known as "El Bronco," was sworn in, this political space closed. Despite the enthusiastic endorsement of "El Bronco" from much of Nuevo León's civil society, and promises that he would be transparent and ethical, this did not translate into a commitment to maintaining the political space opened by de la Garza. El Bronco appointed Roberto Flores Treviño to the position of State Attorney General. Flores, who was later accused of nepotism and resigned his post less than two years later, immediately reassigned the most effective case co-ordinator to a far-flung region of Nuevo León, effectively removing him from the investigation of disappearances, and the other case coordinators were given the equivalent of desk duty. Morales, head of CADHAC, reflected on Flores' tenure in 2019 "You can bring all the pressure you want—but if the man is bad—he's not going to work" (Consuelo Morales, interview with author, Nuevo León, Mexico: August 2019). The participatory investigations ceased, and with this, the window of opportunity to advance the right to justice seemingly closed. Less visible independent searches for remains have continued with the assistance of some allies within the state, but participatory investigations have ceased.

In sum, this case exemplifies what is possible when unstable alliances between DTOs and state allies coincide with a high-ranking state official who is perceived by many to be acting in solidarity with victims of disappearances. We see here the most open legal and political opportunity structure of any of the cases, allowing for a growing number of civil society organizations and victims' collectives to draw upon their diverse experiences and engage in a variety of activist and advocacy strategies. In this case, an advocacy organization partnered with sympathetic state official to establish participatory investigations. These processes were then fueled to produce results by a vocal activist organization. Especially in comparison to the other cases, significant progress was made in the right to truth, justice, and non-repetition, and taken as a whole represent the most significant inroads against impunity of any case profiled in this book. Instructively, these results were not achieved at a time of party alternation, but rather during a time of chaos between local DTOs. These investigations, notably, were devoted to criminal investigations of those responsible for disappearances, and considered finding the remains of the victim secondarily. In Chapter 6, I look in depth at the judicial results of these investigations.

IV. Conclusion

The experience of struggle has transformed the ways in which victims of violence think about navigating the state. In this chapter, we saw victims' collectives in Tamaulipas finding ways to advance their right to truth by constraining themselves to ask for truth—not justice—from a violent state overrun by DTOs. In Veracruz, we saw victims' collectives put the issue of disappearances front and center in the electoral campaign following Governor Duarte's brutal and corrupt administration. When the cynical attorney general channeled political will against impunity into politically motivated prosecutions and sidelined victims' collectives, they sought solidarity from federal officials to provide them with protection and political cover to be able to search for their loved ones. In Nuevo Leon, a spike in violence spurred by DTOs sparring for control of the *plaza*, followed by a relative calm, opened space for both government and civil society to address impunity. In this context, we saw one local organization pivot their strategies as they realized that they had a high-level ally within the state—and work to exploit and institutionalize the investigatory strategies which became possible; while other, more critical, organizations emerged to heighten the pressure for accountability.

This chapter focuses on how victims collectively make sense of political threats and opportunities, and in the process, teaches us two lessons about the political dynamics of criminal governance and impunity. First, these dynamics illustrate the political consequences of *búsqueda,* searching for the disappeared and matching remains with victim identities, are entirely separate from *criminal investigations* into those responsible for the commission of disappearances. This means that *búsquedas* may occur in the context of stable protection rackets. If successful, *búsquedas* can fulfill a central right and demand of victims, and therefore provides police and prosecutors with some degree of political benefit without significantly threatening DTO's central demand of freedom from prosecution. In Chapter 6, I continue this line of argument, showing that *búsqueda* in Mexico has been intentionally institutionally separated from investigation: To identify and match remains, different personnel, different laws, and different databases have been set up that make it difficult for information to be shared or linked with investigations. In short, *búsqueda* in Mexico is generally not linked to criminal prosecution and therefore doesn't threaten DTO impunity, making it possible to advance victims' right to truth even with stable protection rackets.

Second, though I highlight the futility of many participatory investigations in advancing the right to justice, they are also the basis for the cracks in collusive impunity we see in many other states. Recent literature on participatory institutions (Amengual 2016; Baiocchi, Heller, Silva, and Silva 2011; González 2019; Mayka 2019a, 2019b, 2019c; Rich 2019a, 2019b) has highlighted the importance of alliances between civil society and state bureaucrats in allowing civil society groups to influence both policy and judicial outcomes. In this chapter, I have drawn on these ideas to understand how participatory investigations may be a key to challenging state-sponsored protection rackets, exploring when participatory institutions are able to take hold (Mayka 2019a), as well as how and when reform-minded bureaucrats can make use of social movements to legitimate and establish participatory institutions (Rich 2019a). In sum, I describe the various political configurations that can lead to the empowerment of participatory investigations and their corresponding ability to push for advances into the investigation of disappearances.

6

To What Effect?

How Sustained Mobilization Erodes Impunity

I met Yoltzi Martinez Corrales in January 2020 at Centro ProDH, arguably the most important human rights organization in Mexico. She was waiting to board a bus to Veracruz to spend two weeks searching for unmarked grave sites and human remains alongside more than a hundred victim activists and allies. The search was the fifth that had been organized by Familias en Búsqueda (Searching Families), the organization Juan Carlos Trujillo's family played a leading role in founding.

Yoltzi told me that her sister, Yatzil, disappeared nine years earlier, near her home in Acapulco Guerrero. The disappearance devastated her family. Her father tried to commit suicide, and her mother was institutionalized at a psychiatric hospital. The family didn't talk about what had happened: her sister's existence became a shared, and somehow shameful, secret. Yoltzi told me that she felt unimaginably isolated, and just exhausted. She had trouble getting out of bed.

Yoltzi recounted to me how in early 2019, a chance meeting changed her life. She went to church and asked God to help her forget her sister. Yoltzi had had troubling sleeping since her sister's disappearance and incessantly asked herself whether there were things she could have done differently to prevent the tragedy. That same day, she happened on Familias en Búsqueda—they were in Acapulco conducting their Fourth Citizens' Search Brigade.

> I came up to them like a hungry child. And it was the first time I said: "I have a disappeared sister." . . . [F]or me, it was like flipping a switch. . . . Before I joined this group, I felt that I had died. Now I feel like I'm surviving. But we need to feel like we're living . . . and that's what I feel like they're teaching me to do.
>
> They tell me we aren't alone. There are things you can do. My sister is not a case file number. My sister is not a forgotten photo. My sister isn't a person that we shouldn't think about. They taught me to say: my sister has a

Bootstrap Justice. Janice k. Gallagher, Oxford University Press. © Oxford University Press 2023.
DOI: 10.1093/oso/9780197649978.003.0006

name. She is Yatzil. She is a mother. I learned to talk about her in the present
tense—not in the past. . . and as long as I look for her—she is present.

The beginning of Yoltzi's story—of loss, profound personal and familial desperation stemming from the disappearance of a loved one—was achingly familiar to me. After 10 years accompanying and researching the experiences
of family members of people who had been disappeared, these themes were a
tragic constant. As Yoltzi continued to talk about her journey out of isolation
and depression and into community and a sense of agency, however, I was
struck by how different her experience was from those of Juan Carlos, Nancy
and Lucía, and Alfonso.

Many involved in the search for the disappeared can feel like nothing has
been accomplished. Nearly every one of the hundreds of family members
I have met over the past 10 years hasn't achieved what they most desperately
wanted and which drew them to mobilize: finding their loved one alive and
bringing them home. Given this central and devastating failure, what can we
conclude about the achievements and significance of the individual and collective actions detailed throughout this book? In this chapter, I argue that
sustained mobilization has led to measurable advances in the struggle against
impunity, including gains in the right to justice, the right to truth, the right
to reparations, and the right to non-repetition. These gains in rights attain-
ment are evident in different institutional and non-institutional contexts and
at different levels of analysis: from individuals doing their own work to understand a new detail about where their loved one was last seen; to national
legislation criminalizing enforced disappearance throughout the Mexican
territory. Presenting these results coherently, therefore, is a challenge. In this
chapter, I organize these results into four categories: legislative, institutional,
judicial, and movement outcomes. *Legislatively*, I discuss two significant
pieces of legislation that are directly attributable to the victims' movement.
Institutionally, these laws created new judicial and governing bureaucracies
charged with attending to the crisis of disappearances. *Judicially*, I show how
in the most auspicious environment for accountability, Nuevo León, sustained mobilization has resulted in significant inroads into impunity, but also
demonstrates the limits of what is currently possible to achieve in Mexico's
justice system. I also closely review the case results of Nancy, Juan Carlos
and Lucía, and Alfonso, detailing how their mobilization affected the judicial
status of their cases and their conceptions of justice. Next, I show how the capacity of *movements* has grown in the past decade, establishing repertoires of

contention, building networks of support, developing the ability to provide psycho-social support, and creating the capacity to conduct independent searches. I argue that, taken as a whole, the impact of sustained mobilization has reconfigured the experience and possibilities of family members of the disappeared, enabling them to become rights-conscious, and to a greater extent than they may have imagined possible, rights-bearing citizens. It has also moved the needle on perhaps the most vexing and intractable problem in Mexico: impunity.

This chapter contributes to our understandings of social movement and criminal governance outcomes and sheds light on policy feedback within this context. Social movements literature has historically focused more on the causes of mobilization than on outcomes, something that scholars have sought to rectify in the past decade or so (Amenta et al. 2010; Bosi and Uba 2009; Vestergren et al. 2017). When outcomes are considered, they are most often at one level of analysis—and most commonly, they consider macro political outcomes like policy change and electoral victories (or losses). A sub-set of social movement scholars—most within sociology (led by Doug McAdam [1986],[1] and within the adjacent legal mobilization literature [McCann 1994])[2]—have considered the effect of mobilization on individuals. Criminal governance literature, as I discuss in Chapter 5, almost universally focuses on violence as the outcome of interest, while considering impunity as a function of the dynamics of protection rackets. In this chapter, as in the book overall, I consider the many facets of impunity as an outcome—which spans from the individual level of analysis up through judicial and policy outcomes. This synthetic approach provides a more holistic, and complete, understanding of the outcomes of the efforts to combat impunity in Mexico.

Woven throughout this chapter are reflections on how things changed during the course of this study, which began in 2010, which in turn shaped the subsequent actions of activists, advocates, and state actors. Policy

[1] McAdam (1986) pioneered the study of the impact that mobilization has on life trajectory. Drawing on a natural experiment in which he could trace the life trajectories of people who did and didn't participate in the Civil Rights Movement's 1964 Freedom Summer voter registration drive, he shows that participating in a summer of activism fundamentally shifted their life trajectories, with movement participants tending to be more involved with social movements throughout their life than non-participants.

[2] In McCann's foundational law and society work (1994, ch. 7), he dedicates his final empirical chapter to "look beyond the narrow terms of policy impacts, which dominate most scholarly analyses, to the broader political significance" of the movement he studies, the wage equity movement, "for the people it most concerns" (227).

feedback literature helps us think through these dynamics of how "policies, once created, reshape politics" (Mettler and SoRelle 2018; see also Skocpol 1992; Pierson 1993).This literature is often employed to understand outcomes like the behavior of mass publics, policymaking institutions, and the decision-making of political elites— most often in research in the United States and Europe. It is rarely used in thinking through the ways in which policies meant to advance human rights (re)configure politics and shape the incentives of policymakers, judicial officials, and the victim claimants. The longitudinal nature of this study affords me the opportunity to have seen the formation and implementation of policies designed to address impunity in the case of disappearances but also to follow their early implementation and to offer ideas about the ways in which they have shaped subsequent claim-making and judicial practice.

Legislative and Institutional Outcomes

Mexico has passed two major pieces of legislation in response to the crisis of violence and disappearances and as a result of sustained mobilization.[3] The first is the 2013 General Law for Victims, which defined the rights of and provided remuneration to victims of crime (Garcia 2015). The second is the 2017 General Law on Enforced Disappearance, which defined and criminalized "enforced disappearance"[4] throughout Mexico's 32 states and required the immediate investigation and coordination of information needed to search for the missing. Each law, in turn, mandated new federal- and state-level agencies tasked with carrying out key provisions of the law: the Victims' Law established the Commission for Attention to Victims (CEAV), which is tasked primarily with distributing financial support to victims' families; and the Law on Enforced Disappearance spawned the creation of Comisiones de Búsqueda, or Search Commissions.[5]

---

[3] This section draws from Anaya and Gallagher (forthcoming).

[4] See Ansolabehere et al. (2021) for an in-depth discussion of the content and process of drafting Law on Disappearances.

[5] In Mexico, these "General Laws" are passed at the federal level, and authorizing legislation needs to be passed in each state for the laws to apply. Additional laws have also been passed in response to the crisis of disappearances, including laws making the "declaration of absence" of a disappeared person easier. I focus on these general laws because they are the highest impact laws passed in Mexico in response to the crisis of disappearances.

These legislative and institutional changes are due directly to the mobilization of victim activists and advocates. As I discussed in Chapter 3, while a significant increase in disappearances began in 2007, civil society did not begin to mobilize significantly at the state level until 2009 and at the national level until 2011 with the emergence of the Movement for Peace with Justice and Dignity (MPJD). Beginning in 2011, a consistent though shifting coalition of transnational and domestic activists and advocates exerted significant pressure on the Mexican government to investigate and provide redress to victims of disappearance.[6] The adoption of the Victims' Law, which defined the rights of victims of crime and human rights violations and promised them financial assistance, and the creation of the CEAV in 2013 was a response from the government to this pressure. Along with their allies in the Mexican Congress and civil society,[7] the MPJD was the primary advocate for this law. I witnessed the constant strategizing and negotiation between MPJD leaders and members of the Senate who were coordinating to obtain the votes needed, with frequent phone calls and tweaks to the language of the bill to bring additional congresspeople on board. While Calderón had promised to sign the law before leaving office, he demurred and sent the law back to Congress, citing concerns over how the mandate would be funded. Peña Nieto signed the bill into law soon after taking office in January 2013.

The Law on Enforced Disappearance, signed into law in 2017, defines and criminalizes "enforced disappearance" nationwide and requires the immediate investigation and coordination of information needed to search for the missing. Importantly, its full name is the "the General Law on the Enforced Disappearance of Persons, Disappearances Committed by Individuals, and the National Missing Persons System."[8] As the name implies, the law applies to disappearances committed by state and non-state actors—a vital provision given the nature of disappearances in Mexico. The idea for the law originated with the March 2011 visit of the Working Group on

[6] Based on extensive participant observation, and interviews Alejandro Anaya conducted with Alán García, Jaime Rochín, Alejandra Nuño, Pablo Romo, and Angélica de la Peña, and review of the text of numerous proposed reform bills.

[7] Among the key domestic actors who exerted pressure on the government, leading to these legal reforms, were the leaders of the MPJD, most prominently Javier Sicilia and the NGOs Centro Nacional de Comunicación Social (CENCOS) and Servicios y Asesoría para la Paz (Serapaz). They also partnered with other leading national and local human rights NGOs, such as the Centro de Derechos Humanos Miguel Agustín Pro [Centro Prodh], CMDPDH, iDHeas, and the Centro de Derechos Humanos Fray Juan de Larios).

[8] In Spanish, the law's name is "La Ley General en Materia de Desaparición Forzada de Personas, Desaparición Cometida por Particulares y del Sistema Nacional de Búsqueda de Personas."

Enforced and Involuntary Disappearance of the United Nations. Their report recommended that "the offence of enforced disappearance should be included in the criminal codes of all states and that a comprehensive law on enforced or involuntary disappearances should be adopted without delay" (A/HRC/19/58/Add.2; VII., B. 86; p. 17), that there be a reliable registry of the disappeared, and that Mexico implement legal reforms meant to standardize the provision of justice. Victims' collectives spawned by the MPJD had, by 2013, begun to use these recommendations as an organizing tool. Thirty-five victims' collectives, including several made up of Central American mothers looking for their missing migrant children, together with 40 human rights NGOs, formed the "Movement for Our Disappeared" with the singular goal of drafting Enforced Disappearance legislation. In 2015 they carried out a series of forums in different regions affected by violence in Mexico and were supported by the United Nations High Commissioner for Human Rights (UNHCHR).

While I have highlighted the importance of allies within the legal bureaucracy throughout this book, allies have also been key legislatively. Whereas the federal government has acted to deter both of the significant victim-led pieces of legislation, the Senate Human Rights Commission has played a supportive and proactive role. During the debate of the Victims' Law, for example, they organized and hosted forums with advocates, academics, and the UNHCHR to discuss the law's adoption and reform. For the Law on Enforced Disappearance, President Peña Nieto presented his own iteration of the law, which was viewed by civil society advocates as regressive and which omitted many of the key points that civil society valued, including bureaucratic support for searching and a provision for citizen oversight.[9] The Senate Human Rights Commission, however, was tasked with adapting and drafting the proposed legislation in 2016 and negotiated in good faith with the Movement for Our Disappeared. Peña Nieto intervened again to install an attorney general who took aim at some of the provisions that sought to establish legal accountability throughout the judicial bureaucracy and streamline the searching process:[10] however, many of the strengths of the new law

---

[9] Information on the drafting of the Law on Enforced Disappearance draws heavily from March 2018 author interview with Michael Chamberlin, a long-time organizer and participant in this drafting process (Michael Chamberlain, interview by author, New York: March 2018).

[10] For example, the Movement for Our Disappeared had negotiated to have direct access to judges at the time of a disappearance in an effort to bypass the layers of judicial police and investigators who often dragged their feet during the first crucial hours of investigations. The attorney general who Peña Nieto appointed, Raúl Cervantes, eliminated this provision of the law.

that was drafted in concert with the Senate Human Rights Commission remain.

(In)Effectiveness of Legal and Institutional Changes

What have been the results of these laws and judicial bureaucracies? Victims' Attention Centers (CEAVs) and Comisiones de Búsqueda (Search Commissions) now exist in nearly every state, though the resources at their disposal vary greatly. As I have touched on in previous chapters, victims are eligible for resources from the CEAV and Comisiones de Búsqueda only in the jurisdiction where their case is filed. This has created red tape and a new set of incentives for victims to navigate. Because mobilized victims do have some agency in determining where their case will "reside"—they can petition for their case to be transferred to the Federal Unit on Disappearances from the state jurisdiction, for example—they now need to also consider which entity has the most receptive and well-funded CEAV and Comisión de Búsqueda bureaucracy. There has been widespread frustration that CEAV favours some victims over others and has been slow to perform its key function—to disperse financial compensation to the family members of those that have been victims of violence.[11]

The primary goal of the Victims' Law was to allocate resources to people who have been victimized in some way by the drug war. Despite this stated intention, the implementation of the law has fallen short. Only victims whose cases are in the federal system are eligible to receive assistance from the federal CEAV (Commission for Attention to Victims), the state agency charged with implementing the law, leaving most victims in the care of the state-level CEAVs, which often have limited funds and capacity. In addition, the nature of disappearances often effectively excludes many victims from services. For example, a young man from the state of Queretaro went on vacation in Veracruz. While on vacation, he was disappeared and his body was later discovered in Veracruz. His family, under the law, are considered "victims" eligible for benefits, including financial assistance and psychological support. However, CEAV in Queretaro told the family they couldn't help them in any

---

[11] In 2017, CEAV staff successfully promoted a reform of the Victims' Law, with support from the Ministry of the Interior and the Senate. Victim advocates claim these reforms undermine some of the key provisions of the law and have contributed to their overall disillusionment with how CEAV has worked in practice.

way since he had been killed in Veracruz. In Veracruz, the CEAV was happy to assist them—but only for therapy sessions and other benefits rendered within Veracruz—a more than five hours' drive from the family's home. This Kafkaesque system of victim "support" is just one example of hundreds in which state processes that appear to help victims in fact mire them in a web of red tape without benefits.

While the Victims' Law was never designed to fight impunity, the Law on Disappearances and the implementation of the oral/adversarial justice system (the constitutional reform to passed in 2008 and implemented by 2016) were designed to facilitate the prosecution of perpetrators of enforced disappearances as well as disappearances committed by non-state actors. The implementation of the adversarial system remains incomplete and fraught with institutional barriers. A 2019 evaluation report found that

> Entrenched old practices and continued shortcomings in investigative and technical capacity continue to cripple Mexico's efforts to combat violence and corruption and hold government officials accountable for human rights violations. More than 11 years since Mexico passed the 2008 justice reforms, impunity remains the norm. (Hinojosa and Meyer 2019, 9)

While it is perhaps too early to render judgment on the implementation of the 2017 Law on Disappearances, early evidence from states that have had laws against enforced disappearances on the books shows that the barriers to implementing and prosecuting perpetrators under this law will be very difficult to overcome. As I discussed in Chapter 5, victims reported difficulty persuading state officials to classify their report of their missing loved one as "enforced disappearance," preferring instead to register the case as a missing person, kidnapping, or as "illegal deprivation of liberty" even in cases where witnesses clearly identify state actors such as the military or local police as having taken the victims. Despite this, some cases are appropriately registered as "enforced disappearances:" As shown in Table 5.1, according to the Mexican government's own data there were 1,144 reports of enforced disappearances within the state-level justice systems between 2006 and 2018, with just 28 sentences. Within the federal system, there have been only 34 convictions out of 1,121 cases opened for enforced disappearance committed between 2006 and 2018.[12] As Juan Carlos reflected on in Chapter 5, some of

---

[12] Mexican government, National Public Security System. Consulted 199/3/20; Data have since

these unimpressive results in the federal system may be attributable to the scarce resources allocated to the judicial bureaucracy created by this law. The budget allocation to the Search Unit for Disappeared Persons has never exceeded 2 percent of the federal prosecutors' budget and actually decreased in value after 2014, going from $2.1 million in 2014 to $1.4 million in 2017. In comparison, the Organized Crime Investigation unit received 12 percent of the budget in 2017—$103.1 million.[13]

Apart from legislating the ways in which disappearances should be investigated and prosecuted, the Law on Disappearances charges the state with looking for the disappeared in new ways—principally by tasking the Search Commissions with coordinating efforts. This focus on searching has resulted in locating almost 2,000 clandestine graves with the remains of 2,884 bodies and thousands more bone fragments (Guillén et al. 2018)—still a small percentage of the more than 65,0000 disappeared people. Like many other bureaucracies in Mexico, including the state human rights commissions and CEAVs, the performance of state-level Comisiones de Búsqueda vary greatly and depend on both the configuration of the local protection racket, the disposition of state actors, and the funding allotted. I heard anecdotally of both very helpful and utterly useless *comisiones.*

Perhaps the biggest failings of the Disappearances Law concerns producing a single integrated database that tracks all the pieces of information that would be relevant to locating and identifying remains as well as investigating the perpetrators of disappearances, as the law requires. In practice, the data regarding mass graves and the DNA of exhumed bodies has been isolated from the prosecutorial arm of the state. The case file of a disappeared person is held by the state prosecutor's office. If the disappeared person's family members give DNA, this is tracked separately; and if DNA is found in an unmarked grave, matching this DNA with the DNA of families of the disappeared continues to be a struggle. This inefficiency is intentional. Separating data regarding investigations from data about the location and identity of bodies institutionalizes another roadblock to accountability—something that serves to preserve status quo protection rackets.

been removed: https://www.gob.mx/sesnsp/acciones-y-programas/registro-nacional-de-datos-de-personas-extraviadas-o-desaparecidas-rnped.

[13] Original analysis of data from PGR/SIEIDO; see Anaya and Gallagher, forthcoming, for further analysis.

In Sum

These laws have many detractors. Andreas Schedler (2018) wrote:

> I confess I don't see the practical relevance of the [Victims'] Law. It's a rosary of good intentions which ignores the fact that the imposition of the rule of law is a question of power, not a question of positive thinking. It creates and reaffirms an innumerable number of rights on paper and establishes paper bureaucracies to shore up their appearance. Its logic is not political—it's magical. (218)

While I agree that these laws do not address the fundamental asymmetries in power between state and DTO actors and victims, they are a necessary step in addressing the crisis of disappearances. The major legislation promulgated by mobilized victims has created layers of bureaucracy and channeled some resources into victim assistance, investigation, and searching. Prior to these laws, the state was not dedicating resources to the family members affected by the scourge of violence. Enforced disappearance was not a crime on the books in all Mexican states. And there was little to no forensic capacity nor institutional willingness to search for the disappeared.

In a conversation with Yoltzi in 2020, she expressed her frustration that her collective doesn't get any money from the primary federal agencies that give money to victims: because the cases of most of the people in her collective are being investigated in the state, rather than the federal, justice system, they aren't eligible for the larger pots of money at the federal CEAV or Comisión de Busqueda.

Ten years ago, when the family members of Nancy, Juan Carlos and Lucía, and Alfonso disappeared, there was nowhere to turn to demand this assistance. The existence of these laws has given Yoltzi a sense that the state owes her; that she is entitled to assistance as she looks for her sister. Ten years ago, the state was leaning into the narrative that the disappeared were criminals and imputing shame onto their families. While deeply flawed, these laws state an intention to support victims, investigate enforced disappearances, and search for the disappeared. Seen in this context, these are significant—and undoubtedly political, not magical —achievements.

Judicial Outcomes

How has sustained mobilization affected investigations into disappearances? Obtaining reliable data to answer this question is difficult. Despite the aforementioned legislation requiring better information on disappearances, these data are still elusive. Information from state sources registering disappearances, documenting investigatory progress, and giving the public an accurate idea of the number of perpetrators brought to trial, sentenced, and incarcerated remains diffuse and difficult to access or understand. The flourishing of victims' collectives in Mexico has also not resulted in widely available or systematic information about their results. This is due to many factors, including the sensitivity of the information, a lack of resources and knowledge about how to share and systematize information, especially among smaller victim-led collectives, and the absence of a central organization or network that victims' collectives trust to gather and manage this information. Nancy's collective is helpful to think of here: the case results from her collective are organized in cellphone pictures, paper file folders, and summarized in a notebook she keeps with her. This method of record-keeping is no doubt accurate and fairly confidential, but it is difficult for researchers and the larger movement to access.

In prior research (Gallagher 2015; 2017), I presented data comparing the judicial outcomes of cases accompanied by human rights NGOs in Chihuahua and Nuevo León with the larger universe of cases of disappearances and homicides within each state and found that "more than 75 percent of NGO-accompanied cases report concrete investigatory advances as compared to fewer than 35 percent of average cases" (Gallagher 2017, 23). In Chapter 5 I discussed the configurations of state actors, DTOs, and civil society (activists and advocates) that have led to differentiated outcomes. Examining Tamaulipas, I discuss how despite a dangerous organizing environment and a state government that appears to be captured by DTO interests, there have still been successful efforts by victims' collectives and their allies to search for and identify the remains of their loved ones. The exact number of identifications, however, is unknowable as there is no systematic record-keeping, nor record-sharing among the collectives. These collectives place the number of disappeared people whose remains have been identified at between 50 and 150. In Veracruz, few of former attorney general Winckler's convictions obtained through strategic prosecutions remain. The advocates he crowded out of negotiating with the state, and who were inconvenient for his politically driven prosecutions, have returned and continued to search for their loved ones' remains.

In this section I build on these prior results in two ways. First, I return to Nuevo Leon and update the previously analyzed data, allowing me to draw more in-depth conclusions about the possibilities and limits of judicial accountability in Mexico. Second, I discuss at length the data on the outcomes of the three cases profiled throughout this book, ending with a brief reflection of how each of these people have come to define justice after a decade of interacting with the legal system. By looking at judicial outcomes through these two levels of analysis, we see the difficulty of dislodging legal impunity; what is possible with shifting state alliances, allies, and sustained mobilization; and the ways in which these judicial outcomes do (and do not) map onto victims' understandings of what justice is.

Collective Judicial Outcomes

In Chapter 5, I argue that Nuevo León, from 2011 to 2016, had auspicious conditions for eroding impunity. There was instability in state-DTO relations; a perceived ally in the office of the state attorney general; an established advocacy organization with the capacity and willingness to partner with this ally; and an emergent activist organization that exerted continual pressure for accountability. Given these circumstances, Nuevo León 2011–2016 is a crucial case. That is, if there is anywhere we should see the erosion of impunity around disappearances in Mexico, it is in Nuevo León during this time.

The local advocacy organization, Citizens in Support of Human Rights (CADHAC), documented the disappearance of 269 people between 2009 and 2012. Each of these cases was brought to the NGO by a friend or family member of the disappeared person, and CADHAC agreed to accompany cases in which the victims' family member was able to come to regular meetings with other victims of violence and the NGO's staff. Of these 269 disappearances, 37 had a least one indicted perpetrator, and 12 people were found guilty (some of those found guilty were responsible for multiple disappearances). These 37 disappearances occurred in 12 separate events (or cases).[14] Figure 6.1 summarizes all the cases of disappearances that

[14] CADHAC considers cases as crimes, in this case disappearances, that occur in a single event. A "case," therefore, could include a single victim, or many victims. As long as they were disappeared together by the same actors under the same circumstances, they are considered a single case.

	Event	Disappeared Status	Case Status	Legal Registration of Cases
1	4 people disappeared	Still missing	14 members of organized crime indicted	Illegal Deprivation of Liberty with Kidnapping; Organized Crime
2	1 person disappeared	Still missing	2 Members of organized crime indicted	Illegal Deprivation of Liberty
3	1 person disappeared	Still missing	2 municipal police found not guilty	Illegal Deprivation of Liberty with Kidnapping
4	3 people disappeared	Still missing	2 municipal police convicted (1 of which later appealed/overturned)	Illegal Deprivation of Liberty
5	1 person disappeared	Still missing	2 municipal police indicted; 1 in custody	Enforced Disappearance
6	1 person disappeared	Still missing	3 municipal police indicted	Illegal Deprivation of Liberty
7	1 person disappeared	Identified by DNA; family doesn't accept results	3 members of organized crime indicted	*No Information*
8	2 people disappeared	Still Missing	3 municipal police found guilty	Illegal Deprivation of Liberty with Kidnapping; Organized Crime
9	20 disappeared together	3 identified by DNA	7 found guilty, including 6 municipal police	Aggravated Kidnapping
10	1 person disappeared	Identified by DNA	9 indictments	*No Information*
11	1 person disappeared, last scene in state custody	Still missing	4 municipal police indicted, then case was dismissed	Enforced Disappearance
12	1 person disappeared	Still missing	2 municipal police found guilty	Illegal Deprivation of Liberty; Kidnapping; Robbery

Figure 6.1 Judicial results in state-level courts: The 12 cases of disappearances with indictments in Nuevo León 2009–2012

Source: Author analysis of original data provided by CADHAC. Current as of summer 2019.

Presumed Perpetrator of Disappearance, as indicated in CADHAC case file		% of perpetrators out of total identified perpetrators	% of cases also with DTO involvement
Federal Agents	32	15%	
SEDENA (Army)	12	6%	
Marines	9	4%	11%
Federal Police	6	3%	0%
Local Officials	47	22%	28%
Ministerial Police/AEI	27	12%	62%
Organized Crime	124	58%	

Figure 6.2 Probable perpetrator
Source: Analysis of original data

CADHAC documented in which there has been an indictment and/or sentence. Each row contains information from a single disappearance event; the status of the disappeared person or persons; the status of the judicial case; and finally the charges that were filed against the alleged perpetrator(s).

From these results, several patterns are worth noting. First, it is evident that many cases that involve state forces and could be classified as enforced disappearance—and therefore could have been transferred to the federal justice system—are instead being processed in the state-level courts as either kidnapping or illegal deprivation of liberty.

Second, the only state actors we see being indicted here are local official, and specifically municipal police. As can be seen in Figure 6.2, local officials are credibly identified as the perpetrators in 22 percent of cases, and federal forces (marines, federal police and army) in 15 percent of cases.[15] Despite this, 100 percent of the indictments of government employees are members of local (as opposed to federal) security forces. Echoing the strategic prosecutions dynamic, most of these indicted municipal policemen, the lawyers from CADHAC told me, were from a municipality that abuts the

[15] By far the most common perpetrators are members of organized crime, who were involved in 58 percent of cases.

People Found Alive, Same Year	21	8%
People Found Alive, Different Year	2	1%
Remains Identified through DNA	27	10%
Still Missing	213	79%

Figure 6.3 Status of disappeared persons: At least five years after disappearance event 2009–2013: 269 people disappeared
Source: Author analysis of original data

capital and had different DTO allegiances from the municipal police of Monterrey (the capital city). As we might expect, the levels of documented collusion between local state security forces and organized crime—cases for which there was a credible report of both state official and DTO members working together—are much higher than with federal forces: in 28 percent of the cases in which local officials were involved, the case file or interviews with the lawyers indicated that members of DTOs were also involved.

Third, tragically, indicting perpetrators in these cases has not led to the location of the disappeared people in nearly all cases. When disappeared people are identified, it is through DNA. Very few people are found alive. As can be seen in Figure 6.3, this trend—very few people found, and those that are found identified through DNA results—is true for all cases that CADHAC has received. For those disappeared people found alive, while dates were not always available, in nearly every case that listed the date of when a person was found, it was within several days of the disappearance. Said differently, if a person wasn't found alive quite soon after their disappearance, there was less than a 1 percent chance they would be found alive. This conforms with my experience in hundreds of interviews and in years of participant observation: it is incredibly rare to hear of someone being found alive after being disappeared for more than a week.

Individual Cases: Legal Outcomes and Conceptions of Justice

Nancy, Lucía and Alfonso, and Juan Carlos have engaged in sustained mobilization for more than a decade. In this section, I detail what they have discovered about the whereabouts of their loved ones as well as the judicial status of their cases. Their experiences draw into sharp focus the mismatch between aggregate and one-dimensional data on justice in cases of disappearances with victims' own conceptions and evolving understandings of what constitutes a just and meaningful outcome. This section centers the voices of victims in defining their own successes in their struggle against impunity.

Nancy

Fernando, the director of the drug treatment center where Nancy's 17-year-old son disappeared, was sentenced to 45 years for the kidnapping of Elvis Axell in 2014. He recently appealed the conviction, and his sentence was actually increased by the judge to 70 years after reviewing the case. Her son's whereabouts remain unknown.

From the beginning, Nancy felt that Fernando had played a central role in Elvis's disappearance. Despite the initial refusal of officials to investigate him and suspiciously consistent patterns of action in which investigators dropped their inquiry into Fernando after meeting with him, Nancy's persistent efforts finally paid off. As discussed in Chapter 4, Nancy personally participated in a raid on his clinics in 2013. While it seemed that Fernando had again been tipped off that his properties would be searched, SEIDO [the organized crime division of the federal attorney general's office] nonetheless found incriminating items including counterfeit federal police identification with Fernando's picture and an official vest. Upon further investigation, they concluded that Fernando had been impersonating a federal policeman and using this identity to hide his illicit activities, including selling drugs, and covering up two homicides that had occurred in one of his clinics. They finally found Fernando in jail: he had given a false name after being caught stealing a truck and selling drugs while wearing the uniform of a federal investigator.

After he was caught, Fernando again denied any wrongdoing. Patients from his other three clinics, now all closed and dismantled, began to get in touch. They recounted sexual and physical abuse suffered at Fernando's hand as well as the 2011 death of one patient, who died after a severe beating. They heard stories from young women who were sent out to clubs to sell drugs while they were supposedly receiving drug treatment, with their male fellow patients acting as bodyguards. Nancy heard from former patients and clinic staff that Fernando had put Elvis to work washing cars.

For Nancy, Fernando's incarceration was not the end of her search for justice. She has worked tirelessly to compel Fernando to tell her what happened to her son:

> I thought the last thing I had left was to go beg Fernando to tell me where my son is. So, I asked the Attorney General of the State of Mexico to open the door for me and allow me to speak with Fernando. He arranged this, sent me to the national director of prisons, and he instructed the person in charge of where Fernando is being held to give me access. I was treated very well and everything, but when they tried to retrieve Fernando from his cell to bring him, Fernando refused to see me.

Nancy also asked the judge at Fernando's sentencing to let her speak with him; while the judge acceded, Fernando again refused to speak to Nancy. As a final resort, SEIDO and Mexico State offered to "support"[16] Fernando by getting him transferred to a better prison. But still, Fernando has refused to speak with or talk to Nancy.

While Nancy in many ways accepts that her son is probably not alive, the possibility that he may be guides her ongoing activism:

> If in the investigation into my son there is nothing else to do, I have to look for other ways: maybe speaking to Fernando is a dead end, and searching phone records or searching graves hasn't led anywhere—so, then I'm going to publicize [Elvis's photo]—I need everyone to see my son, that in whatever corner there's a flyer pasted on whatever post—so that maybe if my son is homeless wandering around someone recognizes him and lets me know and says "he's here—and worse still, he doesn't even know his name."

Despite Fernando's incarceration, what Nancy understands as "justice"—as I referenced in Chapter 1—still eludes her:

> For many who have found their loved ones are deceased, now they want justice. This is very respectable. For me, my case is upside down. The person who could be held to account—I've already gotten them sentenced. But— how does this help me?

---

[16] Nancy's exact words: "SEIDO and the State of Mexico told me that if I talked to Fernando, I could even offer him 'support,' in inverted commas, right? I mean, I can't help him out, but I could help him transfer to a better area [of the prison]."

I've been looking for my son for seven years. Today, I don't seek justice—it's already there, but I did not seek it. I forgave this man long ago. . . . I tried to go look for him [my son] in so many ways: marches, sit-ins, searches, looking for clandestine graves, SEMEFO, prisons, clinics, annexes. I went to places where the destitute live, drug dens—and I can't find him anywhere.

I felt like the lawyers were saying to me "Look señora—look what we achieved!" But I answered them—"And? And my son? Where is my son?" It doesn't help me that this man is locked up—I have forgiven him. I am looking for justice; I am looking for my son.

When I prompted Nancy to tell me more about her collective, she humbly told me of their accomplishments when I pushed. The victims' collective she established has found seven people alive and located the remains of six others. Nancy attributes their success in finding those alive to their innovative methods: they have disguised themselves and gone to bars, for example, to try to find young people they suspect may have been trafficked. At the request of one of the mothers who joined their group, they searched a residence where they suspected her daughter may have been taken. Her daughter had gone to an interview and later been held against her will—and was found alive.[17] In another case, a father had taken his two young daughters, changed their names, and been on the run within Mexico with the children. The group was able to track the children down. In other cases, Nancy doesn't know exactly what happened—only that people were found alive.[18] For those whose remains they have found, four were killed by their spouses. Two young women were taken by a gang, who then used their cell phones to ask for ransom for five other people they had disappeared.

Apart from looking for those who are missing, Nancy's collective has committed to focusing on preventive measures. "Right now, our motto is 'what happened to me happens to you too.' We already have a list of prevention

---

[17] At the residence, they also found another woman had been hiding out: she had become pregnant with her abusive boyfriend's child and wanted to hide her pregnancy from her mother. While she initially went to the residence, essentially a boarding house, willingly, she was later not permitted to leave—and was not heard from for a year. She finally had an opportunity to escape when her infant son became ill and she was allowed to take him to the hospital. While at the hospital, she alerted hospital staff that she and her son were being held against their will. Hospital staff then contacted PGR.

[18] Another woman who had worked with the collective and then located her daughter was very vague—she told Nancy that she (the mother) needed to stop working with their collective immediately because it was key to getting her loved one returned. Another group participant called to advise Nancy: "We found my niece! Thank you! I'll be in touch"; but Nancy never heard from her again. Nancy reports that after finding their loved ones alive, nearly everyone stops communicating with the collective.

measures for people of different ages, from a baby to an elderly person. We are working with the CEAV of the State of Mexico to make some [ad campaigns]." Nancy's group has also asked the state to create a central office in EdoMex where all forensic information would be centralized: all identified remains, from the entire country, would be registered there, so that EdoMex residents looking for their loved one would have one place to go to find remains.

Lucía and Alfonso
In the case of Alejandro's disappearance, eight members of the Zetas cartel were charged with "illegal deprivation of liberty" in the federal justice system. However, they were all found not guilty. Three members of the Zetas have been most closely linked to some level of involvement in Alejandro's disappearance, and they are incarcerated for their involvement in other crimes. Alejandro's whereabouts remain unknown.

As I discussed in Chapter 4, Lucía and Alfonso's strategy has centered on meeting with as many state officials as possible in search of truth and justice in Alejandro's disappearance. These meetings have undeniably generated a plethora of paperwork—but what have they learned from this extensive paper trail and analysis? Three members of the Zeta DTO are thought to be responsible for Alejandro's disappearance, and there is some testimony indicating that he was subsequently killed. The three haven't been consistent in their levels of cooperation with the investigation nor their explanation for why Alejandro was taken.

- Enrique Aurelio Elizondo Flores, aka El Arabe, is a lower-level operative with the Zetas and the only person associated with the case who admits taking part in Alejandro's disappearance. El Arabe told investigators that he had initially questioned Alejandro since he was visibly an outsider: Alejandro's accent and whole look (he was dressed professionally when he was disappeared) indicated he wasn't from the north. El Arabe says that after he questioned Alejandro, a higher-ranking Zeta, El Chabelo, talked to him, and then he was taken away to be killed. While not convicted in Alejandro's disappearance, in 2015, El Arabe was sentenced to 186 years in prison for killing more than 75 people in Nuevo León and Tamaulipas, including passengers taken off of buses in Reynosa, Tamaulipas in 2011 (Mosso 2015).

- Marco Garza de León Quiroga, aka El Chabelo, a top Zetas leader in northeastern Mexico, allegedly gave the order to a lower-level assassin (El Indio) to kill Alejandro and burn his body. Several witnesses claim to have subsequently seen Chabelo driving Alejandro's car around Tamaulipas, though he denies this. He was indicted in the federal judicial system for his involvement in the illegal deprivation of liberty in Alejandro's case, as well as collaboration with organized crime and arms possession. He was detained in October 2011, and while he wasn't convicted in Alejandro's disappearance, he is currently incarcerated for charges related to the 2010 murder of 72 migrants in San Fernando, Tamaulipas, and the death of 52 people in Casino Royale in Monterrey (Al Jazeera 2011).
- Miguel Ángel Andrade Martínez, aka El Indio, was accused by El Arabe as the person who actually killed Alejandro. El Indio was previously incarcerated, during which time he admitted to other crimes and was accused by the Nuevo León prosecutors' office of dissolving the remains of more than 50 people—but he completely denied his involvement in Alejandro's disappearance. He was killed while in prison in Monterrey in 2013 (Ramos 2012).

In addition to their involvement in Alejandro's disappearance, El Chabelo and El Arabe are accused of beheading two federal policeman with the support of the municipal police. This killing, according to Francisco Romero, the MPJD pro bono lawyer and *co-ayudvante* in their case, led the army to pursue El Chabelo, and to bring about his eventual detention. The murder of these federal policemen was prosecuted simultaneously with Alejandro's case—something that Romero believes confused the judge and the prosecution and led to them being found not guilty for Alejandro's disappearance.

At times, there have appeared to be other breaks in the case: a woman was found to be using Alejandro's cell phone (an expensive iPhone) in Southern Mexico—but it couldn't be traced past a flea market where it had been purchased in Tamaulipas. There were some leads on finding Alejandro's car—but again, this ultimately was a dead end. Atala Chavez, the psychologist who also works pro bono with various victims' collectives and is the second *co-ayudvante* on the case, worked with federal officials to conduct drone surveillance of several ranches in northern Mexico with the hope of finding evidence of either human remains or of people being held. While they found evidence of human remains, the security situation was too difficult to send troops in. Lucía recounted how "when Chabelo was detained, Alfonso asked—why don't you send him to the federal penitentiary [as opposed to holding him in a state jail]? And he succeeded in getting him transferred [to a federal prison]. And they got him to say where the *narco cocina*[19] was. And from there, the PGR found a lot of remains." This also happened with El Árabe: once detained, he revealed the location of other *narco cocinas*. None of these investigatory advances, however, have led to the discovery of Alejandro's remains. This has compelled Lucía and Alfonso to keep looking.

For Lucía and Alfonso, their motivations and successes most closely reflect Wood's conception of "pleasure in agency." When analyzing why peasants in El Salvador participated in revolutionary movements, she argues that they rebelled "in order to defy long-resented authority, to repudiate perceived injustices . . . and to assert, and thereby to constitute – their dignity" (Wood 2002, 143). The vestiges of the "before the law" perspective the couple had before their son's disappearance have shaped their conception of what dignifying their son's memory means. The ability to access the most elite members of the state, including two presidents, and to wrangle the members of the federal prosecutors office to devote attention to their case: to them, this is their rebellion against the betrayal of the state to do as it promises to do, and in this rebellion, they imbue their son's disappearance with meaning and dignity. Identifying the probable perpetrators has brought them some satisfaction, and the feeling that they have exhausted the state's resources brings them some measure of peace. That they have not located Alejandro, however, continues to plague them. Without this, they both say "there is not justice."

Juan Carlos

In the case of the four disappeared Herrera Trujillo brothers, the results have been the most limited in terms of the investigation of those responsible. For the first disappearance, of Raúl and Salvador in 2008 from Atoyac Guerrero, Raúl's dancer friend and the bartender were briefly detained but then released without charges. The Trujillo Herrera family believes there are two possible scenarios: the bar owner and dancer orchestrated the robbery/disappearance, or their disappearance was part of revenge taken by the local aggrieved DTO. In early September 2008, just a week after Raúl and Salvador were

---

[19] Literally, "narco kitchen": colloquially refers to the ovens that DTOs were using to incinerate bodies after homicides.

disappeared, the truck they were traveling in was found burned. According to Centro ProDH, no forensic analysis was ever conducted on this truck.

In the case of the disappearance of Gustavo and Luis Armando in 2010 from Veracruz, there are no suspects nor any leads. When Juan Carlos obtained the investigative case file for Gustavo and Luis Armando several years after their disappearance was reported, the only thing in the case file was a photo of the antenna of the cell tower which his brothers' cell phone had last pinged off of. Juan Carlos, together with Anais Palacios, the law student from Veracruz, started to analyze the pattern of violence in Veracruz at the time of the disappearance, looking at which municipal police were collaborating with which DTOs. Their results, at the time of this writing, have been minimal.

While the results in their personal cases have been limited, Juan Carlos and his family have been at the forefront of several groundbreaking changes in how the families of the disappeared pursue justice and how Mexico's human rights community approaches disappearances. In 2008 through 2011, Juan Carlos accompanied his mother, and sometimes his brother Miguel, to endless meetings with state officials of all levels. After he came to the conclusion that this wasn't serving him or his disappeared brothers well, Juan Carlos devoted himself to physically searching for his brothers: dead or alive; by carrying their pictures throughout Mexico, the United States and Europe; and through searching for bone fragments and DNA evidence. These efforts coalesced into the creation of both Familias en Búsqueda María Herrera, the Herrera family's own collective dedicated to searching for the remains of their loved ones, and in 2012 the Red de Enlaces, which now brings together more than 164 organizations, including the collective Nancy leads, and thousands of family members searching for their loved ones. As of early 2020, the two organizations had organized five *caravanas de búsqueda*, search caravans, weeks-long citizen-led efforts to search for bodies and bone fragments in clandestine sites. It was on one of these caravans that they met Yoltzi. In the first two citizens' search caravans they did in Veracruz, they did not find the bodies of the Herrera brothers—though they did find 1,200 bone fragments and six identifiable bodies.

As Juan Carlos realized he wanted to devote himself to searching for his brothers and not to learning more about how to be a lawyer, he sought an organization that would provide him with legal accompaniment. As discussed previously, Centro ProDH is among the oldest and most prominent human rights organizations in the country. Until the disappearance of the

Trujillo-Herrera brothers, they had always taken on the litigation of cases in which state agents were clear perpetrators. In 2016, following the Ayotzinapa disappearances, they decided to accede to Juan Carlos's and his mother's request that they become the lawyers on their case[20] and also accompany their work in the Red de Enlaces. Their lead lawyer at ProDH explained how ProDH thinks about the people they accompany:

> We understand them as "political subjects." They walk, and we follow. Sometimes we go to meetings together, and sometimes they're pulling us. This is super important for pushing the case forward.[21]

By delegating the legal accompaniment of his case to Centro ProDH, Juan Carlos has been able to focus on seeking what he understands as justice. He told me:

> Yes, we are making advances, but there is a sickly dehumanization of violence in this country . . . which means the only way to find justice—to truly *know* justice—is to know the truth of what happened . . . and the only way to get this is to work together.

Juan Carlos recognizes his own growth: he has learned to calm down a bit, to delegate tasks, to "be more analytical, and not run around like a crazy person," in his words. When I met with him in August 2021, he was living outside of Mexico City with his large extended family, including his six children. After leaving the gold business, he started a new business running junkyards—he currently has 10, with 32 employees. He sees himself as wiser—and spoke of his activism as a result of the following choice: "You change the country, or it changes you. You decide." He is comfortable with the choice he has made.

* * *

---

[20] When ProDH took over the case, they essentially needed to start the investigation into all four brothers from the beginning. They obtained the investigatory tomes from SEIDO, and combined them with the 9 investigatory tomes from Veracruz, and the 8 from Guerrero. ProDH, at the time of this writing, was attempting to get the case admitted to the United Nations Committee on Enforced Disappearances (CED).

[21] For Juan Carlos, even as his case has been taken up by Centro ProDH, he is critical of their predominant model, which is to accompany a small number of "paradigmatic" legally and politically important cases. In his words, "I don't like the talk that [my case] is a paradigmatic case. I think every mother, every family who has someone disappeared is a paradigmatic case—because it's all the same pain. I want people to understand—the help that is for me is really for the entire society."

In sum, while the practice of injustice is tenacious in Mexico, the experience of collective challenges to legal impunity suggest ways of moving the needle forward. CADHAC's experiences show that under auspicious conditions—a high-ranking institutional ally, a determined advocacy organization, an activist organization demanding accountability, decreasing DTO violence—it is possible to indict and convict some perpetrators, including local members of the state security apparatus. It is unlikely, however, that the crime on the books will indicate that they are being held legally accountable for a disappearance. And while local state officials, in particular municipal police, are vulnerable to prosecution, implicated federal officials appear untouchable.

For each individual profiled in this book, their path has led them to significant, and at the same time deeply unsatisfactory, results. The disappearance of each of their loved ones has been investigated to a much greater extent than an average case in Mexico. Nancy has the most measurable success in these terms: the perpetrator of her son's disappearance is incarcerated for his role in that crime. For Lucía and Alfonso, the three Zeta members implicated in Alejandro's disappearance are dead or behind bars—though not for crimes associated with Alejandro's disappearance. For Juan Carlos, while he feels he understands what happened to his bothers, no perpetrators have been punished.

These individual case results do not line up with the understandings of justice for each of these individuals. Nancy wants to know where her son is—something that hasn't been achieved by the conviction of the perpetrator. She finds meaning in working on behalf of others going through what she went through. Lucía and Alfonso find satisfaction in having a solid idea of what happened to Alejandro and dignity in having the attention of powerful people and institutions focused on their son's fate. Juan Carlos accepts that he may never know what happened to his brothers, but he finds meaning and a road to justice and dignity in searching for them and others. For each of them, what started as a quest for answers and accountability within the formal legal system has led them to develop other means of achieving what they understand as justice.

Scaffolding the Struggle Against Impunity: Movement Outcomes and Feedback Effects

Ten years ago, there was no victims' movement in Mexico. Since then, more than 100 collectives in most Mexican states have emerged. In this section,

I reflect on how these developments in social movement organizing which I reviewed throughout this book have changed the available mobilizing resources and repertoires of contention for victims' collectives; social attitudes toward the disappeared; and the networks of psycho-social support available to victims. I use the story of Yoltzi, whom I introduced at the beginning of this chapter, to frame these changes. The movement environment she encountered in 2019 offers a sharp contrast to the early experiences of Nancy, Lucía and Alfonso, and Juan Carlos discussed in Chapters 2 and 4.

After joining the Fourth Brigade on the spot when she encountered Familias en Búsqueda in 2019, Yoltzi decided that she wanted to continue to participate actively in searching for her sister and others, and also to share what she was learning with others in her situation. When I spoke with her about a year after she first encountered Familias, she had already founded a victims' collective and organized 35 families who are searching for their loved ones. After spending two weeks in Veracruz, she planned to lead her own collective's search for bodies in clandestine graves near their home in Acapulco and Zihuatenejo, two cities in the state of Guerrero.

When I asked Yoltzi to describe the work of her collective early in 2020, she told me that they "do the whole process." For her, there is a clear and defined set of actions she understands as constituting the work of victims' collectives. They accompany people to report their cases in the local prosecutors' office. They engage in participatory investigations with state officials—at the time of our interview, they had held two meetings with them. They do forensic searches in unmarked graves, often working with other collectives and sharing results. And they conduct *búsquedas en vivo*, they search to find people alive. In these *búsquedas en vivo*, they regularly go to jails, where they are both looking for the people who have been disappeared and also for anyone who might have information about what happened to them. They also search in medical and psychiatric hospitals, in drug treatment centers, and among homeless people. They gather in town centers with large photos of their loved ones, hoping someone has seen them. They also attend marches.

Embedded in Yoltzi's account is also a strikingly clear understanding of the available repertoires of contention for those with a disappeared family member. As she ticked off the "whole process" her collective engages in—state engagement; forensic and on-the-ground searching; various forms of mobilization—I was struck by the common sense (Wolford 2006) in this narrative, but also how entirely new it was. In 2011 and 2012, when Nancy,

Juan Carlos and Lucía, and Alfonso were in the early stages of responding to their loved ones' disappearances—all of these forms of mobilization were not common sense. Rather, each action that Yoltzi had quickly learned to include in her contentious repertoire had been tried and adjusted and shared among mobilized victims as they learned what was effective and what was not in the course of their sustained mobilization, and as their thinking about themselves and legality evolved. .

Society's receptiveness to the strategies Yoltzi was employing had also shifted markedly: 10 years ago, mobilized victims were not regularly invited to speak about their experiences. They were criminalized by the state, and many families internalized the shame imputed on them by the state, and as a result were reluctant to speak about their disappeared loved ones. The 2011 MPJD mobilization gained such resonance in part because it provided an outlet for the outrage of those who had endured the aspersions cast on their disappeared loved ones. Yoltzi cited this sense of shame as a reason for not coming forth sooner about her sister's disappearance. By 2020, however, sustained mobilization, along with sympathetic members of the media, had managed to challenge this culture of blame and the practice of blaming and criminalizing victims. Apart from searching for their loved ones, members of the collective Yoltzi are regularly invited to local universities and churches to talk about what it's like to be a family member of someone who has been disappeared; to urge young people to help; and to educate them on what it means not to "revictimize" people directly affected by violence. She teaches people not to say "Oh—that girl, she'll be back, she probably just ran off with her boyfriend . . ." when they hear about a disappearance. For Yoltzi, this is part of the work that needs to be done to make sure such treatment doesn't happen to others: "We're trying to create solidarity among the youth. . . . We have forgotten what happened in the 1970s, which is part of why it's happening again today. We ask for the authorities to be sensitive to us—but sometimes we aren't sensitive among ourselves."

Yoltzi plans to continue to mobilize, though she didn't hesitate to tell me what this has cost her. Like Nancy and Juan Carlos, searching for her sister has put her job at risk. To participate in the Search Brigade, Yoltzi asked for time off from her government job working at a local library. They didn't grant this to her and she wasn't sure she would have a job when she returned home.

I asked her why, despite the risk to her livelihood, she continues to organize, and what she has learned from working with the other victims' collectives. She told me she doesn't feel it is a choice:

I didn't ask to be a victim. I'm a woman—and I *decide* to be a woman because I have right to choose my gender. I *decide* to be a citizen. But I *did not
decide* to be a victim. And as a victim—I have to struggle to live.

Conclusion

When the crisis of disappearances began in Mexico in the late 2000s, there was
little legal, institutional, judicial, or movement capacity equipped to handle
the investigation of these cases or to support the family members of people
who had been disappeared. As I discussed in Chapter 3, the very concept of
disappearances in their current modality did not exist: disappearances were
a type of violence used by state forces during the Dirty War against radicals.
As disappearances began to be a common modality of violence in Mexico's
drug war, and the Mexican state became increasingly fragmented, it became
clear to family members of those being disappeared just how alone they
were. Through thousands of personal processes similar to the ones Nancy,
Lucía and Alfonso, and Juan Carlos went through, groups of family members
began to mobilize throughout Mexico. By 2018, incoming president Lopez
Obrador identified these victims' collectives as the most important voice for
human rights and justice in Mexico.

While victims' collectives have undoubtedly gained political force, this
chapter details some of the ways they have made institutional inroads within
the Mexican state's legal, judicial, and bureaucratic structures as well as the
somewhat intangible shifts in the organizing and movement environment.
While this book is largely about the ways that laws on paper do not automatically translate into practice, I argue that the two major pieces of legislation spurred by the victims' movement—the 2013 Victims' Law and
the 2017 Law on Disappearances—are an important and necessary part of
shifting legal norms around the worthiness of victims as political subjects.
These laws have also led to resources being channeled to the families of the
disappeared. While the bureaucracies these laws created are flawed, creating
these legal entitlements is an important material and symbolic step toward
accountability.

I next reviewed some of the judicial results of cases accompanied by the
leading human rights NGO in Nuevo León as well as the cases of the individuals profiled in this book. Perhaps one of the most marked results in
this section is the scarcity of available data: because of the illegibility and

unavailability of judicial outcomes data, systematic comparison of cases of disappearances is not possible. The data in this section, gathered from close personal involvement with CADHAC's database and with the individuals profiled, does demonstrate that with exhaustive effort and auspicious conditions, it is possible to make meaningful progress on the right to justice. As for Nancy, Juan Carlos and Lucía and Alfonso, I share their reflections on what "justice" means to them—and for all, it is quite distinct from the formal legal processes involved in sentencing the perpetrators of their loved ones' disappearances.

I used the disappearance of Yatzil Martinez Corrales, and her sister Yoltzi's subsequent mobilization, as a way to take stock of just how far the victims' movement has come. Yoltzi was able to learn mobilizing tactics, tap into existing networks of organized victims' collectives, advocate for public education around supporting victims of disappearances, understand how to lead her own collective, and develop a sense of self-efficacy and entitlement that would have been unthinkable 10 years ago.

Taken together, these achievements—pioneering legislation, state resources for victims, convictions and finding some disappeared people within the context of generalized impunity, and movements with significant capacities—have meaningfully eroded impunity by advancing the realization of the right to truth, justice and reparations. These modest but meaningful developments attest to the power of sustained mobilization to enable victims to become if not full rights-bearing citizens, citizens who enjoy greater rights than would have been possible, or perhaps even imaginable, 10 years ago. They are a tribute to the arduous work motivated by deep suffering of an untold number of people whose loved ones remain disappeared.

7

Conclusion

> "For disappearances to end, justice must begin."
> —The Washington Office on Latin America (WOLA) campaign
> slogan, 2021

Figuring out how to study violence and its many related maladies, including impunity, can be overwhelming and fraught. Violence and impunity are arguably the most pressing political, human rights, and public health issues in Mexico—as well as in many countries struggling with lethal violence. The impact of impunity, in particular, is devastating not only to victims of violence and their families, but to society at large as it erodes accountability, trust, and the rule of law. Impunity also disarms the state of perhaps its most important deterrent against violent crime.

Since impunity is clearly such a dire problem, it begs the question: why hasn't more progress been made? By many measures, there has been an immense effort over the past decade to address impunity in in Mexico. Mexico has overhauled its judicial institutions (at great cost to both Mexico and the United States), transitioning from a written to an oral, adversarial system of justice. Mexico's Constitutional Court has elevated the authority of international law, giving it a privileged place in Mexico's legal order that, in theory, overrides Mexico's own constitution. At the same time, a large and powerful trans-national advocacy network has mobilized in response to disappearances demanding justice—most notably in the aftermath of the disappearance of the 43 students from Ayotzinapa. These efforts have resulted in passing historic, if flawed, national legislation both to provide a form of reparations to victims of drug war violence (2013 Victims' Law), and to increase the state's capacity to respond effectively to disappearances (2017 Disappearances Law).

And yet, despite these efforts, impunity appears as bad as ever. The number of disappearances continues to rise, and the state's ability to respond,

Bootstrap Justice. Janice k. Gallagher, Oxford University Press. © Oxford University Press 2023.
DOI: 10.1093/oso/9780197649978.003.0007

document, investigate, and punish those responsible remains abysmal. When I began this project over a decade ago, I focused on understanding the institutional and social movement context and changes, which, I expected and hoped, would meaningfully shift impunity outcomes.[1] I thought this book would be about the importance of institutional reform, or international human rights organizations, or networks of movements in breaking through the wall of impunity.

Instead, I realized that there was a different, and still important, book to be written. Over the course of a decade, I had seen a tenacious commitment by some family members of the disappeared to grapple with impunity on a nearly daily basis. To fight to claim every bit of land amid the sea of impunity—within every level and branch of Mexico's broad judicial bureaucracy. Those islands they did manage to claim—locating and identifying the remains of a deceased person; managing to indict a perpetrator; getting the state to recognize their rights as victims—while humble, were the only solid ground being won in the battle against impunity.

This book endeavors to tell this story: of how those most affected by impunity—family members of people whose loved ones are disappeared—became rights-claiming, and ultimately rights-bearing citizens. I focus on the ways of thinking and being of three families prior to their loved ones' disappearances (Chapter 2); the context of violence, institutional atrophy, and scarce mobilizing resources that they confronted (Chapter 3); the shifts in their ways of thinking and acting as they looked for their loved ones and as they joined with others to form common strategies (Chapter 4); the ways this growing sophistication in perceiving and responding to different political and security opportunities mapped onto collective strategies in three very different contexts (Chapter 5); and finally, the ways in which these organizing strategies have combated impunity, achieving legislative, institutional, judicial, and movement progress, and moving the needle on the right to truth, justice, and reparations in Mexico (Chapter 6). The inroads against impunity are a paradox: both devastatingly insignificant compared to the scale of the problem and the need; and also the most significant advances made by any group in society on a momentous problem.

---

[1] I spent countless hours operationalizing impunity by trying to nail down the numbers of cases of disappearances and their judicial status. I developed a 5-step judicial status classification rubric (Gallagher 2017), which categorized cases according to how far they had progressed in the legal system (and steering us away from all-or-nothing understandings of judicial results).

In the broadest sense, this book argues that impunity—an outcome long considered to lie within the domain of formal legal institutions—has been meaningfully challenged by the sustained mobilization of the family members of the disappeared over the past decade. In their endless meetings with state officials, they have incrementally learned more about what happened to their loved ones, advancing the right to truth. Through their independent investigatory actions—interviewing those who may have seen their disappeared loved ones; pushing the state to check within its jails and hospitals for their loved ones; and searching for their loved ones alive or dead—they have inched forward investigations that would otherwise most certainly be stalled, thus advancing the right to justice. They have worked collectively to pass legislation obligating the state to recognize and finan-cially remunerate direct and indirect victims of violence, advancing the right to reparation.

The right to non-recurrence—that is, the obligation that states have to guarantee that human rights violations do not recur—has proved to be the most difficult to meaningfully advance, shown most tragically in the steady increases in disappearances since 2006. The government's own sta-tistics document over 23,000 disappeared people between 2018 and 2020.[2] While the victims' movement is largely responsible for the groundbreaking 2017 legislation that calls for vital, concrete steps to avoid disappearances—searching immediately for those who are disappeared; clearly and transpar-ently documenting cases in order to detect patterns—it has, unsurprisingly, scarcely been implemented. The reasons for this are both infinitely complex and obvious. In Chapter 5, I argue that when state alliances are stable and state officials operate cynically, impunity will almost certainly be the out-come. That is—I argue that the status quo equilibrium in Mexico is impu-nity, and that while there are ways to disrupt this, the normal operation of institutions guarantees that crimes will not be investigated; perpetrators will not be punished; and no steps will be taken to provide redress to victims or to prevent disappearances in the future. Insofar as violence responds to incentives, until impunity is not the status quo, deterrence will be difficult. As WOLA's recent human rights campaign puts it: "For disappearances to end, justice must begin."

---

[2] WOLA's s analysis shows that in the 15 states that reported their statistics on disappearances between 2018 and 2020, charges were filed against private citizens in 195 of 14,500 cases, with 25 convictions. The statistics for cases of *enforced* disappearances are even worse: only 11 state agents were convicted (WOLA 2021).

Contributions

Methodological

While this book is about impunity—it is also implicitly about how to study, think, and write about diffuse and chaotic, but vitally important, outcomes. My true north in this project has been to center the voice and central question of the victims. Their quest to find out *dónde están*, where are they, focused my inquiry on the fate of cases of disappearances in Mexico. This narrow topic allowed me to take a thin, steep slice, analytical approach. By tightly defining the topic of interest, I made space for an in-depth examination of overlapping and interacting layers of analysis. To show how these different levels of analysis interact and inform each other, I implicitly organized the book as a crescendo and converging between disparate levels of analysis. I start with chapters at opposite ends of the unit-of-analysis spectrum: in Chapter 2, I tell the backstories of the three families profiled in the book and follow them as their prior outlooks shape the way they initially react to the disappearance of their loved ones. In Chapter 3, I situate the struggle against impunity within the broader regional, national, and historical context, and discuss the changing nature of legal opportunities in Mexico. In Chapter 4, I put the three families' stories in relation to one another theoretically and in practice, tracing their increasing convergence in thought and action as they continue to mobilize and engage with social movements. In Chapter 5, I follow these social movements as they forge allies (and sometimes make enemies) with individuals within the state judicial bureaucracy and navigate the local political terrain of shifting political and criminal dynamics. The book ends by integrating these disparate levels of analysis (Chapter 6), discussing what has been achieved by those struggling to end impunity in the legal, institutional, judicial, and movement realms. This converging multi-level approach allows us to understand how micro and macro politics affect each other—the mechanisms through which individuals join movements that then shape policies and systemic outcomes, and the ways in which those polices, in turn, impact individuals and movements. The result is a more integrated, holistic, and robust understanding of the vexing problem of impunity in cases of disappearances in Mexico. Built on 10+ years of evidence, including interviews with the families involved conducted years apart, and longitudinal organizational ethnographies, the evidence gained temporal depth and dynamism.

Conceptual

The concept of sustained mobilization draws from and bridges literatures on individual political participation and collective mobilization. There are two main theoretical takeaways: first, by focusing on the mechanisms and processes that explain how and why individuals come to engage in long-term mobilization, I capture the common but under-studied reality of people entering and exiting different organizations and social movements while simultaneously engaging in independent advocacy during the course of their political trajectories. I am able to analyze how and why their strategies of interacting with the state evolve over time, providing a dynamic theoretical framework that grounds our understandings of collective mobilization in individuals' experiences, growth, and consciousness. While social movements scholarship (Della Porta and Mattoni 2015; McAdam 2010; Tarrow 2011) has provided extensive tools for understanding the emergence of collective mobilization—and regards the "sustained interaction with elites, opponents and authorities"[3] as part of the accepted definition of social movements—consideration of why certain individuals (and not others) mobilize has been left largely to scholars of political participation. By conducting a longitudinal study and bringing in concepts from the legal consciousness and mobilization literature (Ewick and Silbey 1998; Marshall and Barclay 2003; McCann 1994), I make the novel argument that trauma—in this case the disappearance of a loved one—may reconfigure the way people think about themselves and their relationships to others, and to the law. I show how disappearances inspire sustained mobilization and provide the fuel for ongoing struggle, and I demonstrate that ongoing interactions with state officials both inspire and require changes in thinking on the part of the victims themselves.

Second, the contentious politics literature (Tilly 1977; McAdam et al. 2001) usually understands repertoires of contention as comprising visible and public actions: protests; sit-ins; armed resistance. I argue that the bulk of time, energy, and substantive political negotiation that occur over the long period of sustained interaction between elites and victims is quotidian: private meetings between low-level investigators and victims; text messages and calls between and among victims and the different organizations and officials

---

[3] Tarrow (1998) defines social movements as "collective challenges, based on common purposes and social solidarities in *sustained interaction* with elites, opponents, and authorities."

they interact with. These seemingly mundane interactions, which I refer to as claim-making, have material consequences on the provision of justice—a significant outcome for scholars of judicial politics and democratic governance. These findings go to the heart of studies of state-society relations and most closely echo those of Kruks-Wisner (2018), who similarly shows the ways that citizens in India make claims on the state for social welfare—and in so doing, meaningfully shape who receives the scarce resources of the state.[4]

My attention to impunity builds on and contributes to our understandings of criminal governance. Recent works (Arias 2017; Durán-Martinez 2018; Moncada 2016; Trejo and Ley 2020) argue that impunity within protection rackets (Snyder and Durán-Martinez 2009)[5] is the key benefit the state guarantees its criminal allies. If criminals fear they will be prosecuted for their illicit activities, this is an existential threat to their ability to conduct business, control territory, and live freely. Within this literature, impunity is nearly always understood as both automatic and binary: when there are stable protection rackets, there is total impunity; when the protection racket is destabilized, impunity ruptures and prosecutions occur. I complicate this understanding by unpacking impunity as an outcome and specifying the mechanisms involved in determining these diverse outcomes. There are both different *types* of impunity (no prosecution; no information; prosecution only of political enemies), and different *degrees* of impunity. I argue that organized victims and/or state agents take strategic action based on the perceived local political opportunities and that when they can locate allies within the state, or perceive that there are cracks in the alliances within and between the state and DTOs, there will be some degree of impunity erosion. This understanding of impunity calls into question the assumption that broken protection rackets automatically lead to prosecution by inserting civil society action, a diverse array of state actors, and the underlying institutional and political environment as consequential actors and factors.

---

[4] Claim-making is the focus of Gallagher et al. (forthcoming), entitled "Beyond Ballots and Barricades, the Everyday Politics of Claim-Making."

[5] Protection rackets are defined as the "informal institutions through which public officials refrain from enforcing the law or, alternatively, enforce it selectively against the rivals of a criminal organization, in exchange for a share of the profits generated by the organization" (Snyder and Durán-Martinez 2009, 254).

Broader Implications

O'Donnell (1993) recognized Mexico (along with Brazil) as a case of "high territorial and functional heterogeneity." That is, a country in which that state is "unable to enact effective regulations of social life across their territories" (1993: 9). Mexico, in O'Donnell's view, was rife with "brown areas," areas in which despite the presence of elections, parties and legislatures, effective bureaucracy, and "properly sanctioned legality" were scarce (1993: 9). He cautioned that many new democracies have extensive brown areas— which "severely curtails" citizenship (1993: 15). While this book is focused on Mexico, its lessons for how citizens seek to claim and bear rights when faced with state absence, incompetence, and capture are instructive for all states that contain brown areas—including certain parts of the United States in which impunity for homicides, for example, is common.[6] In countries struggling to implement the rule of law throughout their territory, this book maps the bottom-up processes through which citizens seek to bridge the gap between promised and practiced rights.

Implications for Policymakers and Funders

This book redirects scholars and policymakers—who often address problems of injustice with top-down solutions—to a grassroots-led vision of impunity erosion. Whether passing new legislation, training judges and prosecutors in the operations of an adversarial justice system, or seeking to strengthen human rights through international treaties and constitutional reforms, this book inserts an analysis of power and the state into these discussions. This is not an argument against the relevance and importance of formal reforms to state institutions and treaty commitments. Rather, it is a call to consider the incentives, dispositions, and positionality of all the stakeholders in the judicial process, including the victims.

At base, the suggestion of this book is that it is vital to support the victims' collectives and small human rights organizations that are doing the arduous

---

[6] There are pockets of impunity in states that we may think of as high-performing judicially. In a 2018 report, for example, the *Washington Post* identified areas within US cities with exceptionally high impunity rates for homicide: "Some cities, such as Baltimore and Chicago, solve so few homicides that vast areas stretching for miles experience hundreds of homicides with virtually no arrests" (Lowery 2018).

and dangerous work of challenging impunity. Since strengthening the pro-vision of justice and rule of law is a central objective for many governments (particularly the US government) and non-governmental foundations and initiatives, and given these findings, how might these organizations produc-tively intervene in the Mexico's crisis of disappearances?

The most common form of support for these local victims' collectives and human rights organizations is financial assistance. To begin the discus-sion of the impact of financial support on local non-state organizations, take the example of one of the leading victim-led human rights organizations in Chihuahua. The organization has been able to pay rent for a modest office in downtown Chihuahua City and pay a staff of about five people to sup-port their advocacy work. They have received modest grants from several small foundations, including the Global Fund for Women and the Angelica Foundation as well as from the larger Avon Foundation. They have also re-ceived a small grant from the US embassy in Mexico. They have successfully advocated on behalf of the families of missing and disappeared women, accompanying participatory investigations and providing legal and psycho-social support to victim's families. Should international donors double or triple their budget? Should they fund the founder to replicate the project in other states? In other words, what are the normative and policy implications of these findings for supporting local groups?

While I don't have the answers to these important questions, the following insights were gleaned from conversations with both donors and numerous local organizations:

- *Resources increase capacity and impact.* The basic activities engaged in by those undertaking sustained mobilization are strengthened by fi-nancial resources. These include hiring and retaining competent staff, maintaining a physical location that is safe and conducive to work getting done (has internet, computers, air-conditioning in hot places), having a meeting place for family members of victims, providing food for people coming to long meetings from far away, being able to pro-vide transportation to go to and from different government meetings, and publishing reports about the cases they are advocating for and/or critiques of the local manifestations of impunity.
- *Applying to and administering grants requires professionalization and organizational resources.* Most victims' collectives have no budget or staff, all but precluding them from receiving funding. In small human

rights organizations, they may have small, nearly always over-burdened staffs—so when lengthy, demanding grant reports are being written, these are being done by activists and advocates at home and at night. Most grants do not fund services such as preparing grant reports; they are seen as incidental, when in fact there is a direct opportunity cost: grant applications and reports are being written during time that would otherwise be spent on advocacy and activist activities. Being imaginative about how to include these organizations in funding streams in ways that recognize their limited time and resources will be vital to getting funding to the organizations that need it most, as well as decreasing the burden that receiving funding places on them.

- *Organizations that are effective may not document their activities well.* None of the victims' collectives that I worked with clearly document their work and judicial and searching successes. Most of them develop their strategy of working with state officials intuitively and iteratively. When they see that a certain official produces results, they continue to work with him (or her). They are by definition flexible and adaptable organizations, doing whatever they can with the resources they have. The very qualities that make them effective advocates do not lead them to be very good grant recipient candidates: as their activities are shifting depending on the local context, what they promised they would do during a foundation's last grant cycle becomes outdated.

- *Money affects the dynamics between organizations.* Organizations operating in the same political context know when money comes in, and money is often the cause of what can be virulent in-fighting. Though accusations of corruption and "selling out" can be mitigated by transparent accounting practices and documentation of the outcomes produced, there is a limit to these mitigation efforts—and an organization receiving an influx of capital from outside the judicial decision-making site will nearly always be accused of benefiting financially from victims. This must be kept in mind in this funding environment.

- *Money incentivizes local organizations to assume the priorities of funders.* Foundations, embassies, and other funding organizations most often enter into contexts with their funding priorities already defined. Often a lengthy visioning process conducted with the person or corporation that provides the money to the organization has determined these priorities. Though funders often pay lip service to understanding the local context and to respecting the decisions of the local organizations, these pre-determined priorities most often structurally prohibit them from allowing local organizations to frame and carry out their work in what these local entities see as the most effective way. I saw an exception to this pattern in the grant-making of the Global Fund for Democracy, GFD,[7] which funds many of the northern Mexican human rights organizations and victims' collectives. GFD took an implicitly ethnographic approach to grant-making. Grant officers participated in the mobilization and educational activities of the various organizations, established long-term relationships with their grant recipients, and made longer and more regular visits to these small organizations. By speaking with and observing different staff members working through their day-to-day challenges and successes, GFD gained a much more complete picture of the organizations' inner-workings without the tedious and resource-intensive grant reports that most funders required.

In sum, building the capacity of local victims' collectives and human rights organizations is a crucial and fraught part of creating a healthy and functioning victims' movement. While financial resources are undoubtedly necessary for their vitality, money nearly always causes internal distortions and can aggravate the existing and nearly unavoidable conflicts with other local activist and advocate groups. Grant-makers that take the time to understand the local political contexts and explicitly make space for the priorities and practices of their grantees increase the chance that their financial resources will indeed strengthen local non-state actors.

Personal Impact: *"They Gave Me Our Lives"*

Even as this book lauds the contributions of victim activists to advances against collusive impunity, I want to close by paying close attention to the personal costs, transformations, and meanings described by each of the family members profiled in this book. For each of them, the desperation of not knowing what had happened to their loved one has had a profoundly destabilizing impact on their lives. In what follows, I have included their

[7] Ana Paula Hernandez was the grant officer at GFD who carried out this strategy in Mexico and Central America with integrity, compassion, and infinite heart. She was killed in 2019 in a bus accident while doing her job. I am indebted to her friendship and mentorship as well as the funding legacy she left.

thoughts on sustained mobilization in the wake of the tragic disappearances of their loved ones.

Lucía and Alfonso: Vela Diaria

It's not exactly that Alejandro's cozy second-floor bedroom has been frozen in time: Lucía and Alfonso both talked about wanting to give the room life. When his younger brother lived with his parents, he would often go to sleep in Alejandro's bed, though he didn't leave any of his things there. When I visited in January 2020, Alfonso had just cleared off a part of Alejandro's desk and put in a new computer. The computer that Alejandro had set out to bring home from Laredo Texas sat in the center of the room, unopened. Alfonso referred to it with scorn—"for this computer, Alejandro . . ."—and then his voice trailed off.

With some slight adjustments, however, the room has been maintained just as Alejandro left it: his clothes are hanging in the closet, though his dad admits that a couple times he has borrowed a couple of Alejandro's jackets. His extensive collection of *Star Wars* memorabilia, video games, animé DVDs, CDs, and figurines crowd the shelves. Various electronic games, including *Guitar Hero*, *Ace Combat*, and *RockBand*, are stacked to the ceiling on top of his dresser, with a brand new xBox sandwiched in the middle. In the hallway right outside his room, there is a small altar with pictures of Alejandro and the family. Lucía puts a candle there every day as a way of remembering Alejandro and signaling that he is welcome to come home.

Alfonso and Lucía understand themselves as a family that doesn't talk much about emotions.

The impact of Alejandro's disappearance and their subsequent activism is more present in the change in the ways Alfonso's meticulously organized and documented life has changed since the disappearance. From the time he and Lucía were married in 1976, to 2010, there are 21 bound leather photo albums documenting the family's life: trips to the beach, birthdays, graduations. In the first album, a young Lucía and a plump Alejandro appear in the waters of Acapulco, Lucía always elegant and covered up, even at the beach. The three boys—Alejandro and his two brothers—are the center of these volumes.

Up two flights of stairs, behind a retractable table that Alfonso tells me was his and Lucía's first dining room table sits another series of bound leather volumes. These are the case files of Alejandro's disappearance. There are 14 volumes in the house, each several hundred pages long, plus an oversized volume that Alfonso assembled between 2010 and 2014. In this oversized book, tall enough that a full-sized newspaper page can be affixed without folding the edges, Alfonso has clipped and chronologically arranged newspaper articles having to do with Alejandro's disappearance, the battle between the state and DTOs in northern Mexico, and the movements demanding justice. There is a sense that the first four years following Alejandro's disappearance, Alfonso really thought he would find his son, and Lucía energetically and skillfully supported this goal. The other 14 volumes in his attic are the copies of the case files from their Nuevo León. Later that evening, he brings out the hard drive with the digitized investigatory tomes, which he tells us they have never opened in the year since they have had it.

This is consonant with Alfonso's approach to business and his reaction to Alejandro's disappearance: he is deliberate, intentional, and actualized in his plan for his life, business, and family. The failure to resolve what happened to Alejandro has fundamentally and permanently shaken and reshaped his world. Lucía has always helped Alfonso maintain the order in his world—which used to consist of keeping his books and maintaining the house and children. Bringing order to their lives after the chaos of their son's disappearance became an outsized and extraordinary task that necessitated Lucía's developing an entirely new set of skills, relationships, and daily practices. There is some pride in having adapted and persisted for both of them, but close to the surface is deep pain and persistent desperation.

Despite the birth of grandchildren from their other two sons, graduations, weddings, and even a few vacations more recently, after Alejandro's disappearance, there are no more family photo albums.

Nancy: Meaning in Struggle

Nancy has tried to take her own life two times since her son disappeared. She has also founded an organization, met with Mexico's highest-level officials, learned to drive, and obtained a scholarship to continue her education.

Nancy's relationships with her family have been tested and, in some cases, transformed by the disappearance. When Nancy was on a hunger strike in front of PGR, her mother wouldn't speak to her. One day, however, she showed up at the protest site. She told Nancy she was missing her grandson and feared that now she would lose her daughter as well. That is, she thought

Nancy might die from the hunger strike. Nancy reassured her, telling her they had a plan if they started to feel sick, even though they didn't at the time. Nancy's husband was working full-time during the hunger strike and would stop home and feed the dog, iron his uniform, and then come to PGR and sleep in Nancy's tent each night.

Nancy reflected on her reasons for continuing to mobilize:

I look for my son because I love him, because I want to know how he is, where he is, what happened to him, to help him where I can, as I can. I don't look for him because I have a need. . . . And with this I don't want to say I don't want my son; on the contrary, I love him, I love him very much.

I can't listen to music because all the music hurts me. Love songs are like I am singing my love to my son, I know maybe it's meant as couple's music, but I lived with my son for a long time as a single mother, and we were practically like a couple, because the day-to-day was "What do you think son? We do this or go here? Or do we eat this?" I didn't spend more time in my life with anyone [other] than him. We worked together; we went out to sell *gelatinas* [jello drinks] in the street; he helped me to sew. We could sit here for another eight hours and I could tell you all the life we lived together . . . but I look for my son because I love him and I want to know he's okay. . . .

I had a dream [in 2013] where he was dressed in white. He doesn't even like white. But all dressed in white he was saying goodbye. . . . And he was peaceful; pleased. And though I don't believe in signs like this—this makes me think that he has passed. And then there was a time when . . . something happened, something squeezed into my body. . . . I don't know if right then something happened to my son, perhaps he was beaten, sick, tortured . . . and when I had this dream is when I felt he had died. [Up until then], I felt like an anguish in the stomach . . . like when butterflies. . . I felt the—after that dream I no longer felt anything. . . .

From then on, I perceived that my son was killed—so I clung to looking for his remains . . . but to know that there are so so many remains . . . and that they have been hidden, and that there are ash heaps of bodies—that makes me despair. How are we going to find our loved ones amid all that?

Nancy says that "right now if my son saw me he wouldn't recognize me, because back then I was quiet. . . ." Nancy still posts to Facebook sometimes about her struggles with mental health. But overall, she reports that she is doing better—that feeling she is helping others has given her purpose. The day-to-day struggle to find those who have been disappeared occupies her time and her thoughts.

Juan Carlos: "Cleaning Your Own Wounds"

Juan Carlos's understanding of how to respond to his brothers' disappearances has shifted dramatically over the past decade. When Juan Carlos connected with the MPJD for the first time, it was at a meeting where they were setting the agenda for meeting with President Calderón in the summer of 2011. In his recounting of one of these meetings,

> they were talking about who was going to go, who would sit where, what happened if they didn't ask us this or that, if we were able to sit face-to-face with [Calderón]—I didn't really understand what was happening. So, we started working on the attendance list, the document they were going to present, and everyone who was there—or at least the majority—they decided that my mom was going to represent the group. . . . I saw how much love everyone there had for my mom, and I remember my mother said "I can't, I'm not prepared. . . . I don't have [my reading] glasses, I can't read whatever you give me because I didn't bring my glasses—so someone else should do it." And I remember in that moment it rained down like 20 pairs of glasses.

This sense of generous acceptance from other people who were going through the same thing changed Juan Carlos forever. As someone who had begun to confront the disappearance of his brothers almost two years before the emergence of the MPJD and who had succeeded in accessing the state's most powerful officials, Juan Carlos cycled through different modes of resistance quite quickly. His "with the law" perspective pre-disposed him to think strategically about the different forms of looking for his brother he was presented with. Here he reflects on learning about advocacy strategies and why he found something fundamentally flawed in merely pressuring the state:

> So, I would go and review the case file—but I had to learn how to review a case file. And the case file kept growing—and I was understanding it better,

but to understand the case file better, you have to understand the limits of what the official can do, and what they are mandated to do by law. And what the law says, is that you have to have a complete, well put together case file....

If we are able to recover our brothers—it's because God put us on the road to look for them—and to look for them—we have to actually search. It's the only way that they will be found: searching for them.

This strategy of looking for people, with a focus on searching for unmarked graves, has taken a high personal toll. It caused conflict, at some points, between Juan Carlos and his mother, "because my mom still believed a lot in the system." In time, however, Juan Carlos told me he had evolved to embrace the conflicts, his mistakes, and the whole struggle to find his brothers as "a way of cleaning your own wounds. . . . When we put our weaknesses in front—it can actually help you. It can be therapy."

I spoke with Doña Mari and Juan Carlos about the toll the disappearances, the threats, and their subsequent mobilization has had on them. Mari talked about how lucky she feels to have been accompanied all this time by so many people who are in solidarity[8]—but that at the same time, she feels pressured to be a leader. These people have given her strength but also an obligation to lead. When she met with Calderón, afterward people started to seek her out, and hope and expect that she could help them. With the access the family had to high-level state officials, others expected that they would be able to lift them up as well. While neither they nor anyone else in Mexico has been able to deliver formal justice in the cases of disappearances, their work searching for their loved ones, and coordinating a network of victims, has undoubtedly had an impact. As Yoltzi, whose story I discussed in Chapter 6 and who joined the Red de Enlaces in 2019, told me:

They [Juan Carlos Trujillo and the other members of victims' collectives] might think they did nothing—but they gave me our lives. The made us revive as a family. My mother began to live again. The fact that we have a photo of my sister on the wall of our house now—this is a huge achievement. It was a secret in our house. For them, maybe it's nothing. And the families ask me the same thing—how can I express my thanks? And

---

[8] The ReverdeSer Collective, for example, brings together young people to accompany the work of Enlaces Nacionales, and they have also provided organizational and emotional support to Familiares en Búsqueda María Herrera since their founding.

I say—you don't have to thank me, you don't have to pay me. Help someone else who is going through what you're going through. Teach them what you have learned. And this is the way to pay it forward. . . . Our goal is to bring the same hope that they are bringing to us.

Yoltzi decided to name the collective after Juan Carlos's brother, Raúl Trujillo Herrera, in tribute to what she has learned from them.

* * *

The resilience of Nancy, Lucía and Alfonso, and Juan Carlos is undeniable and inspires me to appreciate what is possible in seemingly impossible circumstances. Let us not take their resilience and sustained mobilization for granted, however. The work of the state is to admit that impunity is embedded within the state's institutions and to work diligently so that more families may be reunited with their loved ones; more of the disappeared may be located; more of the perpetrators may be prosecuted; and vitally, more disappearances may be prevented. While the path to these outcomes is complicated, the families most affected by disappearances have charted a path through the desolate judicial bureaucracy of the Mexican state. We would all do well to follow their lead.

Afterword

On August 27, 2021, more than 11 years after I first began my research in Mexico, I went to a state-sponsored meeting about disappearances. Much had changed. The event was held at Los Pinos, long the opulent presidential residence; at this time, on the order of populist and popular president Andrés Manuel López Obrador, often referred to as AMLO, it had become a cultural center open to the public. Alejandro Encinas, the sub-secretary of Human Rights and highest-ranking state official in attendance, spoke to the assembled victim activists, officials, and media:

> It's very significant to be holding this event in this house: here decisions were made to exterminate dissidents; here Calderón and Peña Nieto decided that the pain inflicted by the war on drugs would be borne by civil society, shouldered by victims. And that the victims themselves—most of whom are good people—would be blamed for what beset them. All of this was deemed acceptable collateral damage.

The event was held to launch a photo exhibit honoring the women who search for their loved ones. Encinas, together with other high-ranking state officials[1] charged with searching for the disappeared and prosecuting the perpetrators, alternately fist-bumped and embraced the members of the three victims' collectives who had assembled for the occasion. One official placed the number of disappearances at 91,000 and celebrated the presence of victim's collectives. The leader of a Veracruz-based collective spoke of the putrid work of searching for victims—and bemoaned that for too long the work of searching had been done with the indifference of the authorities.

Gone were the recriminations of state agents against victims, implying that somehow those who had been disappeared deserved their fate. There were also no more denials about the number of disappeared. Instead of elite social movement leaders, the voices of women-run, grassroots victims'

---

[1] Attendees included the national director of the search commission, Karla Quintana, and the former lead prosecutor specializing in enforced disappearances within PGR, Eréndira Cruzvillegas.

collectives took center stage. And while the president wasn't there, he has consistently decried the authoritarianism and repressive excesses of prior administrations.[2]

And yet—for the families profiled in this book, the prospects for justice under AMLO have not shown any great improvement: each one of the pro-filed families agreed that things have gotten worse. López Obrador, a vocal critic of neoliberalism, has nonetheless slashed government spending on state services that directly impact victims. In October 2020, he made good on his campaign promise to eliminate the funding of 109 fideicomisos—autonomous fiduciary bodies created to ensure the consistent and apolitical funding of state services, including funds formerly earmarked for family members of the disappeared. He has also gutted funding for the Search Commissions guaranteed in the General Law on Disappearances.

When we met in late summer 2021, Nancy told me that she felt these cuts: "he [AMLO] has closed the doors on us." She recounted that the little financial support Comisión de Atención a Víctimas. CEAV, the Victims' Attention Commission, did provide has been reduced or altogether cut, making it impossible for several families she knows to continue to mobi-lize. All three families also reported that state protection—granted to many human rights defenders and victims as a result of the law to protect human rights defenders—had been stopped, something deeply concerning for those who had come to rely on that protection. Juan Carlos recognized that while AMLO wants to make a change—he didn't know how to go about it and "needs to learn to listen." Emilio Alvarez Icaza, former MPJD leader, former commissioner of the Inter-American Commission on Human Rights, and current independent senator,[3] told me that López Obrador's resource alloca-tion for addressing disappearances amounted to "using a lily pad to cover a swimming pool."

The pandemic, I was surprised hear, has not stopped the actions and mobilizations of the collectives. Nancy recounted to me that her group has taken advantage of online group therapy offered by the state agencies. Additionally, the participatory investigation meetings with state officials have continued virtually through video conferencing. Nancy expressed with

[2] At the 50th anniversary of the Tlateloco massacre in 2018, for example, he swore to never again use the armed forces or police to oppress the people. " 'Ni perdón ni olvido,' claman en México a 50 años de la masacre de Tlatelolco." https://www.elpais.cr/2018/10/02/ni-perdon-ni-olvido-claman-en-mexico-a-50-anos-de-la-masacre-de-tlatelolco/

[3] Alvarez Icaza is often a lone voice of opposition to AMLO and calls himself "the least powerful of Mexico's 128 senators."

some incredulity that the EdoMex officials had continued diligently to work her case and that of the other collectives. When I asked her why, she attributed it to the empathy that the victims' collectives had sparked in them.

While the rhetoric and discourse of the Mexican state has shifted dramatically in the past decade, the scales have not been tipped toward disrupting systemic impunity. Victims wonder aloud what they can hope for in terms of state response if López Obrador, who most saw as the president most naturally allied with victims' interests, is not meaningfully and systematically addressing disappearances and impunity. In the meantime, victims' collectives continue to multiply and organize in the face of even more disappearances.

References

Abu-Lughod, L. (2000). Locating ethnography. *Ethnography*, *1*(2), 261–267.

Agencia Reforma (2019). Urge CNDH medidas por fosas en Veracruz. *El Mañana*, April 24. https://www.elmanana.com/urge-cndh-medidas-por-fosas-en-veracruz/4807505

Aguayo, S. (Ed.). (2017). *En el desamparo: Los Zetas, el Estado, la sociedad y las víctimas de San Fernando, Tamaulipas (2010), y Allende, Coahuila (2011)*. México, DF: El Colegio de Mexico AC.

Aguayo, S., del Ángel, S., Pérez Aguirre, M., & Askenazi, D. (2016). *Mexico: State of neglect—Los Zetas, the state, society and the victims of San Fernando, Tamaulipas (2010) and Allende, Coahuila (2011)*. México, DF: Centro de Estudios Internacionales, El Colegio de México.

Ahmed, A. (2020). She stalked her daughter's killers across Mexico, one by one. *New York Times*, December 13. https://www.nytimes.com/2020/12/13/world/americas/miriam-rodriguez-san-fernando.html

Ahmed, A., & Villegas, P. (2019). He was one of Mexico's deadliest assassins. Then he turned on his cartel." *New York Times*, December 14. https://www.nytimes.com/2019/12/14/world/americas/sicario-mexico-drug-cartels.html

Al Jazeera (2011). "Zetas cartel boss" captured. *Al Jazeera*, October 17. https://www.aljazeera.com/news/2011/10/17/zetas-drug-cartel-boss-captured-in-mexico

Alanís, R. (2018). Presentan protocolo de búsqueda de desaparecidos en Tamaulipas. *Milenio*, September 28. https://www.milenio.com/politica/comunidad/presentan-protocolo-de-busqueda-de-desaparecidos-en-tamaulipas

Albiston, C. R. (2010). *Institutional inequality and the mobilization of the Family and Medical Leave Act: Rights on leave*. New York: Cambridge University Press.

Alcántara, J. C. (2017). #YoSoy132, social media, and political organization. In *Oxford Research Encyclopedia of Latin American History*. Oxford: Oxford University Press. https://doi.org/10.1093/acrefore/9780199366439.013.484

Amengual, M. (2016). *Politicized enforcement in Argentina: Labor and environmental regulation*. Cambridge: Cambridge University Press.

Amenta, E., Caren, N., Chiarello, E., & Su, Y. (2010). The political consequences of social movements. *Annual Review of Sociology*, *36*, 287–307.

Amnesty International (1979). *Annual report*. London: Amnesty International Publications.

Amnesty International (2017). Mexico: Killing of activist in Tamaulipas highlights government negligence. *Amnesty International*, May 11. https://www.amnesty.org/en/latest/news/2017/05/mexico-asesinato-de-activista-en-tamaulipas-pone-de-manifiesto-la-negligencia-del-gobierno/

Anaya, A., Cavallaro, J., & Marín, P. C. (2021). *La impunidad activa en México. Cómo entender y enfrentar las violaciones masivas a los derechos humanos*. Guadalajara, Mexico: ITESO.

Anaya, A. & J. Gallagher (forthcoming). Willingness: Human rights crises and state response in Mexico. Forthcoming, *Latin American Politics and Society.*

Angel, A. (2020). Impunidemia: Fiscalías resuelven solo 73 de más de 46 mil casos de tortura y desaparición forzada. *Animal Político,* October 8. https://www.animalpolitico.com/2020/10/impunidemia-fiscalias-casos-tortura-desaparicion/

Animal Político (2011). Cae "El Indio," jefe "zeta" en Veracruz y expolicía. *Animal Político,* December 24. https://www.animalpolitico.com/2011/12/cae-el-indio-jefe-zeta-en-veracruz-y-expolicia/

Animal Político (2012a). Movimiento por la Paz propone a los presidenciables un acuerdo de unidad. *Animal Político,* May 28. http://www.animalpolitico.com/2012/05/en-reunion-con-el-movimiento-por-la-paz-josefina-se-disculpa-a-nombre-del-pan/

Animal Político (2012b). Movimiento por la Paz y artistas se ponen "En los Zapatos del Otro." *Animal Político,* January 31. https://www.animalpolitico.com/2012/01/movimiento-por-la-paz-y-artistas-se-ponen-en-los-zapatos-del-otro/

Animal Político (2012c). "El Mañana de Nuevo Laredo decide ya no cubrir temas del narco." *Animal Político,* May 12. https://www.animalpolitico.com/2012/05/el-manana-de-nuevo-laredo-decide-ya-no-cubrir-temas-del-narco/

Ansolabehere, K., Frey, B. A., & Payne, L. A. (Eds.). (2021). *Disappearances in the post-transition era in Latin America.* Oxford: For the British Academy by Oxford University Press.

Arendt, H. (1949). *"The rights of man": What are they?* New York: American Labor Conference on International Affairs.

Arias, E. D. (2017). *Criminal enterprises and governance in Latin America and the Caribbean.* Cambridge: Cambridge University Press.

Asmann, A. (2020). Mexico's navy may accept alleged role in 2018 border kidnappings. *InSight Crime,* July 30. https://insightcrime.org/news/analysis/mexico-navy-kidnappings/

Associated Press (2017). More than 250 skulls found in "enormous mass grave" in Mexico. *The Guardian,* March 14. https://www.theguardian.com/world/2017/mar/14/mexico-skulls-mass-grave-drug-cartel-veracruz

Astorga, L., & Shirk, D. A. (2010). Drug trafficking organizations and counter-drug strategies in the U.S.-Mexican Context. *UC San Diego: Center for U.S.-Mexican Studies.* Retrieved from https://escholarship.org/uc/item/8j647429

Avalos, J. (2016). Jorge Winckler, nuevo Fiscal de Veracruz. *Eje Central,* December 30. https://www.ejecentral.com.mx/jorge-winckler-nuevo-fiscal-de-veracruz/

Bailey, J. (2014) Crimen e impunidad: Las trampas de la seguridad en México. *Estudios 112*(XIII), 181–188.

Baiocchi, G., Heller, P., Silva, M. K., & Silva, M. (2011). *Bootstrapping democracy: Transforming local governance and civil society in Brazil.* Stanford, CA: Stanford University Press.

Bargent, J. (2017). Veracruz, Mexico is LatAm's epicenter of violence against journalists. *InSight Crime,* March 27. https://insightcrime.org/news/brief/veracruz-mexico-latam-epicenter-violence-against-journalists/

BBC News (2013). Mexico estimates 26,000 missing since 2006. *BBC News,* February 27. http://www.bbc.co.uk/news/world-latin-america-21597033.

Beer, C. C. (2012). Invigorating federalism: The emergence of governors and state legislatures as powerbrokers and policy innovators. In R. A. Camp (Ed.), *The Oxford handbook of Mexican politics* (pp. 119–142). Oxford: Oxford University Press.

Beittel, J. S. (2009). *Mexico's drug-related violence*. Washington, DC: Congressional Research Service, Library of Congress.

Beittel, J. S. (2015). Mexico: Organized crime and drug trafficking organizations. Washington, DC: Congressional Research Service, Library of Congress.

Beyerlein, K., & Hipp, J. (2006). A two-stage model for a two-stage process: How biographical availability matters for social movement mobilization. *Mobilization: An International Quarterly, 11*(3), 299–320.

Bob, C. (2010). *The international struggle for new human rights*. Philadelphia: University of Pennsylvania Press.

Bonello, D. (2017). Mexico arrest of fugitive ex-governor is result of politics, not ethics. *InSight Crime*, September 13. https://insightcrime.org/news/analysis/mexico-arrest-of-fugitive-ex-governor-is-result-of-politics-not-ethics/

Bosi, L., & Uba, K. (2009). Introduction: The outcomes of social movement. *Mobilization: An International Quarterly, 14*, 409–415.

Botero, S. (2015). *Courts that matter: Judges, litigants and the politics of rights enforcement in Latin America* [Doctoral dissertation, University of Notre Dame].

Botero S., D. Brinks, & E. Ocantos-Gonzalez (forthcoming). *The limits of judicialization: Progress and backlash in Latin American politics*. Cambridge: Cambridge University Press.

Brinks, D. M. (2008). *The judicial response to police killings in Latin America*. Cambridge: Cambridge University Press.

Buscaglia, E. (2013). *Vacíos de poder en México: El camino de México hacia la seguridad humana*. Mexico: Debate.

Calderón Hinojosa, F. C. (2014). *Los retos que enfrentamos: Los problemas de México y las políticas públicas para resolverlos (2006–2012)*. Mexico: Debate.

Calveiro, P. (2019). *Resistir al neoliberalismo: comunidades y autonomías*. México, DF: Siglo XXI Editores México.

Chávez, A. (2022). *Colectivo 21 de mayo: Experiencias de la búsqueda de personas desaparecidas en Miguel Alemán, Tamaulipas* [MA in Social Psychology Thesis, Universidad Autónoma Metropolitana].

Chua, L. J. (2015). The vernacular mobilization of human rights in Myanmar's sexual orientation and gender identity movement. *Law & Society Review, 49*(2), 299–332.

Chua, L. J. (2018). *The politics of love in Myanmar*. Stanford, CA: Stanford University Press.

Chua, L. J., & Engel, D. M. (2019). Legal consciousness reconsidered. *Annual Review of Law and Social Science, 15*, 335–353.

CNN (2011). Mexican peace activist gunned down. *CNN*, November 29. https://www.cnn.com/2011/11/29/world/americas/mexico-activist-killed/index.html Accessed 11/25/19

Committee to Protect Journalists (2021). *Data archives—Committee to Protect Journalists* [online] Available at: <https://cpj.org/tags/Data/> [Accessed 8 March 2021].

Corcoran, P. (2017). Zetas–Gulf Cartel conflict continues to rock Mexico's northeast. *InSight Crime*, October 30. https://insightcrime.org/news/analysis/zetas-gulf-cartel-conflict-continues-rock-mexico-northeast/

Correa-Cabrera, G. (2017). *Los Zetas Inc.: Criminal corporations, energy, and civil war in Mexico*. Brownsville: University of Texas Press.

Cortés Martínez, B. (2020). ¿Quién es "La Jefa"? lideresa de "Los Zetas" y prima de la fiscal de Veracruz. *Radio Fórmula*, January 22. https://www.radioformula.com.mx/

breaking-news/2020/1/22/quien-es-la-jefa-lideresa-de-los-zetas-prima-de-la-fiscal-de-veracruz-434688.html

Davidovic, M. (2021). The law of "never again": Transitional justice and the transformation of the norm of non-recurrence. *International Journal of Transitional Justice, 15*(2), 386–406.

de Córdoba, J., & Montes, J. (2016). Mexico issues arrest warrant for Veracruz state governor Javier Duarte. *Wall Street Journal*, October 19. http://www.wsj.com/articles/mexico-issues-arrest-warrant-for-veracruz-state-governor-javier-duarte-1476905635

De Dios Palma, A. (2017). Capturan a "El Nene," supuesto líder de la banda Los Granados en Guerrero. *El Universal*, April 12. https://www.eluniversal.com.mx/articulo/estados/2017/04/12/capturan-el-nene-supuesto-lider-de-la-banda-los-granados-en-guerrero

De Greiff, P. (Ed.). (2008). *The handbook of reparations*. Oxford: Oxford University Press.

De Vecchi Gerli, M. (2018). ¡*Vivxs lxs Queremos! The battles for memory around the disappeared in Mexico* [Doctoral dissertation, University College London].

Della Porta, D., & Mattoni, A. (2015). Social movements. In G. Mazzoleni (Ed.), *The international encyclopedia of political communication* (pp. 1–8). Hoboken, NJ: John Wiley & Sons.

Desmond, M. (2014). Relational ethnography. *Theory and Society, 43*(5), 547–579.

Dewhirst, P., & Kapur, A. (2015). *The disappeared and invisible: Revealing the enduring impact of enforced disappearance on women*. New York: International Center for Transitional Justice.

Dresser, D. (2003). Mexico: From PRI predominance to divided democracy. In J. Domínguez & M. Shifter (Eds.), *Constructing democratic governance in Latin America* (pp. 321–347). Baltimore: Johns Hopkins University Press.

Dudley, S. (2011). Zeta testimony solves mystery of Mexico bus massacres. *InSight Crime*, June 27. https://insightcrime.org/news/analysis/zeta-testimony-solves-mystery-of-mexico-bus-massacres/

Dudley, S. (2012). Part II—The Zetas and Monterrey math. *InSight Crime*, March 27. https://insightcrime.org/investigations/zetas-monterrey-math/

Durán-Martínez, A. (2018). *The politics of drug violence: Criminals, cops and politicians in Colombia and Mexico*. New York: Oxford University Press.

El Comercio (2012). México: Lucha antidrogas he dejado 70.000 muertos en últimos seis años. *El Comercio*, December 18. https://elcomercio.pe/mundo/actualidad/mexico-lucha-antidrogas-ha-dejado-70000-muertos-ultimos-seis-anos-noticia-1511471/

El País (1990). Vargas Llosa: "México es la dictadura perfecta." *El País*, August 31. https://elpais.com/diario/1990/09/01/cultura/652140001_850215.html

Engle, K., Miller, Z., & Davis, D. M. (Eds.). (2016). *Anti-impunity and the human rights agenda*. Cambridge: Cambridge University Press.

Epp, C. R. (1998). *The rights revolution: Lawyers, activists, and supreme courts in comparative perspective*. Chicago: University of Chicago Press.

Ewick, P., & Silbey, S. S. (1998). *The common place of law: Stories from everyday life*. Chicago: University of Chicago Press.

Felbab-Brown, V. (2009). *Shooting up: Counterinsurgency and the war on drugs*. Washington, DC: Brookings Institution Press.

Fox, J., & Hernandez, L. (1992). Mexico's difficult democracy: Grassroots movements, NGOs, and local government. *Alternatives, 17*(2), 165–208.

Franklin, J. C. (2008). Shame on you: The impact of human rights criticism on political repression in Latin America. *International Studies Quarterly, 52*(1), 187–211.

Frey, B. A. (2015). Uneven ground: Asymmetries of power in human rights advocacy in Mexico. In J. R. Pruce (Ed.), *The Social Practice of Human Rights* (pp. 121–139). New York: Palgrave Macmillan.

Fu, D., & Simmons, E. S. (2021). Ethnographic approaches to contentious politics: The what, how, and why. *Comparative Political Studies, 54*(10), 1695–1721.

FUNDENL (2014). Gobierno de Nuevo León destruye nombres de Desaparecidos [Press release]. *FUNDENL*, June 17. http://fundenl.org/gobierno-de-nuevo-leon-destruye-nombres-de-desaparecidos/

Gallagher, J. (2015). *Tipping the scales of justice: The role of organized citizen action in strengthening the rule of law* [Doctoral dissertation: Cornell University].

Gallagher, J. (2017). The last mile problem: Activists, advocates, and the struggle for justice in domestic courts. *Comparative Political Studies, 50*(12), 1666–1698.

Gallagher, J. (2019). The judicial breakthrough model: Transnational advocacy networks and lethal violence. In A. Anaya & B. Frey (Eds.), *Mexico's Human Rights Crisis* (pp. 250–271). Philadelphia: University of Pennsylvania Press.

Gallagher, J. (2020). (Enforced) disappearances—when state and criminal perpetrators blur. *Völkerrechtsblog, International Law & International Legal Thought* (blog), January 18. https://voelkerrechtsblog.org/enforced-disappearances-when-state-and-criminal-perpetrators-blur/

Gallagher, J., & Contesse, J. (forthcoming). Critical disconnects: Progressive jurisprudence & tenacious impunity in Mexico. In S. Botero, D. Brinks, & E. Ocantos-Gonzalez (Eds.), *The Limits of judicialization: Progress and backlash in Latin American politics.* Cambridge: Cambridge University Press.

Gallagher, J., Kruks-Wisner, G., & Taylor, W. (forthcoming). *Beyond ballots and barricades: The politics of everyday claim-making.* Cambridge: Cambridge University Press.

Gallagher, M. E. (2006). Mobilizing the law in China: "Informed disenchantment" and the development of legal consciousness. *Law & Society Review, 40*(4), 783–816.

Gallagher, M. E. (2017). *Authoritarian legality in China: Law, workers, and the state.* Cambridge: Cambridge University Press.

García, J. A. (2018). Los escuadrones de la muerte de Veracruz. *El País*, February 24. https://elpais.com/internacional/2018/02/24/mexico/1519432756_158531.html

García, J. A. (2019). Tamaulipas con déficit de 2 mil 500 policías. *Milenio*, June 2. https://www.milenio.com/policia/tamaulipas-deficit-2-mil-500-policias

García, J. J. G. (2015). *Ley general de víctimas, un resultado político del Movimiento por la Paz con Justicia y Dignidad.* México, DF: El Colegio de México.

Gerth, J. (1988). On the Trail of the Kingpins. *New York Times*, November 6. https://www.nytimes.com/1988/11/06/books/on-the-trail-of-the-kingpins.html

Gibler, J. (2017). *I couldn't even imagine that they would kill us: An oral history of the attacks against the students of Ayotzinapa.* San Francisco: City Lights Books.

Gillingham, P., & Smith, B. T. (Eds.). (2014). *Dictablanda: Politics, work, and culture in Mexico, 1938–1968.* Durham, NC: Duke University Press.

Gobierno de México (2016). ¿Qué sabes sobre #DDHH y la Reforma Constitucional de 2011? 11 puntos clave para entender y ejercer tus derechos. *Secretaría de la Gobernación*, January 12. https://www.gob.mx/segob/articulos/que-sabes-sobre-ddhh-y-la-reforma-constitucional-de-2011-11-puntos-clave-para-entender-y-ejercer-tus-derechos

Gobierno de México (2017). ¿Por qué la Reforma Constitucional de Derechos Humanos de 2011 modificó la relación entre el gobierno y la sociedad? *Secretaría de la Gobernación*, June 9. https://www.gob.mx/segob/articulos/por-que-la-reforma-constit

ucional-de-derechos-humanos-de-2011-cambio-la-forma-de-ver-la-relacion-entre-el-gobierno-y-la-sociedad

Goldman, F. (2017). The Atenco warning. *New York Times*, June 29. https://www.nytimes.com/2017/06/29/opinion/atenco-mexico-pena-nieto-yosoy132.html

Gómez, E. (2014) Familiares de desaparecidos reclaman justicia al gobernador de Veracruz. *La Jornada*, February 25. https://www.jornada.com.mx/2014/02/25/estados/031n2est

González, Y. M. (2019). Participation as a safety valve: Police reform through participatory security in Latin America. *Latin American Politics and Society*, 61(2), 68–92.

González, Y. M. (working paper n.d.). From victims to resilient citizens: The policy feedback effects of state violence.

González-Ocantos, E. A. (2016). *Shifting legal visions: Judicial change and human rights trials in Latin America*. Cambridge: Cambridge University Press.

Grillo, I. (2012). *El Narco: Inside Mexico's criminal insurgency*. New York: Bloomsbury.

Haldemann, F., & Unger, T. (Eds.). (2018). *The United Nations principles to combat impunity: A commentary*. Oxford: Oxford University Press.

Hellman, J. A. (1978). *Mexico in crisis*. Teaneck, NJ: Holmes and Meier.

Hernández, R. R. (2008) *El centro dividido: La nueva autonomía de los gobernadores*, México, DF: El Colegio de México.

Herrera, E. (2011), Nepomuceno ante Calderon. *Emergencia.mx*, November 29. https://www.youtube.com/watch?v=3Bp_1a9QG84

Heyer, K. (2015). *Rights enabled: The disability revolution, from the US, to Germany and Japan, to the United Nations*. Ann Arbor: University of Michigan Press.

Hilbink, L. (2007). *Judges beyond politics in democracy and dictatorship: Lessons from Chile* (Cambridge Studies in Law and Society). Cambridge: Cambridge University Press. doi.org:10.1017/CBO9780511511509

Hilbink, L., & Salas, V. (2021). Advancing human rights through legal empowerment of the disadvantaged. In M. F. Davis, M. Kjærum, & A. Lyons (Eds.), *Research handbook on human rights and poverty* (pp. 354–368). Cheltenham, UK: Edward Elgar Publishing.

Hilbink, L., Salas, V., Gallagher, J. K., & Restrepo Sanín, J. (2022). Why people turn to institutions they detest: Institutional mistrust and justice system engagement in uneven democratic states. *Comparative Political Studies*, 55(1), 3–31.

Hinojosa, G., & Meyer, M. (2019). *Mexico's rule of law efforts: 11 years after criminal justice reforms*. Washington, DC: Washington Office on Latin America. https://www.wola.org/wp-content/uploads/2019/11/JUSTICE-REFORMSREPORT-ENG.pdf

Hirschman, A. O. (1970). *Exit, voice, and loyalty: Responses to decline in firms, organizations, and states* (Vol. 25). Cambridge, MA: Harvard University Press.

Holland, A. C. (2017). *Forbearance as redistribution: The politics of informal welfare in Latin America*. Cambridge: Cambridge University Press.

Human Rights Watch (2013). *Mexico's disappeared: The enduring cost of a crisis ignored*. New York: Human Rights Watch. Retrieved from http://www.refworld.org/docid/512748192.html

Humphrey, M., & Valverde, E. (2007). Human rights, victimhood, and impunity: An anthropology of democracy in Argentina. *Social Analysis*, 51(1), 179–197.

Huntington, S. P., & Moore, C. H. (1970). *Authoritarian politics in modern society: The dynamics of established one-party systems*. New York: Basic Books.

Ingram, Matthew. (2016). *Crafting courts in new democracies: The politics of subnational judicial reform in Brazil and Mexico*. New York: Cambridge University Press.

International Crisis Group. (2017). "Veracruz: Fixing Mexico's state of terror." (Latin America Report 61.) Brussels: International Crisis Group.

Janowitz, N. (2018). Code name Jaguar: How a top police official carried out a reign of terror in Mexico. *The Intercept*, May 20. https://theintercept.com/2018/05/20/code-name-jaguar-how-a-top-police-official-carried-out-a-reign-of-terror-in-mexico/

Jourde, C. (2013). The ethnographic sensibility: Overlooked authoritarian dynamics and Islamic ambivalences in West Africa. In E. Schatz (Ed.), *Political ethnography: What immersion contributes to the study of power* (pp. 201–216). Chicago: University of Chicago Press. https://doi.org/10.7208/9780226736785-012

Kapiszewski, D., Levitsky, S., & Yashar, D. J. (Eds.). (2021). *The inclusionary turn in Latin American democracies*. Cambridge: Cambridge University Press.

Keck, M. E., and K. Sikkink (1998). *Activists beyond borders: Advocacy networks in international politics*. Ithaca, NY: Cornell University Pres.

Klandermans, B., & Staggenborg, S. (Eds.). (2002). *Methods of social movement research* (Vol. 16). Minneapolis: University of Minnesota Press.

Knight, A. (2012). Narco-violence and the state in modern Mexico. In W. G. Pansters (Ed.), *Violence, coercion, and state-making in twentieth-century Mexico: The other half of the Centaur* (pp. 115–134). Stanford, CA: Stanford University Press.

Knight, A., & Pansters, W. G. (Eds.). (2005). *Caciquismo in twentieth-century Mexico*. London: University of London Press.

Krause, P., & Szekely, O. (Eds.). (2020). *Stories from the field: A guide to navigating fieldwork in political science*. New York: Columbia University Press.

Krauze, E., Meyer, J. A., & García, C. R. (1977). *La reconstrucción económica*. México, DF: El Colegio de México.

Kristlik, Tomas (2013). The end of the drug war: Its implications and the future of drug trafficking in Mexico. *Georgetown Security Studies Review*, 1(1), 12–18.

Kruks-Wisner, G. (2018). *Claiming the state: Active citizenship and social welfare in rural India*. Cambridge: Cambridge University Press.

Lakhani, N. (2020). Mexico world's deadliest country for journalists, new report finds. *The Guardian*, December 22. https://www.theguardian.com/world/2020/dec/22/mexico-journalists-deadly-cpr-press-freedom

Lessing, B. (2017). *Making peace in drug wars: Crackdowns and cartels in Latin America*. Cambridge: Cambridge University Press.

Ley, S. (2014). *Citizens in fear: Political participation and voting behavior in the midst of violence* [Doctoral dissertation: Duke University].

Ley General de Víctimas (2013). *Diario oficial de la Federación, Cámar de Diputados del H. Congreso de la Unión*, January 9. http://www.diputados.gob.mx/LeyesBiblio/pdf/LGV.pdf

Ley Orgánica de la Fiscalía General del Estado de Veracruz de Ignacio de la Lllave (2016). *Gaceta oficial, Órgano del Gobierno del Estado de Veracruz*, November 8. https://www.legisver.gob.mx/leyes/LeyesPDF/LOFG%20081116.pdf

Lowery, W., Kelly, K., Melink, T. & Rich, S. (2018). Murder with impunity: Where killings go unsolved. *Washington Post*, June 6. https://www.washingtonpost.com/graphics/2018/investigations/where-murders-go-unsolved/

Lutz, E. L. (1990). *Human rights in Mexico: A policy of impunity*. New York: Human Rights Watch.

Magaloni, B., & Rodriguez, L. (2020). Institutionalized police brutality: Torture, the militarization of security, and the reform of inquisitorial criminal justice in Mexico. *American Political Science Review*, *114*(4), 1013–1034.

Maier, Elizabeth. (2001). *Las madres de los desaparecidos: Un nuevo mito materno en América Latina?* México, DF: Colegio de la Frontera.

Marshall, A. M. (2005a). *Confronting sexual harassment: The law and politics of everyday life*. Abingdon, UK: Routledge.

Marshall, A. M. (2005b). Idle rights: Employees' rights consciousness and the construction of sexual harassment policies. *Law & Society Review*, *39*(1), 83–124.

Marshall, A. M., & Barclay, S. (2003). In their own words: How ordinary people construct the legal world. *Law & Social Inquiry*, *28*, 617.

Martínez, P. (2013). Lanzan Unidad de Búsqueda de Desaparecidos con 12 ministerios públicos. *Animal Político*, May 27. https://www.animalpolitico.com/2013/05/pgr-prese nta-hoy-la-unidad-de-busqueda-de-desaparecidos/

Mayka, L. (2019a). *Building participatory institutions in Latin America: Reform coalitions and institutional change*. Cambridge: Cambridge University Press.

Mayka, L. (2019b). The origins of strong institutional design: Policy reform and participatory institutions in Brazil's health sector. *Comparative Politics*, *51*(2), 275–294.

Mayka, L. (2019c). Society-driven participatory institutions: Lessons from Colombia's planning councils. *Latin American Politics and Society*, *61*(2), 93–114.

McAdam, D. (1986). Recruitment to high-risk activism: The case of Freedom Summer. *American Journal of Sociology*, *92*(1), 64–90.

McAdam, D. (2010). *Political process and the development of black insurgency, 1930–1970*. Chicago: University of Chicago Press.

McAdam D., Tarrow S., & Tilly C. (2001). *Dynamics of contention*. Cambridge: Cambridge University Press.

McCann, M. W. (1994). *Rights at work: Pay equity reform and the politics of legal mobilization*. Chicago: University of Chicago Press.

McDonnell, P. J., & Sanchez, C. (2017). A mother who dug in a Mexican mass grave to find the "disappeared" finally learns her son's fate. *Los Angeles Times*, March 20. https://www.latimes.com/world/mexico-americas/la-fg-mexico-disappeared-20170320-story.html

Mendoza Aguila, G. (2012). Familiares de desaparecidos en México terminan huelga hambre. *El Diario NY*, November 13. https://eldiariony.com/2012/11/13/familiares-de-desaparecidos-en-mexico-terminan-huelga-hambre/

Merry, S. E. (1990). *Getting justice and getting even: Legal consciousness among working-class Americans*. Chicago: University of Chicago Press.

Merry, S. E. (2006) *Human rights & gender violence: Translating international law into local justice*. Chicago: University of Chicago Press.

Mettler, S., & SoRelle, M. (2018). Policy feedback theory. In C. M. Weible & P. A. Sabatier (Eds.), *Theories of the policy process* (4th ed.). New York: Routledge.

México Evalúa (2020). *Hallazgos 2020: Seguimiento y evaluación del sistema de justicia penal en México*. México, DF: México Evalúa. https://www.mexicoevalua.org/mexic oevalua/wp-content/uploads/2021/10/hallazgos2020-7octubreok.pdf

Meyer, D. S., & Minkoff, D. C. (2004). Conceptualizing political opportunity. *Social Forces*, *82*(4), 1457–1492.

Meyer, M., & Suárez-Enríquez, X. (2016). *Mission unaccomplished: Mexico's new criminal justice system is still a work in progress*. Washington, DC: Washington Office on Latin America.

Michel, V. (2018). *Prosecutorial accountability and victims' rights in Latin America*. Cambridge: Cambridge University Press.

Migdal, J. S. (1988). *Strong societies and weak states: State-society relations and state capabilities in the Third World*. Princeton, NJ: Princeton University Press.

Miller, M. (1991). Jailed cocaine baron directs drug trade from cell." *Los Angeles Times*, March 13. https://www.latimes.com/archives/la-xpm-1991-03-23-mn-462-story.html

Molina, I. (2018). Más de 5 mil asesinatos en Veracruz en period de Duarte. *Diario de Xalapa*, March 2. https://www.diariodexalapa.com.mx/local/mas-de-5-mil-asesinatos-en-veracruz-en-periodo-de-duarte-1036383.html

Moncada, E. (2016). *Cities, business, and the politics of urban violence in Latin America*. Stanford, CA: Stanford University Press.

Montalvo, T. (2017) Lo que dejó Duarte a Veracruz: Récord en homicidios, fosas, deuda y más pobreza. *Animal Político*, April 17. https://www.animalpolitico.com/2017/04/duarte-veracruz-violencia-deuda-fosas/

Mosso, R. (2015). Condenan a multihomicida de Los Zetas. *Milenio*, May 26. https://www.milenio.com/policia/condenan-a-multihomicida-de-los-zetas

Murdie, A. M., & Davis, D. R. (2012). Shaming and blaming: Using events data to assess the impact of human rights INGOs. *International Studies Quarterly* 56(1): 1–16.

National Security Archive (2006). *Official report released on Mexico's "Dirty War."* Washington, DC: National Security Archive. https://nsarchive2.gwu.edu/NSAEBB/NSAEBB209/#informe

Naval, C., with Salgado, J. (2006). *Irregularities, abuses of power, and ill-treatment in the Federal District*. México, DF: Fundar Centro de Análisis.

Navarro, M. (1989). The personal is political: Las Madres de Plaza de Mayo. In S. Eckstein & M. A. G. Merino (Eds.), *Power and popular protest: Latin American social movements* (updated and expanded ed., pp. 241–258). Berkeley: University of California Press.

Neilson, R. (2020). Recite! Interpretive fieldwork for positivists. In P. Krause & O. Szekely (Eds.), *From the field: A guide to navigating fieldwork in political science* (pp. 36–47). New York: Columbia University Press.

Nielsen, L. B. (2000). Situating legal consciousness: Experiences and attitudes of ordinary citizens about law and street harassment. *Law & Society Review*, 34(4), 1055–1090.

O'Donnell, G. (1993). On the state, democratization and some conceptual problems: A Latin American view with glances at some postcommunist countries. *World Development*, 21(8), 1355–1369.

Olson, J. (2012). Organized crime as human rights issue: Where is the outrage? *ReVista Harvard Review of Latin America*, 11(3).

Olson, M. (2009). *The logic of collective action*. Cambridge, MA: Harvard University Press.

Ostrom, E. (2000). Collective action and the evolution of social norms. *Journal of Economic Perspectives*, 14(3), 137–158.

Pachirat, T. (2015). We call it a grain of sand: The interpretive orientation and a human social science. In D. Yanow & P. Schwartz-Shea (Eds.), *Interpretation and method* (pp. 426–432). New York: Routledge.

Padgett, H. (2016). *Tamaulipas: La casta de los narcogobernadores: Un eastern mexicano*. Barcelona: Ediciones Urano.

Palacio, C., & Olvera, A. J. (2017). Acallar las voces, ocultar la verdad: Violencia contra los periodistas en Veracruz. *Argumentos, 30*(85), 17–35.

Paley, D. (2011). Off the map in Mexico. *Nation, 292*(21), 20–24.

Pansters, W. (Ed.) (2012). *Violence, coercion, and state-making in twentieth-century Mexico: The other half of the Centaur.* Redwood City, CA: Stanford University Press.

Peruzzotti, E., & C. Smulovitz (Eds.) (2006). *Enforcing the rule of law: Social accountability in the new Latin American democracies.* Pittsburgh: University of Pittsburgh Press.

Pierson, P. (1993). When effect becomes cause: Policy feedback and political change. *World Politics, 45*(4), 595–628.

Placencia, J. G. (2017). Actores y redes del movimiento por los derechos humanos en América Latina. *Boletín de Antropología, 32*(53), 158–179.

Pozas-Loyo, A., & Ríos-Figueroa, J. (2016). The transformations of the role of the Mexican Supreme Court. In A. Castagnola & S. L. Noriega (Eds.), *Judicial politics in Mexico: The Supreme Court and the transition to democracy* (pp. 22–54). New York: Routledge.

Przeworski, A., & Teune, H. (1970). *The logic of comparative social inquiry.* Hoboken, NJ: John Wiley & Sons.

Rainsford, C. (2019). Cronies of disgraced Veracruz ex-governor walk free in Mexico. *InSight Crime*, April 5. https://insightcrime.org/news/analysis/cronies-disgraced-veracruz-ex-governor-walk-free-in-mexico/

Ramírez Atilano, D. A. (2014). *Fuerzas Unidas por Nuestros Desaparecidos en Nuevo León (FUNDENL): La acción colectiva en busca de las personas desaparecidas en Monterrey* [MA Sociology Thesis, Universidad de Monterrey].

Ramos, D. (2012). ¿Dónde quedaron los dos jefes zeta que estaban presos en Apodaca? *Animal Político*, February 23. https://www.animalpolitico.com/2012/02/donde-queda ron-los-dos-jefes-zeta-reclusos-en-apodaca/

Rath, T. (2013). *Myths of demilitarization in postrevolutionary Mexico, 1920–1960.* Chapel Hill, NC: UNC Press Books.

Reforma (2017). Tras 3 años, fracasa el plan Tamaulipas. *Reforma*, May 14. https://www.reforma.com/aplicaciones/articulo/default.aspx?id=1113255

Rice, P. (2018). Survivors and the Origin of the Convention for the Protection of All Persons from Enforced Disappearance. In A. Moore & E. Swanson (Eds.), *Witnessing torture: Perspectives of torture survivors and human rights workers* (pp. 157–168). New York: Palgrave Macmillan.

Rich, J. A. (2019a). Making national participatory institutions work: Bureaucrats, activists, and AIDS policy in Brazil. *Latin American Politics and Society, 61*(2), 45–67.

Rich, J. A. (2019b). *State-sponsored activism: Bureaucrats and social movements in demo-cratic Brazil.* Cambridge: Cambridge University Press.

Ríos-Figueroa, J. (2007). Fragmentation of power and the emergence of an effective judiciary in Mexico, 1994–2002. *Latin American Politics and Society, 49*(1), 31–57.

Ríos-Figueroa, J. (2015) Judicial institutions. In J. Gandhi & R. Ruiz-Rufino (Eds.), *Routledge handbook of comparative political institutions* (pp. 195–208). New York: Routledge.

Risse, T., Ropp, S. C., & Sikkink, K. (Eds.). (2013). *The persistent power of human rights: From commitment to compliance.* Cambridge: Cambridge University Press.

Rizzo, S. (2019). Do Mexican drug cartels make $500 billion a year? *Washington Post*, June 24. https://www.washingtonpost.com/politics/2019/06/24/do-mexican-drug-cartels-make-billion-year/

Robben, A. C. (2010). *Political violence and trauma in Argentina.* Philadelphia: University of Pennsylvania Press.

Ron, J., Ramos, H., & Rodgers, K. (2005). Transnational information politics: NGO human rights reporting, 1986–2000. *International Studies Quarterly, 49*(3), 557–587.

Santiago, V. (2019). *Guerracruz: Rinconcito donde hacen su nido las hordas del mal.* México, DF: Aguilar, Penguin Random House Grupo Editiorial.

Sarat, A. (1990). ". . . The law is all over": Power, resistance and the legal consciousness of the welfare poor. *Yale Journal of Law & the Humanities, 2*:343–379.

Sarat, A., & Scheingold, S. A. (2006). *Cause lawyers and social movements.* Redwood City, CA: Stanford University Press.

Sarkis, S (2017). 11 red flags of gaslighting in a relationship. *Psychology Today*, January 22. https://www.psychologytoday.com/us/blog/here-there-and-everywhere/201701/11-red-flags-gaslighting-in-relationship

Schedler, A. (2018). *En la niebla de la guerra (2da. Edición): Los ciudadanos ante la violencia criminal organizada.* México, DF: CIDE.

Schmitz, H. P. (2002, March). *From lobbying to shaming: The evolution of human rights activism since the 1940s* [Paper presentation]. International Studies Association (ISA) Meeting 2002, New Orleans.

Schwartz-Marin, E., & Cruz-Santiago, A. (2016). Forensic civism: Articulating science, DNA and kinship in contemporary Mexico and Colombia. *Human Remains and Violence: An Interdisciplinary Journal, 2*(1), 58–74.

Schwartz-Marin, E., & Cruz-Santiago, A. (2018). Antigone's forensic DNA database: Forensic technologies and the search for the disappeared in Mexico. *Athenea Digital, 18*(1), 129–153.

Scott, R. E. (1964). *Mexican government in transition.* Urbana: University of Illinois Press.

Sheridan, M. B. (2021). A lawyer fought for justice after a Mexican massacre. Then the government made her a suspect. *Washington Post*, November 23. https://www.washingtonpost.com/world/2021/11/23/mexico-disappeared-organized-crime/

Shirk, D. A. (2011). *The drug war in Mexico: Confronting a shared threat.* New York: Council on Foreign Relations.

Sieff, K., & Martinez, G. (2019). Migrants say police in Mexico opened fire on their truck, killing a 19-year-old woman. *Washington Post*, June 19. https://www.washingtonpost.com/world/the_americas/migrants-say-police-in-mexico-opened-fire-on-their-truck-killing-19-year-old-woman/2019/06/18/69eb35c6-9204-11e9-956a-88c291ab5c38_story.html

Simmons, E. S. (2016). *Meaningful resistance: Market reforms and the roots of social protest in Latin America.* Cambridge: Cambridge University Press.

Skaar, E. (2011). *Judicial independence and human rights in Latin America: Violations, politics, and prosecution.* New York: Springer.

Skocpol, T. (1992). *Protecting soldiers and mothers: The politics of social provision in the United States, 1870s–1920s.* Cambridge, MA: Belknap Press of Harvard University Press.

Snyder, R., & Duran-Martinez, A. (2009). Does illegality breed violence? Drug trafficking and state-sponsored protection rackets. *Crime, Law and Social Change, 52*(3), 253–273.

Solera, C. (2015). Ausencias que lastiman: En 2011, Zetas deshacían cuerpos con diesel. *Excelsior*, February 1. https://www.excelsior.com.mx/nacional/2015/02/01/1005903. Accessed June 20, 2019

Swidler, A. (1986). Culture in action: Symbols and strategies. *American Sociological Review*, 51(2), 273–286.

Tarrow, S. (1996). States and opportunities: The political structuring of social movements. In D. McAdam, J. McCarthy & M. Zald (Eds.), *Comparative perspectives on social movements: Political opportunities, mobilizing structures, and cultural framings* (pp. 41–61). Cambridge: Cambridge University Press.

Tarrow, S. (2011). *Power in movement: Social movements and contentious politics.* Cambridge: Cambridge University Press.

Taylor, W. K. (2018). Ambivalent legal mobilization: Perceptions of justice and the use of the tutela in Colombia. *Law & Society Review*, 52(2), 337–367.

Taylor, W. K. (2020). On the social construction of legal grievances: Evidence from Colombia and South Africa. *Comparative Political Studies*, 53(8), 1326–1356.

Tilly, C. (1977). *Repertoires of contention in America and Britain, 1750–1830.*

Trejo, G., Albarracín, J., & Tiscornia, L. (2018). Breaking state impunity in post-authoritarian regimes: Why transitional justice processes deter criminal violence in new democracies. *Journal of Peace Research*, 55(6), 787–809.

Trejo, G., & Ley, S. (2018). Why did drug cartels go to war in Mexico? Subnational party alternation, the breakdown of criminal protection, and the onset of large-scale violence. *Comparative Political Studies*, 51(7), 900–937.

Trejo, G., & Ley, S. (2020). *Votes, drugs, and violence: The political logic of criminal wars in Mexico.* Cambridge: Cambridge University Press.

United Nations (2002). Commission on Human Rights, Civil and Political Rights, Including Questions of: Independence of the Judiciary, Administration of Justice, Impunity. Report on the Mission to Mexico. E/CN.4/2002/72/ADD.1, January 24. https://documents-dds-ny.un.org/doc/UNDOC/GEN/G02/103/44/PDF/G0210344.pdf?OpenElement

United Nations (2005). Updated set of principles for the protection and promotion of human rights through action to combat impunity. E/CN.4/2005/102/Add.1, February 8. https://documents-dds-ny.un.org/doc/UNDOC/GEN/G05/109/00/PDF/G0510 900.pdf?OpenElement

United Nations (2009). Fact Sheet No. 6 Rev. 3, Enforced or involuntary disappearances. UN Office of the High Commissioner for Human Rights (OHCHR). https://www.ohchr.org/sites/default/files/Documents/Publications/FactSheet6Rev3.pdf

United Nations (2010). International Convention for the Protection of All Persons from Enforced Disappearance. UN Office of the High Commissioner for Human Rights (OHCHR). https://www.ohchr.org/en/instruments-mechanisms/instruments/international-convention-protection-all-persons-enforced

United Nations (2012). Report of the Working Group on Enforced or Involuntary Disappearances, Mission to Mexico, A/ HRC/19/58/Add.2, paragraph 17, December 20. https://documents-dds-ny.un.org/doc/UNDOC/GEN/G11/174/92/PDF/G1117 492.pdf?OpenElement

United Nations (2021). Informe del Comité contra la Desaparición Forzada sobre su visita a México en virtud del artículo 33 de la Convención. CED/C/MEX/VR/1. https://tbinternet.ohchr.org/_layouts/15/treatybodyexternal/Download.aspx?symbolno=INT%2fCED%2fINF%2fMEX%2f22%2f33831&Lang=en

Ureste, M. (2019). Durante sexenio de Peña, México se volvió el país más peligroso para ejercer el periodismo en AL: Artículo 19. *Animal Político*, April 2. https://www.animalpolitico.com/2019/04/periodistas-asesinados-mexico/

US Department of Justice (2018, April 20). *Former Mexican governor extradited to the Southern District of Texas* [Press release]. https://www.justice.gov/usao-sdtx/pr/for mer-mexican-governor-extradited-southern-district-texas

Vanhala, L. (2010). *Making rights a reality?: Disability rights activists and legal mobilization*. Cambridge: Cambridge University Press.

Vanhala, L. (2011) Legal mobilization. In *Oxford bibliographies*. Oxford: Oxford University Press. doi.org:10.1093/obo/9780199756223-0031

Vanhala, L. (2012). Legal opportunity structures and the paradox of legal mobilization by the environmental movement in the UK. *Law & Society Review, 46*(3), 523–556.

Vela, D. (2016). En la última década, 9 de 10 desaparecidos en Veracruz, con Duarte. *El Financiero*, July 25. https://www.elfinanciero.com.mx/nacional/en-la-ultima-decada-de-10-desaparecidos-en-veracruz-con-duarte/

Verba, S. (1965). Comparative political culture. In L. W. Pye (Ed.), *Political culture and political development* (pp. 512–560). Princeton, NJ: Princeton University Press.

Vestergren, S., Drury, J., & Chiriac, E. H. (2017). The biographical consequences of protest and activism: A systematic review and a new typology. *Social Movement Studies, 16*(2), 203–221.

Villarreal, A. (2015). Fear and spectacular drug violence in Monterrey. *Violence at the Urban Margins, 9*, 84.

Villarreal, A. (2021). Domesticating danger: Coping codes and symbolic security amid violent organized crime in Mexico. *Sociological Theory, 39*(4), 225–244.

Villarreal Martínez, M. T. (2015). Participación y gestión pública en Nuevo León, México. *Revista Enfoques, 7*(11), 417–439.

Villarreal Martínez, M. T. (2016). Los colectivos de familiares de personas desaparecidas y la procuración de justicia. *Intersticios sociales, 11*.

Villegas, P. (2017). Gunmen kill Mexican activist for parents of missing children. *New York Times*, May 12. https://www.nytimes.com/2017/05/12/world/americas/mexico-mot her-activist-murdered-daughter-tamaulipas.html

Washington Office on Latin America (WOLA) (2021). *For disappearances to end, justice must begin*. https://mexicodisappearances.wola.org/

Weber, M. (1978). *Economy and society: An outline of interpretive sociology*. Oakland: University of California Press.

Wedeen, L. (2010). Reflections on ethnographic work in political science. *Annual Review of Political Science, 13*, 255–272.

Wilson, C., & Weigend, E. (2014). *Plan Tamaulipas: A new security strategy for a troubled state*. Washington, DC: Wilson Center, Mexico Institute.

Wolford, W. (2006). The difference ethnography can make: Understanding social mobilization and development in the Brazilian Northeast. *Qualitative Sociology, 29*(3), 335–352.

Wood, E. J. (2003). *Insurgent collective action and civil war in El Salvador*. Cambridge: Cambridge University Press.

Wood, E. (2002). The emotional benefits of insurgency in El Salvador. In J. Goodwin & J. M. Jasper (Eds.), *The social movements reader: Cases and concepts* (pp. 143–152). Oxford: Blackwell.

Woody, C. (2018). Violence in Mexico is still setting records—and the embattled president just reached a grisly milestone. *Business Insider*, April 23. https://www.business insider.com/mexico-violence-homicides-under-pena-nieto-2018-4

Wright, T. C. (2014). *Impunity, human rights, and democracy: Chile and Argentina, 1990–2005*. Austin: University of Texas Press.

Zamora, S., Díaz, J. R. C., Castro, L. P., Xopa, J. R., & Lopez, D. (2005). *Mexican law*. Oxford: Oxford University Press.

Zavaleta, N. (2018). Se va Yunes, entra Cuitláhuac y la sombra de Duarte sigue. . . . *Proceso*, November 30. https://www.proceso.com.mx/reportajes/2018/11/30/se-va-yunes-entra-cuitlahuac-la-sombra-de-duarte-sigue-216379.html

Zavaleta, N. (2019). Más de dos mil desaparecidos en el bienio de Yunes Linares: Colectivo Solecito. *Proceso*, February 1. https://www.proceso.com.mx/nacional/estados/2019/2/1/mas-de-dos-mil-desaparecidos-en-el-bienio-de-yunes-linares-colectivo-solecito-219605.html

Zepeda Lecuona, G. (2014). *Crimen sin castigo: Procuración de justicia penal y ministerio público en México*. México, DF: Fondo de Cultura Economica.

Zepeda Lecuona, G. (2019). *Índice estatal de desempeño de las procuradurías y fiscalías*. México, DF: Impunidad Cero.

Index

For the benefit of digital users, indexed terms that span two pages (e.g., 52–53) may, on occasion, appear on only one of those pages.

Note: Tables and figures are indicated by *t* and *f* following the page number

accompaniment, 31, 75–76, 96, 110n.60, 143, 221–22
  as a methodology, 31–32
action, collective, 5–6, 8–9, 19–20, 133–34
activists, 10–11, 12–13, 30–31, 74–75, 83–84, 114, 116–17, 133–34, 194, 197, 204
  2006-2012, 88–100
  2012-2018, 100–12
  vs. advocates, 12, 73–74, 74*f*
  before 2006, 77–88
  definition of, 12
  in Nuevo León, 175–76
  in Tamaulipas, 175
  in Veracruz, 175
  violence against, 72, 103–4, 113
advocates, 75–77, 204, 236
  2006-2012, 88–100
  2012-2018, 100–12
  before 2006, 77–88
  vs. activists, 73–74, 74*f*
  definition of, 12
  in Nuevo León, 175–76
  in Tamaulipas, 175, 181
  in Veracruz, 175, 187–91, 210–11
AFADEM (Association of Families of the Disappeared Detained), 82n.11, 84–85
agency, 21–22, 115–16, 123, 162–63, 206
  collective, 29
  pleasure in, 33, 37–38, 39, 119–20, 220
Alfonso. *See* Moreno, Alfonso
Alianza Cívica, 85–86
Álvarez Icaza, Emilio, 72, 194, 246
Amnesty International, 83
AMORES, 192

Angelica Foundation, 235
Arendt, Hannah, 3–4
Argentine Forensic Team, 110
Arraigo, 89
Atoyac de Álvarez, Guerrero, 65–69, 124, 220–21
availability, biographical, 42–44, 56–57, 65, 119*f*, 134
Avilés Rojas, Epifanio, 81–82
Avon Foundation, 235
Ayotzinapa disappearances, 27–28, 73, 104–14, 157, 228

Baca, Alejandro Moreno, 2, 123, 129–31, 238–39
  disappearance of, 62–65
  legal outcomes, 218–20
  life prior to disappearance, 51–53
  possible perpetrators of disappearance, 218–19
  See also Baca, Lucía; Moreno, Alfonso
Baca, Lucía, 1–2, 69–71, 116, 218–20, 223
  engaging in contentious action, 137–39
  legal consciousness, 52, 123, 129–31, 133–34
  life prior to son's disappearance, 50–52
  locating state allies 151–52
  navigating judicial bureaucracy 148–50
  partnering with social movements, 140–41
  personal impact on, 238–39
  reaction to son's disappearance, 62–65
  searching, 159–60
  See also Baca, Alejandro Moreno; Moreno, Alfonso

Baja California, 17–19
Baltazar, Salomon, 154–55
Beltrán Leyva Cartel, 66, 169f, 177, 193
Bermúdez Zurita, Arturo, 185–86
bootstraps, 20, 21f
bordando por la paz, 196
Bravo, Luis Ángel, 185–86, 188
Brigada Nacional de Búsqueda (National
    Citizens' Search Brigade), 110, 155–
    56, 200, 224
El Bronco. See Rodriguez Calderón, Jaime
buscando nos encontramos, 159
búsqueda. See searching

Cabañas, Lucio, 84–85
Caciques, 78
Calderón, Felipe, 24–27, 81, 88–100, 146–
    47, 204
capacity, movement, 36, 201–2, 226, 237
caravans, 32, 99–100, 130, 131–32, 194
    description, 5–6
    participation of Juan Carlos, 221
    in United States, 139
    in Veracruz, 187
cartels. See Drug Trafficking Organizations
Catholic church, 85
caudillistas, 78
CENCOS (National Center of
    Communications), 127–28
Centro ProDH (Center for Human Rights
    Miguel Agustin Pro Juárez), 86–88,
    96–97, 110, 200, 221–22
Chavez, Atala, 150, 219–20
Chihuahua, 50, 62, 98–99, 172–73, 210–
    11, 235
Ciencia Forense Ciudadana (CFC;
    Citizen-led Forensic Science), 106–7
Ciudadanos en Apoyo de los Drechos
    Humanos AC (CADHAC; Citizens
    in Support of Human Rights), 32, 42–
    43, 129–31, 138, 192–98, 211–14, 223
Ciudad Juarez, 99–100
civic organizations, 24, 73, 187
claim-making, 5–6, 8–9, 21–22,
    44, 232–33
co-adyuvante, 150
Coahuila, 96, 129, 176, 225
Cold War, 6–7

colectivos, 2–3
Colinas de Santa Fe, 185–86
Colombia, 24, 31, 79
Coludido, 64, 147–48
Comisión de Búsqueda (National Search
    Comission), 206, 209
Comisión Mexicana de Defensa y
    Promoción de los Derechos
    Humanos, A.C. (CMDPDH;
    Mexican Commission for the
    Promotion and Defense of Human
    Rights), 86, 87–88
Comité Cerezo, 96
Comité pro Defensa de Presos,
    Perseguidos, Desaparecidos y
    Exiliados Políticos de Monterrey
    (Monterrey's Committee for Political
    Prisoners, Persecuted, Disappeared
    and Exiled), 82–83
Comisión Ejecutiva de Atención a
    Víctimas (CEAV; Commission for
    Attention to Victims), 154, 203–9,
    217–18, 246
Comisión Nacional de Derechos
    Humanos (CNDH; National Human
    Rights Commission), 171t, 186–87
contention, repertoires of, 36, 81, 118–19,
    135, 161, 232–33
contingente carriola, 107–8
cooptation, 23–25
crises, economic, 80
Cuernavaca, 129–30

de la Garza, Adrián, 193–98
de Wallace, Isabel Miranda, 97–98
defensa integral, 96–97
Delgadillo, Ana Lorena, 181
democratization, 12, 34–35, 73, 113
density of exposure, 120, 162–63
denuncia, 62–63, 65
descabezando, 90–91
Deudos y Defensores por la Dignidad de
    Nuestros Desaparecidos, 160–61
Dirty War, 23–25, 74–75, 78–79, 81–85,
    87, 226
disappearances, 1
    definition, 1n.1
    General Law on, 109, 204–6, 246

justice in cases of, 2–3, 7–8, 16, 103–4, 165, 214–23
legal classifications of, 172–73
in Mexico post-2006, 88–94
modalities/strategic use of, 30, 168–70
prevalence, 2–3, 25f
victim profile, 25
DNA, 14–15, 106–7, 182, 186–87, 208, 214
Doña Mari. *See* Herrera, María
Doretti, Mercedes, 181
Drug Trafficking Organizations (DTOs), 13–14, 66
growing power of, 24, 79–80, 88
relationships with officials, 14, 24–25, 35–36, 95, 101, 103–4
See also Cartel Jalisco Nueva Generación; Gulf cartel; Sinaloa cartel; Zetas
Drug War, 32, 73, 91, 93, 206–7, 226, 228
Duarte de Ochoa, Javier, 154–55, 175, 183–91
dysfunction, judicial, 3–4, 7–8, 15–16, 19–20, 234

Encinas, Alejandro, 245
Estado de México, 48, 101–3
estamos hasta la madre, 27–28, 99, 131
ethnographic methods, 28–33
ethnography, 8, 30–33, 37, 45–46, 162–63, 236–37
Eureka Committee of the Disappeared, 82–83
executions, extrajudicial, 82

Familia Michoacana, 66, 169f
Familiares en Búsqueda María Herrera, 158
La Federación Latinoamericana de Asociaciones de Familiares de Detenidos-Desaparecidos (FEDEFAM; Latin American Federation of Associations for Relatives of the Detained-Disappeared), 83
Federal Judicial Police, 80
Federal Search Unit, 144
femicide, 98–99
Fernandez Garcia, Mauricio, 193

fideicomisos, 246
Fiscalía Especializada en Investigación de Desaparición Forzada (Special Prosecutor for Enforced Disappearances), 148–49
Flores Treviño, Roberto, 197–98
Fox, Vicente, 24, 80
Fray Juan de Larios, 96
FrayBa, 87–88, 95
Fuerza Unidas por Nuestros Desaparecidos Coahuila (FUUNDEC; United Forces for Our Disappeared in Coahuila), 16–17n.16, 96
Fuerza Unidas por Nuestros Desaparecidos Mexico (FUUNDEM; United Forces for Our Disappeared in Mexico), 16–17n.16
Fuerza Unidas por Nuestros Desaparecidos Nuevo León (FUNDENL; United Forces for Our Disappeared in Nuevo León), 196–97

Garcia Abregó, Juan, 177
García Cabeza de Vaca, Francisco Javier, 179
García Jiménez, Cuitlahuác, 190
García, Eliana, 152–53
Garralda, Jorge, 126
gatekeeper organizations, 87–88, 97, 98–99
General Law on the Forced Disappearance of Persons, Disappearances Committed by Individuals. and the National Missing Persons System, 109, 114, 203–6, 207–8, 226, 246
General Victims' Law, 1, 2–3, 104–5, 138–39, 153–54, 203–9, 226, 228
Global Fund for Democracy, 236–37
Global Fund for Women, 235
goods, public, 23–24, 39–40
Granados. *See* Familia Michoacana
grievance, 10, 21–22, 33, 40–42, 117, 119–20
Grupo Interdisciplinario de Expertas y Expertos Independientes (GIEI; Interdisciplinary Group of Independent Experts), 109

Guerrero, 23–24, 66, 81–86, 106–12, 124–25, 200, 224
Gulf Cartel, 169f, 176–79, 184–85, 192–93
Guzmán, Joaquin "El Chapo," 101

Hijos por la Identitad y la Justicia contra el Olvido y el Silencio (HIJOS; Children for Identity and Justice against Oblivion and Silence), 84
Han Visto a ("Have you seen. . .") initiative, 153–54
Hernández Giadáns, Verónica, 190–91
Hernández, Eugenio, 178
Herrera Beltrán, Fidel, 183
Herrera, María, 29n.27
Human Rights Watch, 19, 93
hunger strike, 5–6, 81, 136–37, 141–42, 144, 188–89, 239–40

Ibarra, Rosario, 82–83
I(dh)eas, Litigio estratégico en derechos humanos, A.C., 110n.60
immigration, 32, 55
impunity
    definition of, 6–7, 8, 233
    eroding, 5, 8, 13–14, 13f, 15–16, 29–30, 35–36, 167, 192–98, 200–27
    measuring, 36, 228
    United Nations convention on, 83
independence, judicial, 4
inequality, 80, 234
inertia, bureaucratic, 72
Institutional Revolutionary Party (PRI), 23–24, 77–81, 84–86, 91–92, 170, 177–79, 183, 193–94
Inter-American Court of Human Rights (IACtHR), 84–85, 97, 101–3
International Criminal Court, 41
International Crisis Group, 184–85
interpretivism, 28–29, 30–33
investigations, participatory, 5–6, 15–16, 27–28, 104–7, 111–12, 187–88, 194–95, 197–99
    description, 16–19
    notes from, 17–19
    in Nuevo León, 192–98

origins, 105
in Veracruz, 182–91

Jalisco New Generation Cartel (CJNG), 183–85
Jarab, Jan, 75–76, 107–8, 179
jefe de la plaza, 66–67, 124, 183
Jesuits, Society of, 86
Journalists, violence against, 103, 184–85
Juan Carlos. See Trujillo Herrera, Juan Carlos
judges, 4–5, 89, 172
judicial decision-making site (JDMS), 74–75

Laredo, 2, 62
Law on Disappearances. See General Law on the Forced Disappearance of Persons, Disappearances Committed by Individuals. and the National Missing Persons System
legal consciousness, 5, 9–11, 33, 37
    definition of, 45
    forms of, 45, 49–55
    impact of trauma on, 10–11, 117, 162–63, 232
    relation to mobilization, 5, 10–11, 33, 35, 36, 44–46, 117–18, 120–25, 135
liberation theology, 86
litigio estratégico, 96–97
Lopez Obrador, Andrés Manuel, 88–89, 245–47
Lopez Portillo, José, 82–83
Los Otros Desaparecidos, 111, 157–58
Lucia. See Baca, Lucia

Madres de la Plaza de Mayo (Argentina), 41
Martí, Alejandro, 97–98
Martinez Corrales, Yatzil, 200, 227
Martinez Corrales, Yoltzi, 200–1, 209, 223–26, 227, 242–43
mass graves, 14–15, 39–40, 111, 181, 185–86, 190, 208
Medina de la Cruz, Rodrigo, 193–94
Mérida Initiative, 90–91
mesas de trabajo. See investigations, participatory

Mexican Dirty War. *See* Dirty War
Mexico City, 1, 23–24, 26, 65, 72, 148–49
México Unido Contra la Delincuencia,
    MUCD, Mexico United Against
    Delinquency, 99n.50
Michoacán, 53, 65–69
ministerio público (public prosecutor),
    17–19, 35–36, 63–64, 122, 123,
    172, 193–94
mobilization, legal, 44, 116–17, 202, 226
mobilization, sustained, 5–6, 6f, 11–12,
    29, 116–20
money laundering, 32, 178
Monterrey, Nuevo León, 62–65, 82–83, 93,
    129–31, 151, 192–97
    arrival of caravan to, 130, 194
    government response to violence, 88–
        91, 100–5
    See also Ciudadanos en Apoyo de los
        Derechos Humanos AC (CADHAC)
Morales, Hermana Consuelo, 129–30
Morales, Marisela, 141
Moreno, Alfonso, 1–2, 69–71, 116, 218–
    20, 223
    engaging in contentious action, 137–39
    legal consciousness, 52, 123, 129–
        31, 133–34
    life prior to son's disappearance, 50–52
    locating state allies 151–52
    navigating judicial bureaucracy 148–50
    partnering with social
        movements, 140–41
    personal impact on, 238–39
    reaction to son's disappearance, 62–65
    searching, 159–60
    See also Baca, Alejandro Moreno;
        Baca, Lucía
Moreno Nuñez, Nepomuceno, 103–4
Mother's Day March, 39
Movimiento por Nuestros Desaparecidos
    (Movement for Our Disappeared),
    87n.27, 204–5
Movimiento por la Paz con Justicia y
    Dignidad (MPJD; Movement for
    Peace with Justice and Dignity), 1
    as brokers in Nuevo León, 99–100
    caravans, 32, 99–100, 130, 131–32, 139,
        152–53, 187, 194

interactions with Juan Carlos and Doña
    Mari, 131–34, 139, 142, 146–47, 241
interactions with Lucia and Alfonso,
    129–31, 138–39, 140–41
interactions with Nancy, 127–29, 133–
    34, 136–37, 145, 152
origins of, 27–28, 99–100, 204
role in Victims' Law, 1, 104n.53, 204
in Veracruz, 99–100, 187
movements, victim-led, 4–5, 12,
    105, 226
Murillo Karám, Jesús, 154–55

naming and shaming, 4–5, 23–24, 74–
    75, 76–77
Nancy. *See* Rosete, Nancy
neoliberalism, 80, 246
Nuevo Laredo, 62–64, 123, 159–60
Nuevo Laredo Human Rights
    Committee, 180
Nuevo León, 17–19, 32, 36, 123, 175–76,
    192–98, 201–2, 211–14
Núñez Mendieta, Iván Baruch, 93

Odebrecht, 101
Oficina del Alto Comisionado por los
    Derechos Humanos (OACNUDH;
    Office of the United Nations High
    Commissioner for Human Rights),
    40–41, 129
Olson, Joy, 92
Olvera, Alberto, 183–84
opportunity structure, legal/political, 73,
    76, 167, 198
Organization of American States (OAS),
    2–3, 107–8
Otra Campaña, 84
outcomes, 36, 201–2
    institutional, 203–9
    judicial, 210–14
    legislative, 203–9
    movement, 223–26

Pajacuarán, 53, 54–55, 67, 131
Palacios, Anais, 187–88, 221
Palacios, Maria Lourdes, 155–56
Partido de Acción Nacional (PAN;
    National Action Party), 80, 179

Partido de la Revolución Democrática (PRD; Party of the Democratic Revolution), 83–84, 88–89
Partido Revolucionario Institucional (PRI; Institutional Revolutionary Party), 23–24, 77–81, 91–92, 170, 177, 179, 193–94
Peña Nieto, Enrique, 27–28, 72–73, 91, 100–12
    changes in institutional response, 100–3, 109
    homicides and disappearances during administration, 104–9
    mobilization under, 27–28, 109–12
    role in San Salvador Atenco case, 101–3
Plan Tamaulipas, 178–79, 182
Plantón, 138
Ponte En los Zapatos del Otro, 127–28
positionality, 31, 234
positivism, 28–29
Poza Rica, 68–69
protection rackets, 166–67, 199, 202, 208, 233
protest, 5–6, 9, 105, 232–33
psycho-social support, 36, 98–99, 201–2, 223–24

Radilla, Rosendo, 84–85, 89–90, 97
Ramos, Raymundo, 180
Red de Enlaces Nacionales, 111, 158, 221
Red de Todos los Derechos para Todos (RedTDT; Network of All Rights for All People), 87, 96–97
ReverdeSer Collective, 242
rights, 3–4, 19–20
    -bearing, 22–23, 36, 37, 170–71, 201–2, 227, 229
    -claiming, 3–4, 22, 37
    relation to impunity 8, 22
Ríos Alvarado, Flavino, 184–85
Rodriguez Calderón, Jaime, 197–98
Rodríguez, Miriam Elizabeth, 103–4, 181
Romero, Francisco, 219
Rosete, Nancy
    engaging in contentious action, 136–37
    legal consciousness, 49–50
    life prior to son's disappearance, 46–49

locating state allies 152–54
navigating judicial bureaucracy 144–46
partnering with social movements, 141–42
personal impact on, 239–41
reaction to son's disappearance, 59–62
See also Torres Rosete, Elvis Axell

Sabinas Hidalgo, Nuevo León, 63–64
Salinas de Gortari, Carlos, 80
Salva Tu Vida, 2, 58
San Fernando massacre, 181
San Pedro, Nuevo León, 193
San Salvador Atenco, 101–3
searching, 159–60
Secreraría de Gobernación (SEGOB; Ministry of the Interior), 136–37, 141–42, 144, 146
SEIDO, 67, 125–49, 146, 148, 153, 189, 215
Servicio Médico Forense (SEMEFO; Medical Forensic Service), 164, 217
Servicios y Asesoría para la Paz A.C. (SERAPAZ), 87n.27, 128
Sicilia, Javier, 27–28, 99–100, 127–28, 136, 194
Sicilia, Juan Francisco, 27–28, 99
Sinaloa Cartel, 168–70, 169f, 177, 183–84, 193
social media, 17–19, 34–35, 128–29, 164–65
social movements, 9, 26–27, 29–30, 42–46, 73–75, 95, 113, 143, 162–63, 202
socio-spatial positioning, 44, 118–19, 162–63
Sonora, 54–55, 103–4
state alliances, 12–15, 13f, 168, 175, 211, 230
state officials, motivation of, 12–15, 13f, 117–18, 143, 168
strategic prosecution. See litigio estartégico
strategies
    activist, 12, 15, 83–84, 105, 135
    advocacy, 12, 15–16, 135, 198, 241

Tamaulipas, 35–36, 103–4, 123, 164–65, 175, 176–82
Tijuana, 17–19, 55

Tlachinollan Centro de Derechos
    Humanos de La Montaña
    (Tlachinollan Mountain Center for
    Human Rights), 87–88
Tlatelolco Massacre, 23–24
Tlatlaya, 103
Torre Cantú, Egidio, 178
Torres Rosete, Elvis Axell
    disappearance of, 58–62
    drug addiction and treatment, 58–59
    legal outcomes, 215–18
    life prior to disappearance, 48–49
    possible perpetrator of
        disappearance, 215
    See also " Rosete, Nancy"
transnational advocacy networks
    (TANs), 4–5
trauma, 10–11, 31–32, 117, 120–21, 162–
    63, 232
Trujillo Herrera, Juan Carlos
    engaging in contentious action, 139
    legal consciousness, 55–56
    life prior to brothers'
        disappearance, 53–55
    locating state allies 154–56
    navigating judicial bureaucracy 146–48
    partnering with social
        movements, 142–43
    personal impact on, 241–43
    reaction to brothers' disappearance,
        67–69, 124–25
    threats against, 124, 188, 242
    work in Veracruz, 69, 124,
        158–59
Trujillo Herrera, Gustavo
    disappearance of, 68
    family's reaction to disappearance of,
        68–69, 124–25, 187–88
    legal outcomes, 221
    possible perpetrator of
        disappearance, 221
Trujillo Herrera, Jesús Salvador
    disappearance of, 66–67
    family's reaction to disappearance
        of, 67–68
    legal outcomes, 220–21
    possible perpetrator of
        disappearance, 220–21

Trujillo Herrera, Luis Armando
    disappearance of, 68
    family's reaction to disappearance of,
        68–69, 124–25, 187–88
    legal outcomes, 221
    possible perpetrator of
        disappearance, 221
Trujillo Herrera, Miguel, 68, 158, 221, 242
Trujillo Herrera, Rafael, 66–69, 124
Trujillo Herrera, Raúl
    disappearance of, 66–67
    family's reaction to disappearance
        of, 67–68
    legal outcomes, 220–21
    possible perpetrator of
        disappearance, 220–21
Turati, Marcela, 181

Unidad de Búsqueda, 144
United Kingdom, 106–7
United Nations High Commission for
        Human Rights. See Oficina
        del Alto Comisionado por
        los Derechos Humanos
United Nations Principles to Combat
        Impunity, 7
United Nations Working Group
        on Enforced or Involuntary
        Disappearances, 92, 204–5
Universal Declaration of Human
        Rights, 92–93

Vargas Llosa, Mario, 77–78
Vasquez Mota, Josefina, 140–41
Veracruz, 35–36, 110, 124, 175, 182–91,
        206–7, 210–11
Vergara, Mario, 158
victim, blaming the, 12, 74–75, 93, 99–
        100, 121–22
victim claimants, 5, 202–3
víctimas, 1–2
Victims' Law. See General Victims' Law
Victims' Monument, 97–98

Washington Office on Latin America
        (WOLA), 92, 103, 228
Weapons, 32, 88, 139, 176
Weber, Max, 4

Winckler, Jorge, 185
Workers Revolutionary Party, 83–84

Xalapa Lencero Police Academy, 183–84

Yarrington, Tomás, 178
#YoSoy132, 101–3

Yunes Linares, Miguel Ángel, 185

Zapatistas, 80n.10, 84, 87n.27
Zedillo, Ernesto, 80
Zetas Cartel, 30, 62, 124, 154–55,
    168–70, 169f, 175–78, 183–85,
    193, 218–19